Pearl Jam and Philosophy

Pearl Jam and Philosophy

Edited by Stefano Marino and Andrea Schembari

BLOOMSBURY ACADEMIC
NEW YORK • LONDON • OXFORD • NEW DELHI • SYDNEY

BLOOMSBURY ACADEMIC
Bloomsbury Publishing Inc
1385 Broadway, New York, NY 10018, USA
50 Bedford Square, London, WC1B 3DP, UK
29 Earlsfort Terrace, Dublin 2, Ireland

BLOOMSBURY, BLOOMSBURY ACADEMIC and the Diana logo are trademarks of Bloomsbury Publishing Plc

First published in the United States of America 2022
This paperback edition published 2023

Copyright © Stefano Marino and Andrea Schembari, 2022

Each chapter copyright © by the contributor, 2022

Cover design: Louise Dugdale
Cover image © Pearl Jam perform at Lollapalooza 2007 in Grant Park, Chicago on August 5, 2007.
Photo by Kevin Mazur/WireImage via Getty

All rights reserved. No part of this publication may be reproduced or transmitted in any form or by any means, electronic or mechanical, including photocopying, recording, or any information storage or retrieval system, without prior permission in writing from the publishers.

Bloomsbury Publishing Inc does not have any control over, or responsibility for, any third-party websites referred to or in this book. All internet addresses given in this book were correct at the time of going to press. The author and publisher regret any inconvenience caused if addresses have changed or sites have ceased to exist, but can accept no responsibility for any such changes.

Whilst every effort has been made to locate copyright holders the publishers would be grateful to hear from any person(s) not here acknowledged.

Library of Congress Cataloging-in-Publication Data

Names: Marino, Stefano, 1976- editor. | Schembari, A. (Andrea), 1978-editor.
Title: Pearl Jam and philosophy / edited by Stefano Marino and Andrea Schembari.
Identifiers: LCCN 2021018353 (print) | LCCN 2021018354 (ebook) | ISBN 9781501362781 (hardback) | ISBN 9781501362798 (epub) | ISBN 9781501362804 (pdf) | ISBN 9781501362811
Subjects: LCSH: Pearl Jam (Musical group) | Music and philosophy. | Rock music–Philosophy and aesthetics.
Classification: LCC ML421.P43 P4 2021 (print) | LCC ML421.P43 (ebook) | DDC 782.42166092/2—dc23
LC record available at https://lccn.loc.gov/2021018353
LC ebook record available at https://lccn.loc.gov/2021018354

ISBN:	HB:	978-1-5013-6278-1
	PB:	978-1-5013-8579-7
	ePDF:	978-1-5013-6280-4
	eBook:	978-1-5013-6279-8

Typeset by RefineCatch Limited, Bungay, Suffolk

To find out more about our authors and books visit www.bloomsbury.com and sign up for our newsletters.

Contents

Foreword *Theodore Gracyk*		vii
Introduction *Stefano Marino and Andrea Schembari*		1
1	Contingency, (In)significance, and the All-Encompassing Trip: Pearl Jam and the Question of the Meaning of Life *Stefano Marino*	13
2	"Just Like Innocence": Pearl Jam and the (Re)Discovery of Hope *Sam Morris*	43
3	Who's the Elderly Band Behind the Counter in a Small Town? *Radu Uszkai and Mihail-Valentin Cernea*	61
4	Making a Choice When There Is No "Better Man" *Laura M. Bernhardt*	79
5	That's Where We're Living: Determinism and Free Will in "Unthought Known" *Enrico Terrone*	95
6	No Code Aesthetics *Alberto L. Siani*	109
7	Can Truth Be Found in the Wild? *Paolo Stellino*	123
8	"They Can Buy, But Can't Put On My Clothes": Pearl Jam, Grunge, and Subcultural Authenticity in a Postmodern Fashion Climate *Stephanie Kramer*	139
9	Pearl Jam's Ghosts: The Ethical Claim Made From the Exiled Space(s) of Homelessness and War—An Aesthetic *Response-Ability* *Jacqueline Moulton*	165
10	Pearl Jam: Responsible Music or the Tragedy of Culture? *Cristina Parapar*	183
11	Pearl Jam/Nirvana: A Dialectical Vortex that Revolves Around the Void *Alessandro Alfieri*	205

12 The Tide on the Shell: Pearl Jam and the Aquatic Allegories
    of Existence *Andrea Schembari*   219

Notes on Contributors   239
Copyright Notices   243
Index   261

Foreword

Theodore Gracyk

The "summer of love" began on April 11, 1967, with the first appearance of poppies in San Francisco's Golden Gate Park.

Or was it, as some cultural historians contend, on April 14?

Actually, I'm making a joke there. Cultural phenomena are not born, nor do they die, on specific days, nor, for the most part, in specific years. They do not work that way. For the most part, their beginnings and endings are fuzzy phenomena.

The cultural phenomenon inextricably linked to Pearl Jam is grunge, which emerged in the late 1980s and then reached its cultural peak in 1990–92. After that, it became mainstream and its identity frayed. But just as the Grateful Dead remained relatively intact and musically vital for decades after the summer of love, so it is with Pearl Jam following the heyday of grunge. This collection of essays about Pearl Jam addresses them as a *living* concern. This is not a work of historical remembrance, as would be the case with a new book about Big Brother and the Holding Company, one of the few bands from the San Francisco scene of the 1960s still performing together. But in order to maintain that there's a difference between such cases, Pearl Jam must be examined within a cultural context that is broader and more lasting than either grunge or post-punk alternative rock, which, I propose, is a case that's easily made.

I don't think I exaggerate too much if I say that Pearl Jam matters because it's one of a handful of great rock bands active today. This is not to disparage the many rock musicians who still make great music alongside the diverse set of other genres that make up contemporary popular music. (No need for fans of The Strokes and Drive-By Truckers to send me angry emails for overlooking them!) I am, instead, making the point that much of what's interesting in popular music in the early 2000s isn't rock music.

The obvious question, then, is what I mean by rock music. I have no original proposal to make here, nor will I repeat the ideas that I've previously defended. Instead, I will borrow from a debate that was playing out in the rock press at the very time that Eddie Vedder was contributing his vocals to that famous demo tape made by Jeff Ament, Stone Gossard, and Mike McCready. Because, ironically, Pearl Jam formed at just the moment when the American rock press plunged into a self-examination of the "rockism" of both their favored music and their critical standards for praising that music. The term and the debate had originated in the United Kingdom in the second half of the 1980s, but only gained international attention and wide American usage around 1990, when Robert Christgau wrote a long essay about rockism for the *Village Voice*. Soon after, Christgau included Pearl Jam in a list of alternative rock bands who were clearly rockist.

Using the broadest of strokes, we might represent rockism as a core set of values extracted from the most revered rock bands of the 1960s: (1) Good rock music is more than disposable ear candy. (2) It cannot be produced by musicians whose primary motivation is commercial success. (3) It reflects and expresses the progressive values of the musicians who make it. (4) It also reflects the values of its audience. (5) Through a process of mutual recognition between musicians and fans, it functions as a unifying, progressive public gesture. (6) There should be guitars.

For the rockist, the intertwined assumptions that rock musicians can only engage in personal disclosure while remaining indifferent to commercial success meant that the musicians wrote and performed their own music. Thus, the Beatles were a rock band, but the Monkees (who didn't write their material and who sang over tracks they didn't perform) were pure pop. And even if Janis Joplin wrote few of the songs that made her famous, it was clear enough that she was pouring out her personal torment in the face of systemic misogyny. In retrospect, rockism confirms Frank Zappa's view that the Shaggs were one of the all-time great rock bands.

The point of identifying rockism was to identify, and then defend, an alternative set of values: those of the sheer joy of the dance track, the radio-friendly single, the gaudy video. In short, to open the door to the possibility that the Monkees merit just as much critical attention as the Beatles, and that the collected works of Metallica are no more interesting than the latest Taylor Swift single. To presume otherwise is "rockist" snobbery that sneers at most of the music that most people like (and, generally, under-values genres favored by everyone who isn't an American white heterosexual male). In short, rockism values artists within popular music who behave like the great artists of aesthetic modernism, and the point of putting a name to it is to reassert the value of popularity and entertainment in popular music. The critical purpose of identifying rockism was to announce that rock bands and rock musicians were no longer the central figures in popular music. Given the timing of events, the major grunge bands look like the last gasp of rockism.

Although the term wasn't in Kurt Cobain's vocabulary, he famously endorsed rockism when he posed for *Rolling Stone* magazine while wearing a shirt that read "Corporate Magazines Still Suck." But he also showed the narrow-mindedness that can come with rockism when he publicly dismissed Pearl Jam as "careerists."

Why do I review all of these points? Because philosophers have long discussed the core set of values that characterize rockism, but under another name: romanticism. Remove the assumption that we're talking about late twentieth-century popular music and what we have left is a recycling of nineteenth-century romanticism.

Although I was writing a little too early to use the term "rockism," I challenged its distortions of rock history in my first book, *Rhythm and Noise: An Aesthetics of Rock* (1996). I emphasized the harm done by bringing the clichés of romanticism into popular music criticism. Romanticism was an important cultural movement within nineteenth-century philosophy and art, but, just like rockism, it encouraged a narrowly elitist disdain for much of what was good and most popular in the art of that era.

At this point, I'll take a page from the work of a contemporary philosopher of art, Jenefer Robinson, who argues that romanticism's deficits as a *general* account of art shouldn't lead us to think that romanticism *never* functions to explain the importance of select artworks and artists. In other words, it is a mistake to over-generalize romanticism and to think it tells us something about all art, but it's also a mistake to think that it doesn't apply to any art.

And so it is with rockism as an updating of romanticism: rockism gets us the wrong results when applied to most popular music. Yet rockism was the guiding philosophy of grunge. We can then go one of two ways with this insight.

We can say that Cobain was right about Pearl Jam. If their supposed careerism was contrary to the grunge scene, that would just mean that after Pearl Jam arose from the ashes of Mother Love Bone, they left grunge behind.

However, that's not the path that I want to follow. As anyone who loves the band knows, their legal challenge of Ticketmaster for price-gouging fans was one of many public actions that mere "careerists" would never have undertaken. And "careerists" wouldn't have channeled a chunk of their profits into their own non-profit charity, the Vitalogy Foundation.

And now I want to go the final step, and say that although rockism shouldn't be applied to all of popular music, in Pearl Jam's case, it fits. Pearl Jam's greatness is best measured by the values of rockism. And they're one of the few remaining rock bands to proudly wave that flag.

Personally, one of my favorite episodes in Pearl Jam's career is their brief association with Neil Young, who is arguably the *other* great remaining embodiment of rockism. Ironically, Pearl Jam's contribution to Young's *Mirror Ball* yielded more interest in that album than any that Young had released in over twenty years, and it was one the last of Young's albums to go "gold" in sales. In hindsight, it was probably his last uniformly good album.

In the end, what do I mean by saying that we should value Pearl Jam, like Young, as exponents of rockism? We could do much worse than highlight dignity, commitment, and playing in the moment. I do not pull those three values out of thin air. When Eddie Vedder gave the 1995 induction speech for Neil Young's entry into the Rock and Roll Hall of Fame, Vedder said that Pearl Jam learned a lot from Young. And then Vedder reeled off those three values: "dignity, commitment, and playing in the moment." Today, twenty-five years later, as I survey Pearl Jam's continuing body of work, I find that they provide a pretty good summary of that career.

Popular music is diverse. Rock's time at center stage has waned. But there are still plenty of music fans who respond to rock music, and to rockist values. For us, Pearl Jam is one of the last great rock bands.

Introduction

Stefano Marino and Andrea Schembari

Picture this frame, imagine this scene, a real *immagine in cornice* (to freely use the title of the live-concert film documenting Pearl Jam's 2006 Italian tour): it is June 24, 2017, and the two editors of the present book are at the Eddie Vedder concert in Firenze. While having a conversation and drinking a few beers in the middle of the crowd at about twenty meters from the main stage, waiting for the concert of our long-time favorite songwriter and singer to begin, we realize that, as academic scholars of philosophy and literature, we have published many articles and books on various topics but we have never written anything about the rock band that, especially in our youth, "changed" or even "saved" our life: Pearl Jam. In saying this, what we are referring to is something comparable to what has been famously claimed by (among others) Wim Wenders, Lou Reed, or Eddie Vedder himself about the way in which certain musical experiences can veritably change your life, and can especially support you and help you when you go through times of trouble. "My life was saved by rock 'n' roll," was famously stated by Wim Wenders.[1] In fact, as Wenders once recalled:

> The next thing that arrived was rock 'n' roll when I was around 10 or 12 years old. I had not been interested in music so much before because the German songs my mother listened to on the radio didn't interest me at all. But when rock 'n' roll arrived I realized that this was the best music in the world ... I bought all these records, but because my parents hated this rock 'n' roll I had to keep my records at a friend's place. But if you have to defend something that you like, it makes you to like it even more. And what I like most is that all these interests were really mine. My parents hated the comic strips, they hated rock 'n' roll, and

---

[1] Wim Wenders, quoted in *The Cinema of Wim Wenders: Image, Narrative, and the Postmodern Condition*, Roger F. Cook and Gerd Gemünden (eds) (Detroit: Wayne State University Press, 1997), 219n.

when they found out what movies I was going to they also were against that. So everything I loved I had to defend.[2]

It is possible to compare these quotations by Wim Wenders to a legendary song by Lou Reed precisely entitled "Rock 'n' Roll" (from the Velvet Underground's 1970 album *Loaded*), which famously sings of a girl named Jenny whose life "was saved by rock 'n' roll" because "[d]espite all the amputations / We could dance to a rock 'n' roll station." And, again, it is possible to compare these words by Wim Wenders and Lou Reed to Eddie Vedder's emotional statements in his Foreword to the book *Join Together (With The Band)* about The Who:

> I believe that music can save a life. And I have proof ... For myself, every invite to play with The Who turned into some of life's most galvanized moments. This goes back to what was written earlier about music not only having restorative properties but life-saving capabilities. For I am an example. I am proof. Somehow through my worst trials and tribulations, when there was no one to turn to and a troubled adolescence had me drowning alone at sea, their music came along like a Coast Guard ship with a searchlight beacon and pulled me out of numerous desperate predicaments that would have been otherwise unsurvivable. Their music and words infused strength enough in me to combat the complete powerlessness I was feeling at the time and set me on course towards a life beyond one's imagination or dreams. Am I grateful? Yes. With every cell in my body and neuron and synapse firing in my brain? Affirmative. Every second of every day? Absofuckinglutely. With that being said, you can imagine it was overwhelming the first few times meeting with them. Yet something incredible happened. Due to their generosity, friendship, and acceptance, suddenly I grew up beyond the fucked up elements of the past and was empowered and enable to move beyond it all. It was still part of the story, but no longer defined me.[3]

For us, the two editors of the present book, in our more or less troubled teens spent in a city like Siracusa, in Sicily, that was thousands miles away from Seattle where many exciting things were happening in the musical scene, it was especially Pearl Jam that displayed those "restorative properties" and "life-saving capabilities" that Vedder, in his personal experience, found in the music of The Who, and that many people probably found in Bob Dylan, Neil Young, Bruce Springsteen, Patti Smith, The Clash, R.E.M., U2, Nick Cave, Sonic Youth, Fugazi,

---

[2] Wim Wenders, "Everything I Loved I Had to Defend," *The Talks*, January 29, 2014.
[3] Eddie Vedder, "Foreword," in William Snyder and Eddie Vedder, *Join Together (With the Band)* (Chicago: Press Syndication Group, 2018), 86.

Tori Amos, Radiohead, and still other artists and bands. In a sense, this is probably comparable to what Neil Young meant when he sang in "After the Gold Rush": "There was a band playin' in my head / And I felt like getting high"—clearly referring here to a concept of 'getting high' as broadly, plainly and, so to speak, soberly understood as indicating great passion, thrill, euphoria, exaltation, excitement, and enthusiasm. Although this may probably seem overemphatic to readers who are not familiar with this kind of experience, we must admit that such words as: "Restless soul / Enjoy your youth . . . / All that's sacred comes from youth";[4] or: "Troubled souls unite / We got ourselves tonight . . . / We will find a way, we will find our place . . . / Delight in your youth";[5] or: "I listen for the voice inside my head . . . / Help me from myself";[6] or: "I'll ride the wave / Where it takes me / I'll hold the pain / Release me";[7] these words really had the power of a "profane revelation" and "redemption"[8] for us and our friends in that far "small town" community of Pearl Jam fans in the mid-1990s.[9] In the typical age of nonconformity and, often, of rebellion against all forms of authority, the powerful and protean sound of the band, and the peculiar timbre of Vedder's voice, took over the voices of fathers, mothers, teachers. For many of us this meant channeling energies and hopes into music, writing, and every sort of artistic expression; or it even just stimulated the capacity of introspection, necessary to give shape and name to one's personality. From a certain point of view, especially in some difficult periods of our youth, Pearl Jam somehow "saved" our lives.

So, let us return to the abovementioned picture, to our specific and unique *immagine in cornice*. As we said, we were at the Eddie Vedder concert in Firenze and we suddenly had this kind of "illumination," as it were: that is, we looked at each other and realized that one fine day we would have had to plan and publish

---

[4] Peal Jam, "Not for You," in *Vitalogy* (1994).
[5] Pearl Jam, "Leash," in *Vs.* (1993).
[6] Pearl Jam, "State of Love and Trust," in *Rearviewmirror: Greatest Hits 1991–2003* (2004).
[7] Pearl Jam, "Release," in *Ten* (1991).
[8] On the philosophical concept of "profane redemption" applied to an interpretation of the experience of rock music (more specifically, Fugazi), see Colin J. Campbell's essay "Carry My Body: 'Profane Redemption' and Fugazi," in *Adorno and Popular Music: A Constellation of Perspectives*, Colin J. Campbell, Samir Gandesha, and Stefano Marino (eds) (Milano-Udine: Mimesis International, 2019), 105–22.
[9] Luca Aiello, Antonio Bordone, Daniele Casciana, Emiliano Colomasi, Carmelo Copani, Luigi Di Pasquale, Fabio Farrugia, Piero Fillioley, Rosanna Garufi, Chris Iemulo, Gabriele Leonti, Alessandra Limer, Francesco Maione, Marco Midolo, Luisa Miano, Livia Mignosa, Ennio Muscolino, Alessia Navantieri, Valeria Nucifora, Andrea Romano, Bruno Scalia, Emanuele Siracusa, Gabriele Siracusa, Marco Venuti, Simone Venuti, etc.: Yes, we mean you!

a book on our favorite band, Pearl Jam. More precisely, as academic scholars working in the fields of philosophy and literature, and specifically interested in the various ways in which philosophical thinking can profitably intersect with popular culture (including rock music[10]), we instantly agreed that our book would have had to deal with the "philosophy of Pearl Jam." As the refrain of "Even Flow" correctly and, so to speak, very philosophically claims, sometimes "[t]houghts arrive like butterflies,"[11] and that afternoon, a few hours before Eddie Vedder went on stage and enchanted the audience with (among other masterpieces) one of the most unforgettable and moving versions ever of "Black," the "butterfly-thought" that arrived in our minds was the intuition about the book that we are happy to present now. It was in that precise moment that the very idea about *Pearl Jam and Philosophy* took shape in our minds, thanks to the inspiration favored by the indeed unique atmosphere of that outstanding concert (as massive and crowded as it was comforting and intimate), and it is a great pleasure for us to remember that moment now in introducing our newly published book to the readers.

Pearl Jam, finally inducted into the Rock & Roll Hall of Fame in April 2017, have undoubtedly established themselves as one of the greatest rock bands of all time. They are the only "survivors" of the first and glorious wave of so-called grunge bands (after the tragic deaths of lead members of the other bands of that awesome period: Kurt Cobain of Nirvana, Layne Staley of Alice in Chains, Chris Cornell of Soundgarden). They have an outstanding discography that includes such now classic titles of rock music as *Ten* (1991), *Vs.* (1993), *Vitalogy* (1994), *No Code* (1996), *Yield* (1998), *Binaural* (2000), *Riot Act* (2002), *Pearl Jam* (2006), *Backspacer* (2009), *Lightning Bolt* (2013), and finally *Gigaton* (2020), plus hundreds of other songs published in collections, B-sides, live recordings, etc. Added to this are a few important side-projects of the band's members, including Temple of the Dog, Mad Season, Three Fish, Brad, and most notably, Eddie Vedder's solo career, including the original soundtrack for Sean Penn's film *Into the Wild* (2007). They have a long-lasting and stable line-up that the community of Pearl Jam fans perceive as something resembling a kind of "family," and they

---

[10] On this topic, see for instance Theodore Gracyk's important trilogy of philosophical books on the aesthetics of rock music: *Rhythm and Noise: An Aesthetics of Rock* (Durham, NC: Duke University Press, 1996), *I Wanna Be Me: Rock Music and the Politics of Identity* (Philadelphia, PA: Temple University Press, 2001), and *Listening to Popular Music: Or, How I Learned to Stop Worrying and Love Led Zeppelin* (Ann Arbor, MI: University of Michigan Press, 2007).

[11] Pearl Jam, "Even Flow," in *Ten* (1991).

have played a now legendary series of world tours with very long and deeply emotional concerts whose track-lists ranged from early songs to recent hits and also included covers from Neil Young, The Who, John Lennon, Tom Petty, and many others. Beside the millions of records sold throughout the decades, one of the factors that have contributed to conferring on them a unique profile and status in the broad realm of contemporary rock music is their capacity to create a real and genuine sense of community with their fans, a genuine atmosphere of intersubjective recognition that one can immediately feel at their concerts and immediately associate with them whenever listening to their music. This sense of community, similar to ones surrounding artists like Bruce Springsteen or Neil Young, is rare in the rock and roll business.

With the present volume on the "philosophy of Pearl Jam," published in 2021 on the occasion of the thirtieth anniversary of Pearl Jam's legendary debut album *Ten*, it was our aim to collect contributions from academic scholars who shared with us a real interest in philosophy and literature, and at the same time a genuine passion for Pearl Jam. While there are of course many books on Pearl Jam, to our knowledge they are mostly biographies or historical reconstructions of the grunge era in general or collections of their lyrics (with or without comment and interpretation[12]): no book has been published yet which addresses Pearl Jam's music, lyrics, social context, activities, and engagement from a philosophical point of view. As academic scholars and at the same time long-standing Pearl Jam fans, we believe that there is good reason for a band of this magnitude, longevity, and significance to be a case study within the expanding literature on philosophy and popular culture. Within academic writing, Pearl Jam are surprisingly under-represented, and with this volume we aim to realize a timely application of critical analysis to the music and lyrics of an iconic rock band worthy of the treatment that has already succeeded in relation to comparable artists such as Bob Dylan, Leonard Cohen, U2, Metallica, Radiohead, and many more. The general scope of the book is to investigate, interpret and decipher the philosophical contents and meanings (at various levels: existential, spiritual, ethical, political, purely aesthetic, etc.) that are present in the production

---

[12] See, for example, Ronen Givony, *Not For You: Pearl Jam and the Present Tense* (New York: Bloomsbury Academic, 2020); Jann Wenner (ed.), *Pearl Jam: The Ultimate Guide to Their Music & Legend* (New York: Rolling Stone, 2017); Thomas E. Harkins and Bernard M. Corbett, *Pearl Jam FAQ: All That's Left to Know About Seattle's Most Enduring Band* (Milwaukee: Backbeat Books, an imprint of Hal Leonard Corporation, 2016); Luca Villa and Daria Moretti, *Pearl Jam Evolution* (Tricase: Youcanprint, 2016); Simone Dotto, *Pearl Jam. Still Alive. Testi commentati* (Roma: Arcana, 2014); Kim Neely, *Five Against One: The Pearl Jam Story* (New York: Penguin Books, 1998).

of Pearl Jam, perhaps the greatest rock band of recent decades, celebrating thirty years of recording and live activity in 2021. From this point of view, the book aims to originally and uniquely unite a genuine passion and enthusiasm for Pearl Jam's music with a rigorous and in-depth capacity of philosophical and also literary analysis, thus proving to be potentially important for both Pearl Jam fans who are also interested in good books and new ideas and also for readers of philosophical books at all levels who are also interested in good music and contemporary popular culture.

This is the first book, to our knowledge, to investigate from a philosophical point of view the music, the life, and the activities of Pearl Jam, combining in a systematic and rigorous way historical reconstructions, original philosophical and also literary interpretations, and genuine passion for their music. While not all Pearl Jam songs can be considered strictly "philosophical" as far as the subjects and contents of the lyrics are concerned, many of them indeed can, inasmuch as they deal with important topics of various kind that have attracted the attention of Western and also non-Western philosophers for centuries, and inasmuch as they actually raise profound questions and then search for answers, although sometimes having to admit (in a very philosophical fashion, indeed): "Questions rise and answers fall, ... / Insurmountable";[13] or: "The questions linger overhead."[14] The topics and keys of interpretation that readers of *Pearl Jam and Philosophy* will find in the contributions offered by Alessandro Alfieri, Laura M. Bernhardt, Mihail-Valentin Cernea and Radu Uszkai, Theodore Gracyk, Stephanie Kramer, Sam Morris, Jacqueline Moulton, Cristina Parapar, Alberto L. Siani, Paolo Stellino, Enrico Terrone, and ourselves, include (but are not limited to): the answerable/unanswerable character of the fundamental human questions about meaning in life and history; the critique of existing society and of modernity; the sense of individuality and the search for authenticity; the sense of community and the importance of "being-with-others"; the nature of ethics and the importance of political commitment and engagement in society; the meaning and significance of love and friendship; resistance, resilience, and the struggle to resist to conformism and pressures; individuality, subjectivity, personal identity, and the question concerning free will; the existence or not of progress in human history; the mystery of death and the finiteness of the human

---

[13] Pearl Jam, "Love Boat Captain," in *Riot Act* (2002).
[14] Pearl Jam, "Thumbing My Way," in *Riot Act* (2002).

condition; spirituality and the human being's (often problematic) openness to the divine; the relationship with mass society, the culture industry, the star system, and fashion; the relation between Pearl Jam and other musicians and bands of the "grunge" movement or style, especially Nirvana.

Added to this, central issues in Pearl Jam songs and also in their choices and behavior towards the music industry also concern the condition of the artist in late capitalist society: the fight against censorship; the struggle to develop more democratic attitude and values; the adoption of a "straight edge" philosophy and lifestyle; and the attempt to be in the society and in the culture industry but without being passively subjugated to it. Finally, many of their extra-musical activities, such as their commitment to politics, ecology, education, feminism, and human rights are also worthy of being included in the list of the topics that deserve being paid attention to in the context of an inquiry into the "philosophy of Pearl Jam." In fact, these extra-musical parts of the life of the band have contributed in many ways and have played a huge role throughout the decades in defining the band's identity and the unique sense of community that, as noted above, is so strong and deeply rooted among Pearl Jam fans.

Finally, from a methodological point of view, we would like to explain to the readers of *Pearl Jam and Philosophy* that the aim of our essays is to offer different interpretations of what we may call the "philosophy of Pearl Jam" or, more precisely (and less emphatically), of some philosophical aspects and implications that are present in many of Pearl Jam's songs. In the contributions collected in the present book the authors have thus intentionally adopted an interpretive approach that, while it aims to be faithful to the lyrics of Pearl Jam songs, the "spirit" of their music, and the history of the band, nevertheless ventures an attempt at drawing explicit comparisons between rock songs and philosophical writings, sometimes deviating from the *mens auctoris*, i.e., the original meaning that the authors appear to have intended. Of course, this might raise some questions of literary hermeneutics and validity in interpretation, but it was not our intention, as authors of this book and philosophical interpreters of the songs of Pearl Jam, to specifically examine these problems here.[15] So, our aim in the contributions collected in the present book is not that of presenting the contents of the songs of Pearl Jam, from *Ten* (1991) to *Gigaton* (2020), as if they formed a

---

[15] See Maurizio Ferraris, *Storia dell'ermeneutica* (Milano: Bompiani, 1988), 361–87.

sort of complete philosophical system, which would be obviously silly and would easily fall prey to an objection of "overinterpretation."[16] Nevertheless, all authors have attempted to identify and bring to light a certain philosophical spirit that, in our view, is present in many Pearl Jam songs. In lieu of the search for systematic unity and absolute coherence, which would be out of place in the case of a philosophical interpretation of the lyrics of rock songs (not to mention the verses of a poem, or the figures of a novel), what we have tried to construct is rather something like a figure, in which certain concepts "enter ... into a constellation."[17] In doing this, some of the authors of *Pearl Jam and Philosophy* have been especially inspired by the conception of philosophical interpretation offered by Theodor W. Adorno, which relies, among other things, on the important role played by "exact fantasy" and which understands interpretation as the authentic methodology of philosophy, in contrast to "the idea of science [which] is research": "[t]he point of interpretive philosophy," as Adorno argues, "is to construct keys, before which reality springs open."[18]

The lyrics of many of Pearl Jam songs are philosophically and also literarily rich, i.e., with profound concepts and meanings, rich in metaphors and in references to the things and events that can make a life meaningful or meaningless, worthy of being lived or not. With the present book it is thus our aim to bring together the contributions of some distinguished academic scholars able to cut in a unique way across different topics, contents, questions, and approaches, contributing to the idea that, on the one side, popular music can be (and indeed should be) a subject of great interest for philosophy today, while on the other side, philosophy can be (and indeed should be) of great interest for all listeners of popular music and for fans of single artists or bands. In fact, rigorous and at the same time original philosophical interpretations can shed light on aspects and dimensions of certain songs or certain live performances or certain music events that otherwise, i.e., without an accurate and adequate interpretation, would remain unintelligible or obscure even to the most passionate and careful "aficionados."

* * *

---

[16] See Umberto Eco, *Interpretation and Overinterpretation* (Cambridge: Cambridge University Press, 1992).
[17] Theodor W. Adorno, "The Actuality of Philosophy," *Telos* 31 (1977): 126, 130–1.
[18] Ibid., 126, 130–1.

We would like to thank Leah and Rachel, our editors at Bloomsbury, for their patience and enthusiasm in bringing our idea to life, Alessandra Limer for her precious help in finding the right image for the book cover, and Karen Pals for her kind and generous assistance. We are also grateful to our group of authors, who honored us with their participation, professionalism, and competence. Stefano Marino would like to dedicate this book to his mom Enrica and his dad Giuseppe, who taught him to love music in his childhood, supported and encouraged him to play drums and form a rock band in his teens, and tolerated some of his excesses and "teenage angst" during his sometimes troubled youth. Andrea Schembari would like to dedicate the volume to his mother Pina (even though in 1996 she prevented him from leaving for Rome to attend what should have been his first Pearl Jam concert), and his father Paolo: their cheerful and delicate humming the songs of their youth at home still accompanies him at present, and it reminds him where his love for words in music comes from. Together, we would also like to thank all our dearest friends and colleagues scattered between Sicily, Bologna, and Szczecin, who enthusiastically encouraged, followed and helped us in the creation of the volume: their names cannot all appear here, but they are well established in our thoughts.

Bibliography

Adorno, Theodor W. "The Actuality of Philosophy," translated by Benjamin Snow. *Telos* 31 (1977): 120–33.

Campbell, Colin J. "Carry My Body: 'Profane Redemption' and Fugazi." In *Adorno and Popular Music: A Constellation of Perspectives*, edited by Colin J. Campbell, Samir Gandesha, and Stefano Marino, 105–22. Milano-Udine: Mimesis International, 2019.

Cook, Roger F. and Gerd Gemünden (eds). *The Cinema of Wim Wenders: Image, Narrative, and the Postmodern Condition*. Detroit: Wayne State University Press, 1997.

Dotto, Simone. *Pearl Jam. Still Alive. Testi commentati*. Roma: Arcana, 2014.

Eco, Umberto. *Interpretation and Overinterpretation*, edited by Stefan Collini. Cambridge: Cambridge University Press, 1992.

Ferraris, Maurizio. *Storia dell'ermeneutica*. Milano: Bompiani, 1988.

Givony, Ronen. *Not For You: Pearl Jam and the Present Tense*. New York: Bloomsbury Academic, 2020.

Gracyk, Theodore. *Rhythm and Noise: An Aesthetics of Rock*. Durham, NC: Duke University Press, 1996.

Gracyk, Theodore. *I Wanna Be Me: Rock Music and the Politics of Identity*. Philadelphia, PA: Temple University Press, 2001.

Gracyk, Theodore. *Listening to Popular Music: Or, How I Learned to Stop Worrying and Love Led Zeppelin*. Ann Arbor, MI: University of Michigan Press, 2007.

Harkins, Thomas E. and Bernard M. Corbett. *Pearl Jam FAQ: All That's Left to Know About Seattle's Most Enduring Band*. Milwaukee: Backbeat Books, an imprint of Hal Leonard Corporation, 2016.

Neely, Kim. *Five Against One: The Pearl Jam Story*. New York: Penguin Books, 1998.

Vedder, Eddie. "Foreword." In William Snyder and Eddie Vedder, *Join Together (With the Band)*, 86. Chicago: Press Syndication Group, 2018.

Villa, Luca, and Daria Moretti. *Pearl Jam Evolution*. Tricase: Youcanprint, 2016.

Wenders, Wim. "Everything I Loved I Had to Defend." *The Talks*, January 29, 2014. Available online: http://the-talks.com/interview/wim-wenders (accessed March 26, 2021).

Wenner, Jann (ed.). *Pearl Jam: The Ultimate Guide to Their Music & Legend*. New York: Rolling Stone, 2017.

Sources

All lyrics of Pearl Jam and Eddie Vedder songs quoted in this book are based either on the versions available on the band's official website (https://pearljam.com/music/songs) or on album liner notes.

Pearl Jam

Studio Albums

Ten (Epic Records, 1991).
VS. (Epic Records, 1993).
Vitalogy (Epic Records, 1994).
No Code (Epic Records, 1996).
Yield (Epic Records, 1998).
Binaural (Epic Records, 2000).
Riot Act (Epic Records, 2002).
Pearl Jam (J Records, 2006).
Backspacer (Monkeywrench Records, 2009).
Lightning Bolt (Monkeywrench Records, 2013).
Gigaton (Monkeywrench Records, 2020).

Compilations

Lost Dogs (Epic Records, 2003).
Rearviewmirror (Greatest Hits 1991–2003) (Epic Records, 2004).
Pearl Jam Twenty (Columbia Records, 2011).

Eddie Vedder

Into the Wild (J Records, 2006).

1

Contingency, (In)significance, and the All-Encompassing Trip: Pearl Jam and the Question of the Meaning of Life

Stefano Marino

For Valeria, with love: for our *Pearl Jam concert in Milano, June 22, 2000.*

For Emi and Simo, with friendship: for the hundreds of times that we listened together to "State of Love and Trust."

Introduction: Interpretations and constellations

As has already been explained in the final paragraphs of the Introduction to this book, the essays collected in the present volume—including this essay—aim to offer interpretations of what we may call the "philosophy of Pearl Jam." And, as has already been said, a philosophical enterprise of this kind should not be understood as the search for systematic unity and absolute coherence in the lyrics of the songs of Pearl Jam from *Ten* to *Gigaton*, but rather as the attempt to construct something like a figure in which certain concepts enter into a *constellation* (following here some insights on philosophical interpretation provided by Theodor W. Adorno). In the specific case of the present contribution on the "philosophy of Pearl Jam," the constellation that I will try to construct is formed by such concepts as contingency, (in)significance, the question of the meaning of life, and the idea of the all-encompassing. This conceptual constellation orbits around the question concerning questioning itself, and we will see that it ultimately leads in the direction of a way of thinking that promises a post-metaphysical rehabilitation of the dimension of time: what Eddie Vedder and Pearl Jam, according to my interpretation, have invoked in their music as the present tense.

The all-encompassing trip: Existential, historical, and metaphysical implications

"Are we getting something out of this all-encompassing trip?"[1] This is the looming question posed by Pearl Jam in "Present Tense," perhaps the most explicitly philosophical song in a catalogue that is abundant with songs rich in philosophical questions. In fact, in a previous song, "Garden," Pearl Jam had suggested precisely that their intention was not to question the meaning of human existence as such. My interpretation of the lines "I don't question / Our existence / I just question / Our modern needs"[2] is that they limit themselves to questioning the needs and values of human beings who live in increasingly reified and commodified societies, ones that favor the adoption of an unnatural and artificial way of life: namely, in societies in which apparently (and needlessly) it has become harder to "find an approach and a way to live."[3]

However, what apparently emerges from the third line of "Present Tense" is a broader and more ambitious proposition than a simple question concerning our modern needs. It is a more totalizing question ("I don't know anything, I question everything,"[4] as Pearl Jam also sing in a recent song) and, above all, it is a genuinely existential question, i.e., something that directly questions our existence and dares to pose the very question of the meaning of life. We could venture a philosophical comparison here: first, to relate the fundamental question of "Present Tense" to Martin Heidegger's *Being and Time*, with its radical way of formulating "the question of the meaning of being" by starting from the "guiding look at being [that] grows out of the average understanding of being in which we are always already involved and *which ultimately belongs to the essential constitution of Da-sein itself*."[5] And second, to connect the more limited question of "Garden" to Hans-Georg Gadamer's *Truth and Method*, with its less radical and more "urbanized" version of philosophical hermeneutics, one that shifts attention from the question of the meaning of being in all its vastness to the more limited question concerning the significance of the humanist

---

[1] Pearl Jam, "Present Tense," in *No Code* (1996).
[2] Pearl Jam, "Garden," in *Ten* (1991).
[3] Pearl Jam, "Present Tense."
[4] Pearl Jam, "Superblood Wolfmoon," in *Gigaton* (2020).
[5] Martin Heidegger, *Being and Time* (Albany, NY: SUNY Press, 1996, §2), 3, 6.

tradition in the increasingly disenchanted techno-scientific civilization of the present.[6]

The question about getting something out of the all-encompassing trip of life is undoubtedly a very deep one, which explicitly addresses existential problems but which is also potentially rich in philosophical-historical or metaphysical implications. A lot depends, among other things, on the way in which one understands the concept of the all-encompassing trip. If we understand it as referring to the life of an individual, then it is easy to interpret the question as focused on whether or not our singular life, the individual life of each and every one of us, appears to have some meaning or not, i.e., appears as meaningful or meaningless to he/she who is living it. From this point of view, as I said, the question raised in "Present Tense" can be summarized and briefly defined as the question concerning the meaning of life. The question formulated in these very simple terms might perhaps fall prey to the objection of a certain naivety, but it is one that a rigorous philosopher like Theodor W. Adorno nevertheless recognized in the mid-1960s as one of those fundamental questions that lead human beings to philosophize, even in an age of disillusion and nihilism like ours: "[t]he metaphysical categories live on, secularized, in ... the question of the meaning of life."[7]

However, we can also understand the all-encompassing trip as metaphorically referring to the wholeness of human history from its inception to the present age, or even as referring to what we may call "the totality of existent things (*das Ganze des Seienden*)."[8] After all, the encompassing (or the embracing: *das Umgreifende*) was precisely the concept coined by Karl Jaspers to designate reality as a whole in its fullness and richness, i.e., the ultimate experienceable horizon, which is surely hard to describe in its essence and to conceptualize— even to the extent of being ineffable and unspeakable—but which we nevertheless know as a real presence and by which we feel constantly surrounded.[9] If so, then

---

[6] Hans-Georg Gadamer, *Truth and Method* (London-New York: Continuum, 2004), 3–37. I borrow the concept of "urbanization," as applied to the relationship between the philosophies of Heidegger and Gadamer, from Jürgen Habermas' famous essay "Hans-Georg Gadamer: Urbanizing the Heideggerian Province" (in Habermas, *Philosophical-political Profiles* [Cambridge, MA: The MIT Press, 1983], 189–98). On these topics, I allow myself to remind the reader of my works *Gadamer and the Limits of the Modern Techno-scientific Civilization* (Bern: Peter Lang, 2011) and *Aesthetics, Metaphysics, Language: Essays on Heidegger and Gadamer* (Newcastle upon Tyne: Cambridge Scholars Publishing, 2015).
[7] Theodor W. Adorno, *Negative Dialectics* (London-New York: Routledge, 2004), 376.
[8] Gadamer, *The Gadamer Reader: A Bouquet of the Later Writings* (Evanston, IL: Northwestern University Press, 2007), 382.
[9] See Karl Jaspers, *Von der Wahrheit* (München: Piper, 1947). On this topic, see Ludovica Neri's recent book *Il problema della "logica filosofica" nel Nachlass di Karl Jaspers* (Milano-Udine: Mimesis, 2021).

it becomes clear that the question asked by Pearl Jam in "Present Tense" can be interpreted not only in an existential way, strictly focusing on the meaning of our individual lives, but also in a philosophical-historical way, or even in a metaphysical way: namely as an ambitious question, focused on whether human history in its entirety, or even being in its totality, has any meaning.

Are we learning something about this immense journey? What are the conditions and limits, and above all what is the meaning, of the life of human beings in this world, i.e., of our "being-in-the-world"? How did this all-encompassing trip start and where will it lead us? We are the "first mammal[s] to wear pants," of course, but can we "do the evolution"?[10] Or are *evolution* and *progress* only ideologies and illusions, and our lives (both as individuals and as humankind) directionless and meaningless? As critical philosophers of history like Walter Benjamin and Theodor W. Adorno suggest, we should probably be more careful and indeed suspicious than we usually are in conceiving of human history as automatically guided by the progress of rationality and the achievement of our goals. Perhaps we "only [see] the progress in mastering nature" and "not the retrogression of society"[11] that simultaneously occurs, and so, "[w]hen progress could be plausible / In reverse we curse ourselves / By thinking we're infallible / We are tempting fate instead."[12] If progress is not linear, straightforward, one-sided, and guaranteed, as we often like to think, but is instead uncertain and contradictory, then it makes sense to claim with Benjamin that "[t]here is no document of culture which is not at the same time a document of barbarism"[13] (an idea which can be profitably compared to some views on history offered by critical historians like Howard Zinn[14]). Pearl Jam's lyrics, "[t]ell the captain / 'This boat's not safe / And we're drowning.' / Turns out / He's the one making waves,"[15] might be metaphorically compared to Horkheimer's and Adorno's incisive interpretation of Odysseus, the hero of Homer's *Odyssey*, as the perfect personification of instrumental rationality. His behavior as captain of the ship

---

[10] Pearl Jam, "Do the Evolution," in *Yield* (1998). As is well-known, this song was influenced by the ideas presented in Daniel Quinn's philosophical novel *Ishmael* (1992) (see Simone Dotto, *Pearl Jam. Still Alive. Testi commentati* [Roma: Arcana, 2014], 181–6). Eddie Vedder cited Quinn's book as an influence on the lyrics of *Yield*, and Quinn, in turn, responded to the album's significance in relation to the book on his website.
[11] Walter Benjamin, "On the Concept of History," in *Selected Writings. Volume 4* (Cambridge, MA-London: Harvard University Press, 2006), 393.
[12] Pearl Jam, "Infallible," in *Lightning Bolt* (2013).
[13] Benjamin, "On the Concept of History," 392.
[14] See Eddie Vedder's note on the passing of Zinn published on the band's official website.
[15] Pearl Jam, "Green Disease," in *Riot Act* (2002).

"in face of the Sirens" represents "a prescient allegory of the dialectic of enlightenment" in which reason, due to its dialectical and paradoxical nature, is "the vehicle of both progress and regression"[16] at the same time.

Faced with the abovementioned existential, metaphysical, and *geschichtsphilosophisch* problems and doubts, it appears reasonable as well as honest to admit: "Got all these questions / Don't know who I could even ask."[17] As is well-known, according to Immanuel Kant "[h]uman reason . . . is burdened with questions which it cannot dismiss, since they are given to it as problems by the nature of reason itself, but which it also cannot answer, since they transcend every capacity of human reason."[18] In Pearl Jam's original treatment of this topic, it always feels like "a question is forming and the answers far,"[19] so that, at the end of the day, "[q]uestions rise and answers fall, . . . insurmountable."[20] For such finite, fallible, and imperfect creatures as we are, with our limited intellect and "[our] small self,"[21] perhaps it is no great surprise to discover that "[t]he questions linger overhead."[22]

Questions rise, answers fall: The primacy of questioning

Whatever the precise interpretation of Vedder's concept of the all-encompassing trip really is, what is of prime importance to this essay is the centrality of questioning that clearly emerges, not only from the abovementioned line of "Present Tense," but also from the song as a whole and from many other songs by Pearl Jam. Precisely questioning can be considered as the very essence of philosophy, both from a purely theoretical and a strictly historical point of view, inasmuch as the origin of Western philosophy itself lies in the unprecedented inclination of the first Greek philosophers to raise questions. As noted by Karl Jaspers in a 1950 talk on the concept of the encompassing (which, again, may remind us of the all-encompassing trip sung by Pearl Jam): "Philosophy began with the question: What is?"[23] In a similar way, Ernst Cassirer noted that:

---

[16] Max Horkheimer and Theodor W. Adorno, *Dialectic of Enlightenment* (Stanford, CA: Stanford University Press 2002), 27.
[17] Pearl Jam, "I Got Id," in *Merkin Ball* (1995).
[18] Immanuel Kant, *Critique of Pure Reason* (Cambridge: Cambridge University Press, 1998, AVII), 99.
[19] Pearl Jam, "Gone," in *Pearl Jam* (2006).
[20] Pearl Jam, "Love Boat Captain," in *Riot Act* (2002).
[21] Pearl Jam, "Sometimes," in *No Code* (1996).
[22] Pearl Jam, "Thumbing My Way," in *Riot Act* (2002).
[23] See Karl Jaspers' 1950 talk on the encompassing (*das Umgreifende*), available on YouTube.

Aristotle called Socrates the discoverer of the concept, because he first recognized the relation between the particular and the general—which is expressed through the concept—as worthy of examination. In the *question* of the τί ἔστι, which he addressed to the concept, he saw the germ of a new *meaning* of the general *question* concerning being.[24]

A very quick look at the observations on this topic offered by some leading figures in twentieth-century philosophy is instructive. For Hans-Georg Gadamer, for example, the hermeneutical experience, i.e., the experience of the simultaneous universality and finitude of the human understanding, and the "historically effected consciousness" that is especially disclosed by language, "implies the primacy of dialogue and the structure of question and answer."[25] According to Gadamer, "there is in fact an infinite dialogue in questioning as well as answering, in whose space word and answer stand. Everything that is said stands in such space."[26] In other words, everything that characterizes human thinking and language stands in the space disclosed by a *question* that searches for its answer(s). In a similar philosophical context (namely, that of a phenomenological-hermeneutical ontology) but more radically than Gadamer, Heidegger famously thought that in philosophy "everything is placed ... in relation to *questioning*," and he even interpreted the entire development of Western metaphysics in light of the distinction between two fundamental questions: "the basic question (*Grundfrage*)," i.e., "the question of being (*das Sein*) [which] is the question of the truth of being (*das Seyn*)," and "the guiding question (*Leitfrage*)," i.e., "the question of beings (*das Seiende*)."[27]

Ludwig Wittgenstein, with his very different but no less rigorous philosophical style, stressed the central role of *questioning* in human life and especially in philosophy, arguing that "[t]he philosopher's treatment of a question is like the treatment of an illness"[28] and that philosophy is typically "tormented by questions which bring *itself* in question" (so that, for him, a "real discovery" in philosophy

---

[24] Ernst Cassirer, *Kant's Life and Thought* (Yale, NH: Yale University Press, 1981), 276 (my emphasis). Cassirer clearly refers here to Aristotle, *Metaph.* I 6, 987b 1–4; XIII 4, 1078b 18–31; XIII 9, 1086b 3–5 (see *The Complete Works of Aristotle. Vol. 2* [Princeton, NJ: Princeton University Press, 1991], 13, 189, 202). I would like to thank Laura La Bella, a very expert scholar of Aristotle, for her help in finding the exact reference to these passages from Aristotle's *Metaphysics*.
[25] Gadamer, *Truth and Method*, 363.
[26] Gadamer, *Philosophical Hermeneutics* (Berkeley-Los Angeles-London: University of California Press, 1976), 67.
[27] Heidegger, *Contributions to Philosophy (Of the Event)* (Bloomington, IN: Indiana University Press, 2012, §2), 8, 10.
[28] Ludwig Wittgenstein, *Philosophical Investigations* (Oxford: Basil Blackwell, 1986, §255), 91.

would be "the one that makes me capable of stopping doing philosophy when I want to," i.e., "[t]he one that gives philosophy peace"[29]). For Wittgenstein, questioning, beside other experiences and human practices, is "as much a part of our natural history as walking, eating, drinking, playing,"[30] namely, something that defines the very nature of human beings and which is a peculiarly defining feature for philosophers: that is, for those bizarre persons whose "thoughts are too big for [their] size"[31] and whose minds are often overwhelmed by "thoughts [they] can't help thinking."[32] Pearl Jam provide, in the lyrics just cited, two striking portraits of precisely what distinguishes the philosopher, whether an ancient thinker like Socrates or modern philosophers like Kierkegaard or Nietzsche.

What I have defined so far as "questioning," interpreting it as the primary component of all genuine philosophical thinking, also seems to be a fundamental aspect of Pearl Jam's catalogue of songs. In general, questioning—that is, raising questions, posing issues, opening up the logical space for questioning things, disclosing a free space for thinking that allows us to develop a critical spirit and radically put the existing reality into question—thus seems to correspond to a, or the, fundamental dimension of philosophizing. Indeed, if there is something characteristic of philosophy in all places and all times, it is probably the primacy of questioning. Apropos of questioning, for example, Heidegger writes:

> Questioning arouses immediately the suspicion of amounting to an empty, obstinate attachment to the uncertain, undecided, and undecidable. Questioning appears as a backtracking of "knowledge" into idle meditation. It seems to be narrowing and hampering, if not even negating. Nevertheless: in questioning resides the tempestuous advance that says "yes" to what has not been mastered and the broadening out into ponderable, yet unexplored, realms. What reigns here is a self-surpassing into something above ourselves. To question is to be liberated for what, while remaining concealed, is compelling.[33]

Heidegger's philosophy challenged the popular understanding of questioning as "idle meditation," as something "narrowing and hampering, if not even negating." It is true, of course, that the power of negation (or more precisely, in terms of post-Hegelian dialectical philosophies, "determinate negation") fuels

---

[29] Ibid. (§133), 51.
[30] Ibid. (§25), 12.
[31] Pearl Jam, "Off He Goes," in *No Code* (1996).
[32] Pearl Jam, "Nothingman," in *Vitalogy* (1994).
[33] Heidegger, *Contributions to Philosophy* (§4), 10.

philosophical reasoning, responding to a natural tendency to critically question everything and pursuing what Marcuse called "[the] negation of the realistic-conformist mind."[34] But philosophy's resistance, its egalitarian insistence ("not one man [can be] greater than the sum"), is in the end "not a negative thought" but "positive."[35] In other words, the negative dimension of philosophical questioning may surely lead us to radically put into question our common assumptions about ourselves and every aspect of the existing reality, as Plato's allegory of the cave, Descartes' hyperbolic doubt, and many other famous examples taken from the whole history of Western philosophy clearly show. However, after doing this, i.e., after putting into question our usual criteria of orientation, philosophical questioning is also aimed at finding new orienting principles to explore the reality and to better cope with it—perhaps even to change it. From this point of view, genuine philosophical questioning is never merely destructive or negative but always entails also a constructive (or "positive, positive, positive") dimension.

If few thinkers in the history of Western philosophy have prioritized the centrality of questioning in the way that Heidegger or Gadamer did, in a somehow analogous way we might say that few artists in the history of contemporary popular music have emphasized the centrality of questioning the way Pearl Jam have done. Just a few examples taken from their discography show an abundance of songs rich in philosophical content, and especially questions. The lines, "Come to send, not condescend / Transcendental consequence / Is to transcend where we are / Who are we? Who we are,"[36] for example, express what we may call the question of personal identity and definition of the human ("Who are we?"). Regarding the same or closely analogous questions, resounding with philosophical implications at various levels, we hear: "What is human? . . . What is more?"[37]; "I'll find my way from wrong, what's real?"[38]; "O who planted all the

---

[34] Herbert Marcuse, *The Aesthetic Dimension: Toward a Critique of Marxist Aesthetics* (Boston: Beacon Press, 1978), 9. To be precise, Marcuse's discourse on "[the] negation of the realistic-conformist mind" is specifically referred in this context to "the aesthetic form" of the work of art: however, this discourse is also appropriate and coherent if referred to the critical function of philosophical questioning-thinking. If, for a philosopher like Marcuse, "[t]he truth of art lies in its power to break the monopoly of established reality (i.e., of those who established it) to define what is real" (Ibid.), we can say that the same holds true also for philosophy, according to the model of critical theory that, after Horkheimer's seminal essay from 1937, thinkers like Marcuse and Adorno also adopted as their own. See Horkheimer, *Critical Theory: Selected Essays* (New York: Continuum, 2002), 188–243.
[35] Pearl Jam, "Dance of the Clairvoyants," in *Gigaton* (2020).
[36] Pearl Jam, "Who You Are," in *No Code* (1996).
[37] Pearl Jam, "Severed Hand," in *Pearl Jam* (2006).
[38] Pearl Jam, "Low Light," in *Yield* (1998).

devils seeds? / And what's the truth?"[39]; "Always something and never nothing / Isn't that the way we're taught to be?"[40]—all of which unintentionally and unconsciously summarize centuries of meditation on nothingness from Parmenides to contemporary philosophy: "Why is there something rather than nothing?"[41] In this context, a song like "Education"—with its characteristic invitation to question "my education" or "my own equation," and with its typical insistence in asking whether my education is "who I am now" and "what does it show," or whether my own equation is "relevant somehow"—appears as a particularly significant example of what I am trying to describe as Pearl Jam's radical and uncompromising poetics of questioning: "A wild world, figuring out the answers / I'll be in my own dance and I, I, yeah, I, I . . . / Could be, the truth it becomes you / I'm a seed, wondering why it grows."[42]

Apropos of this, it must be noted that, quite significantly and also surprisingly, the very beginning of the career of Pearl Jam, or at least of their worldwide success in the early 1990s alternative-rock scene, depended to a great extent on a song intrinsically characterized by what we may call a strictly philosophical question. In "Alive," Pearl Jam's famous hit single from their debut album *Ten* (1991), the main character of the song, after hearing the words announcing him that he is still alive, abruptly and dramatically says: "Oh, and do I deserve to be / Is that the question / And if so . . . if so . . . who answers . . . who answers . . ."[43] It is clear that the question whether we deserve to be alive or not, whether we have an intrinsic and innate right to live or not, whether we can go on living or not, is an existentially decisive question, above and beyond its delimited meaning in the specific context of the story narrated in "Alive." This is clear enough in our sense that horrible things that happen every day in all parts of the world, that "the horror goes on anyway, ad infinitum," a knowledge which makes "our feelings resist any claim of the positivity of existence as sanctimonious, as wronging the victims."[44] It is also clear that nobody can claim to have a final answer for such a question, not least because it seems unlikely that anyone could (or should) establish once and for all a definitive criterion for who and what is worthy of existence. Hence it is right that the question should remain open, and

---

[39] Pearl Jam, "Wash," in *Lost Dogs* (2003).
[40] Pearl Jam, "Lightning Bolt," in *Lightning Bolt* (2013).
[41] See Roy Sorensen, "Nothingness," *The Stanford Encyclopedia of Philosophy* (Spring 2020 Edition), Edward N. Zalta, ed.
[42] Pearl Jam, "Education," in *Lost Dogs* (2003).
[43] Pearl Jam, "Alive," in *Ten* (1991).
[44] Adorno, *Negative Dialectics*, 286, 361, 363.

that this famous passage from one of Pearl Jam's most iconic songs ends with a dramatic question: "Who answers?"

Centuries and centuries of philosophical and religious meditations on this topic, from Greek tragedies and biblical books, to ancient and medieval metaphysics, up to modern and contemporary philosophical and theological speculations, have left unanswered the question as to whether we deserve to be alive or not, and what it even means, precisely, "to deserve" in this context. Looking at contemporary philosophy, in developing his meditations on the changed significance of metaphysics in the contemporary situation (i.e., for him, in the post-Auschwitz human condition), Adorno emphatically and dramatically claimed: "The guilt of a life which purely as a fact will strangle other life … is irreconcilable with living."[45] A very different philosopher from Adorno, Robert Nozick, in an analogous context (i.e., in the chapter on the Holocaust of his book *The Examined Life*) claimed that in our time, after an event like the Shoah, which is "so momentous an event that we cannot yet grasp its full significance"—so that "it is not clear what responses would serve: remembering it, constantly being haunted, working to prevent its like from ever occurring again, a sea of tears?"—"[it] would not be a *special* tragedy if humankind ended."[46] "I do not mean that humanity *deserves* this to happen," Nozick explains; rather:

> earlier, it would have constituted an *additional* tragedy, one beyond that to the individual people involved, if human history and the human species had ended, but now that history and that species have become stained, its loss would now be no *special* loss above and beyond the losses to the individuals involved. Humanity has lost its claim to continue.… Although we are not all responsible for what those who acted and stood by did, we are all stained.… That species, the one that has committed *that*, has lost its worthy status. Not—let me repeat—that the species deserves to be destroyed; it simply no longer deserves *not* to be. Humanity has desanctified itself.… Only human action could redeem us, if anything can. But can anything? … Perhaps what we need to do is help produce *another*, better species or make way for it; can we regain the status of deserving to continue only by stepping aside?[47]

Viewed from a philosophical and indeed a metaphysical perspective, the question raised by Pearl Jam as to whether one deserves to be alive or not is

---

[45] Adorno, *Negative Dialectics*, 364.
[46] Robert Nozick, *The Examined Life: Philosophical Meditations* (New York: Simon & Schuster, 1990), 236–8.
[47] Ibid., 238–40.

something like Nozick's unanswerable question. If they are interpreted as being included in a conceptual constellation of this kind, lyrics like "[t]he answers are fatal"[48] or "I won't wait / For answers / You can't keep / Me here"[49] are clearly understandable and make perfect sense. However, the unanswerable character of the question raised by a song like "Alive" (and, in a different way, by the philosophical texts of such thinkers as Adorno, Nozick, and many others) clearly does not depend on a logical mistake, a trivial misunderstanding, or a subjective incapacity to find an answer. Rather, it depends on the objective stringency and the philosophically demanding character of the question itself. As once noted by Franco Volpi in his outstanding monograph on nihilism, "real philosophical questions have a history but have no answer."[50] As recently noted by Hans-Peter Krüger with specific reference to another leading figure of twentieth-century philosophy, namely Helmuth Plessner, philosophy and, more generally, "[t]he humanities as sciences cannot dispense with a 'guarantee of answerability' of their questions in the sense that their questions have to be formulated so as to be 'reasonable' and to 'allow for decisions.'"[51] At the same time, though, "they must dispense with a guarantee of 'being answered' through experiment and measurement," as it typically happens in the field of natural sciences: "Compared with the natural-scientific guarantee of answer, the questions of the humanities are 'open questions.'"[52]

On this basis, it makes perfect sense to leave open the question dramatically asked in "Alive," and instead of providing a positive but fictitious answer, to honestly limit oneself to repeating the question: "Who answers?" As it happens, a few years later the existential question raised by "Alive" would be evoked and further problematized in the song "I'm Open," where we hear: "A man ... [is] alive, but feels absolutely nothing / So, is he?"[53] What does it exactly mean to be alive in a context like this? And, once again, who can answer such questions? These are, for me, the radical questions that a song like "I'm Open," following in the footsteps of "Alive," raises. This is a profound dimension of *questioning* that

---

[48] Pearl Jam, "Fatal," in *Lost Dogs* (2003).
[49] Pearl Jam, "Can't Keep," in *Riot Act* (2002).
[50] Franco Volpi, *Il nichilismo* (Roma-Bari: Laterza, 2005), 7.
[51] Hans-Peter Krüger, "Modern Research Procedures and their Conflicts in View of Dignity: Helmuth Plessner's First Transformation of the Kantian *Critique of the Power of Judgment*", in *Kant's 'Critique of Aesthetic Judgment' in the 20th Century: A Companion to Its Main Interpretations*, Stefano Marino and Pietro Terzi, eds (Berlin: De Gruyter, 2020), 111.
[52] Ibid.
[53] Pearl Jam, "I'm Open," in *No Code* (1996).

the "philosophy of Pearl Jam" ambitiously and significantly discloses. The question remains thematic, even in a more positive and constructive song like "Grievance," which a few years later would attempt to offer an answer to the question about being alive: "I will feel alive ... as long as I am free ..."[54]

The meaning of living in the present tense

In the context of this general primacy of questioning, a special role is played, both in philosophy and in the songs of Pearl Jam, by the frequently asked question concerning the meaning of life. However, returning to "Present Tense," it is interesting and intriguing to note that the song is essentially characterized by the contrast between the verses—which open up some existential (or even metaphysical) questions with reference to the inspiration offered by gazing at a "tree [that] bends," to the innate tendency of the human being to wonder "how [our] life ends," and to the belief (or perhaps the hope and desire) that "the road ahead" may ascend "off into the light"[55]—and the refrains, which provide a fascinating, and yet to some extent problematic, answer to those questions. In fact, the answer to such questions that we find in the refrains of "Present Tense" has to do—to put it briefly—with ceasing to spend one's time in solitude and isolation, re-digesting one's regrets, and deciding not to abandon oneself to bitterness, resignation, and remorse. The refrains of the song appear, in other words, to propose a shift in attitude, one that consists of coming to terms with oneself (including one's own fragility, vulnerability, limitedness, and imperfection), of realizing that it is possible to accept and forgive oneself, and of understanding that it ultimately "[m]akes much more sense, to live in the present tense."[56]

Now, if observed from the point of view of the different dimensions of temporality, namely the past, the present, and the future, Pearl Jam's answer to the question of what makes sense in the all-encompassing trip that our life is (i.e., the question of what is capable of conferring some meaning on human life) appears rigorously focused on the dimension of the present tense. A song like "Present Tense" discloses a perspective that is philosophically fascinating,

---

[54] Pearl Jam, "Grievance," in *Binaural* (2000).
[55] Pearl Jam, "Present Tense."
[56] Ibid.

stimulating, and original, but which may also appear existentially/metaphysically unusual and problematic, inasmuch as it seems to challenge some fundamental assumptions and views that have been quite typical in the tradition of Western culture. What is apparently challenged by the strong emphasis put on the dimension of the present in a song like "Present Tense" is especially the primacy of the temporal mode of the future in determining the perspective, and indeed the very possibility, of a meaningful experience of life, history, and being. In fact, although it would be obviously be a disproportionate generalization to claim that the whole tradition of Western philosophy has been characterized by a sort of primacy conferred to the temporal mode of the future, it is nevertheless possible to identify a widespread tendency, especially in the modern age, to emphasize the centrality of being projected to the future in the assessment of the value and meaning of existence.

This general view is obviously not valid for, nor applicable to, all the philosophical conceptions theorized by all Western thinkers in modernity. However, with the notable exceptions of such philosophers as Hegel—whose philosophical system is characterized by a circular logic and whose conception of the effective reality (*Wirklichkeit*) includes both the actuality of the present and the necessity of the past—or Nietzsche—who challenged the linear conception of time and provocatively restored a circular logic of temporality under the name of the eternal recurrence of the same—I think that the abovementioned primacy of the temporal mode of the future can be reasonably defined as one of the main trends in modern philosophy and culture.[57] This is especially true with regard to the typically modern centrality of (indeed, the veritable obsession with) progress that, as I have said, such Pearl Jam songs as "Do the Evolution" explicitly put into question.

Limiting myself to just a few examples of outstanding philosophers and historians of modern thought apropos of the question of temporality and what I have previously defined the primacy assigned to the dimension of the future, even a quick look at Heidegger's masterpiece *Being and Time* shows richly how much the belief in the very possibility of answering the question of the meaning of being and hence of finding some significance (rather than insignificance) in human existence depends on the *Dasein*'s ontologically grounded openness to

---

[57] I would like to thank Rolando Vitali for having offered me many stimulating insights about Hegel and Nietzsche on temporality in an email exchange that we had while I was writing the present essay on Pearl Jam.

the future. In particular, in such a fundamental section of *Being and Time* as Section 65 on temporality as the ontological meaning of care, Heidegger writes:

> What does *meaning* signify? Our inquiry encountered this phenomenon in the context of the analysis of understanding and interpretation. According to that analysis, meaning is that in which the intelligibility of something keeps itself, without coming into view explicitly and thematically. Meaning signifies that upon which the primary project is projected, that in terms of which something can be conceived in its possibility as what it is. Projecting discloses possibilities, that is, it discloses what makes something possible. To expose that upon which a project is projected, means to disclose what makes what is projected possible... With the question of the meaning of care, we are asking *what makes possible the totality of the articulated structural whole of care in the unity of its unfolded articulation*? Strictly speaking, meaning signifies the upon-which of the primary project of the understanding of being.... Beings "have" meaning only because, as being that has been disclosed beforehand, they become intelligible in the project of that being, that is, in terms of the upon-which of this project. The primary project of the understanding of being "gives" meaning.... What makes possible this authentic being-a-whole of Da-sein with regard to the unity of its articulated structural whole? Expressed formally and existentially, without constantly naming the complete structural content, anticipatory resoluteness is the *being toward* one's ownmost, eminent potentiality-of-being. Something like this is possible only in such way that Da-sein can come toward itself *at all* in its ownmost possibility and perdure the possibility as possibility in this letting-itself-come-toward-itself, that is, that it exists. Letting-come-toward-itself that perdures the eminent possibility is the primordial phenomenon of the *future*. If authentic or inauthentic *being toward-death* belongs to the being of Da-sein, this is possible only as *futural* ... Anticipation makes Da-sein *authentically* futural in such a way that anticipation itself is possible only in that Da-sein, *as existing*, always already comes toward itself, that is, is futural in its being in general.... We call the unified phenomenon of the future that makes present in the process of having been *temporality*. Only because Da-sein is determined as temporality does it make possible for itself the authentic potentiality-of-being-a-whole of anticipatory resoluteness which we characterized. *Temporality reveals itself as the meaning of authentic care.*[58]

At a more historical-philosophical level, relevant examples that can be mentioned in this context are, for instance, Karl Löwith's seminal book on modern

---

[58] Heidegger, *Being and Time* (§65), 297–300.

philosophies of history *Meaning in History* or Reinhart Koselleck's influential work on the semantics of historical time *Futures Past*. As convincingly explained by Löwith, indeed, "the idea of progress"—that surely represents one of the defining features of the modern worldview—"could become the leading principle for the understanding of history only within [a] primary horizon of the future," and the latter, in turn, is grounded on the religious conception of time as *kairos* that "opens the horizon for past as well as for future":

> The viewpoint of a Christian interpretation of history is fixed on the future as the temporal horizon of a definite purpose and goal; and all modern attempts to delineate history as a meaningful, though indefinite, progress toward fulfillment depend on this theological thought.... True, modern historical consciousness has discarded the Christian faith in a central even of absolute relevance, yet it maintains its logical antecedents and consequences, viz., the past as preparation and the future as consummation, thus reducing the history of salvation to the impersonal teleology of a progressive evolution in which every present stage is the fulfillment of past preparations.[59]

Koselleck, for his part—relying on the primacy assigned in the modern age to the temporal mode of the future, to the point of defining the disclosure of a particular horizon of expectation as the quintessential feature of modernity in general—explains:

> the more a particular time is experienced as a new temporality, as "modernity," the more that demands made of the future increase. Special attention is therefore devoted to a given present and its condition as a superseded former future. If a particular contemporary becomes aware of an increase in the weight of the future in his range of experience, this is certainly an effect of the technical-industrial transformation of a world that forces upon its inhabitants ever briefer intervals of time in which to gather new experiences and adapt to changes induced at an ever-increasing pace.... It was the philosophy of historical process which first detached early modernity from its past and, with a new future, inaugurated our modernity.... Progress opened up a future that transcended the hitherto predictable, natural space of time and experience, and thence—propelled by its own dynamic—provoked new, transnatural, long-term prognoses.[60]

---

[59] Karl Löwith, *Meaning in History* (Chicago-London: The University of Chicago Press, 1949), 84, 160, 186.

[60] Reinhart Koselleck, *Futures Past: On the Semantics of Historical Time* (New York: Columbia University Press, 2004), 3, 21–2. I would like to thank Alessandro Volpi for his valuable suggestions apropos of a potential use of Koselleck's semantics of historical time in the present context, i.e., in the context of an essay on Pearl Jam.

Of course, what I have defined so far as the primacy assigned at an existential or historical level to the temporal dimension of *future* in modern philosophy and culture—with an unprecedented emphasis on the faith in planning, possibility, progress, and fulfillment of our expectations as the only guarantee that something like meaning in life and history is possible[61]—does not imply the forgetting of the contemporaneousness of past, present, and future at the level of our inner-time consciousness. In fact, at least since St. Augustine, philosophers have been fully conscious of the inextricable intertwinement between the different dimensions of time, due to the fact that "the past is no more and the future is not yet," whereas "if the present were always present and never flowed away into the past, it would not be time at all, but eternity"[62]—something which, quite significantly, we can metaphorically find a secret and unconscious trace of in Pearl Jam's recent song "Dance of the Clairvoyants," where we find the somehow cryptic line: "the past is the present and the future's no more."[63]

Anyway, as I said, what I am focusing my attention on in this part of my essay is simply a certain primacy assigned in different epochs and different contexts to one or another dimension of temporality, which has been mostly the future in the modern and contemporary age. Whereas the "philosophy of Pearl Jam," in my interpretation, although obviously not ignoring the relevance of the past and the future, seems to privilege and favor the temporal mode of the present in relation to the question of the meaning of life. This is a temporal mode that, following St. Augustine's philosophy of time, could be even declared impossible or nonexistent, inasmuch as he famously writes:

> What then *is* time? If no one asks me, I know; if I want to explain it to a questioner, I do not know. But at any rate this much I dare affirm I know: that if nothing passed there would be no past time; if nothing were approaching, there would be no future time; if nothing were, there would be no present time... But if the present is only time, because it flows away into the past, how can we say that it *is*? For it is, only because it will cease to be. Thus we can affirm that time *is* only in that it tends towards not-being.[64]

---

[61] On this topic, see also Gadamer, "Notes on Planning for the Future," in *Hans-Georg Gadamer on Education, Poetry, and History: Applied Hermeneutics* (Albany, NY: SUNY Press, 1992), 165–80.
[62] Augustine, *Confessions* (Indianapolis-Cambridge: Hackett Publishing Company, Inc., 2006, Book 11, §XIV), 242.
[63] Pearl Jam, "Dance of the Clairvoyants."
[64] Augustine, *Confessions* (Book 11, §XIV), 242–3.

Beside the primacy that has been often assigned to the dimension of the future, when it comes to the question of the meaning of life, another usual assumption in modern philosophy is the one concerning the problematic character of our limitedness as human beings. In short, the undeniable fact of our imperfect, contingent, ephemeral, and limited nature sometimes appears as an obstacle for the achievement of something truly meaningful in our existence, i.e., of something that may allow us to claim that there is really meaning in human life and history. As noted by Richard Shusterman, for example, philosophers sometimes tend "to conclude the unreality of something from its ephemerality," which, as an argument, is clearly "[a] *non sequitur*" and cannot withstand a serious analysis but nevertheless "may seem convincing not only because it has a grand philosophical pedigree extending back to Parmenides, but also because it serves an equally strong psychological motive—our deep desire for stability."[65] As also observed by Robert Nozick, human beings typically expect their lives to have some value and meaning, and for him:

> [v]alue involves something's being integrated within its own boundaries, while meaning involves its having some connection beyond these boundaries. The problem of meaning itself is raised by the presence of limits. Thus, typically, people worry about the meaning of their lives when they see their existences as limited, perhaps because death will end them and so mark their final limit. To seek to give life meaning is to seek to transcend the limits of one's individual life. [However] [e]ven when we consider the universe as a whole, we can see it is limited. Thus, some people wonder how anything about human existence can have meaning if eventually, millions of years from now, it all will end in some massive heat death of the galaxy or universe. About any given thing, however wide, it seems we can stand back and ask what its meaning is. To find a meaning for it, then, we seem driven to find a link with yet another thing beyond its boundaries. And so a regress is launched. To stop this regress, we seem to need something that is intrinsically meaningful, something meaningful in itself, not by virtue of its connection with something else; or else we need something which is unlimited, from which we cannot step back, even in imagination, to wonder what *its* meaning is. Thus it was that religion seemed to provide a stopping place for questions about meaning, an ultimate foundation of meaning, by speaking of an infinite being which was not properly seen as limited, a being

---

[65] Richard Shusterman, *Pragmatist Aesthetics: Living Beauty, Rethinking Art* (Lanham-Boulder-New York-Oxford: Rowman & Littlefield, 2000), 179.

from which there could be no place to step back in order to see its limits, so that the question about *its* meaning could not even begin.[66]

Metaphysically redeemed: Contingency, finitude, and (in)significance

After having introduced in the previous sections these philosophical insights offered by some leading thinkers of the twentieth century—Heidegger, Gadamer, Wittgenstein, Löwith, Koselleck, Benjamin, Adorno, and Nozick—it is now time to return to the "philosophy of Pearl Jam" and draw some conclusions from what has been said until now and from other lines of their songs that are rich in philosophical content. According to my interpretation, there is something like a *fil rouge* in Pearl Jam's attempt to answer the question of the meaning of life, a line that connects the abovementioned primacy of the temporal mode of the present to their explicit acknowledgment of immanence, limitedness, imperfection, mortality, and contingency as defining elements of the human condition. As a matter of fact, strongly emphasizing the primacy of the temporal dimension of the present also means, at least implicitly, to stress and give prominence to the character of uncertainty, precariousness, ephemerality, and fleetingness of human life.

The fact that human life actually unfolds in the present (moment after moment, minute after minute, day after day), with the strong sensation that everything is transient and nothing really lasts, and thus with no real guarantees or certainties about the future, is captured by many penetrating lines from Pearl Jam songs, such as: "days like frame by frame, where do they go?"[67]; or: "[t]his life I love is going way too fast"[68]; or: "[n]o time to question … why'd nothing last … / Grasp and hold on … we're dyin' fast … / Soon be over."[69] After all, all that we know for certain about our own life can be condensed in the following simple but very forceful words: "I know I was born and I know that I'll die / The in between is mine."[70] What we authentically are, as finite and mortal human beings, is thus an "in between," i.e., something transitory and not at all marked by

---

[66] Nozick, *The Examined Life*, 166–7.
[67] Pearl Jam, "God's Dice," in *Binaural* (2000).
[68] Pearl Jam, "Superblood Wolfmoon."
[69] Pearl Jam, "Last Exit," in *Vitalogy* (1994).
[70] Pearl Jam, "I Am Mine," in *Riot Act* (2002).

necessity or eternity, which can also be expressed metaphorically through the powerful image of the waves: "I had a false belief / I thought I came here to stay / We're all just visiting / All just breaking like waves."[71]

This strong emphasis on ephemerality and impermanence undoubtedly confers a sort of stigma of frailty and vulnerability to human life, which clearly emerges in many Pearl Jam songs dealing with topics such as death, the loss of a loved person, or, in general, "the end." It emerges in a particularly moving way, for example, from the lines of "Sirens" that explain how the "life we lead" is really "a fragile thing," so that if we start thinking too much about it we seriously run the risk of being emotionally overpowered "by the grace / By which we live our lives / With death over our shoulders."[72] After all, just like the butterfly with broken wings that a recent song like "Seven O'Clock" sings about, also we, human beings, are simply "Gods' creation[s]" (or, say, finite and limited beings) that are "destined to be thrown away"[73] one day.

Now, on the basis of what has been said before, honestly acknowledging this fact may also prove to be fearful and threatening, inasmuch as "the shadow of nihilism"[74]—that is, the shadow of the potential meaninglessness and insignificance of human existence—may easily appear to our minds and frighten us. In a sense, suggesting that the answer to the question about getting something out of the all-encompassing trip of our life is to be found by focusing on contingency and the temporal dimension of the present, or even on the impermanence of the moment, runs the risk of letting us fall into an abyss of insignificance. And, as I said, it also runs the risk of conflicting with certain inveterate and deeply rooted ideas of all Western metaphysics, or at least of modern philosophy and culture.

In my interpretation, the fascinating philosophical challenge that Pearl Jam explicitly confront us with is that of fearlessly acknowledging "our insignificance"[75] and, at that point, rather than taking a step back and searching for answers to the questions that trouble and disorient us either in the past (for example, in the presumed existence of something "originary"—of an origin of all things that may safeguard the meaning of the real) or in the future (for example, in an

---

[71] Pearl Jam, "Push Me, Pull Me," in *Yield* (1998).
[72] Pearl Jam, "Sirens," in *Lightning Bolt* (2013).
[73] Pearl Jam, "Seven O'Clock," in *Gigaton* (2020).
[74] I borrow this fitting expression from Gadamer's essay on the hermetic poetry of Paul Celan entitled "Under the Shadow of Nihilism," in *Hans-Georg Gadamer on Education, Poetry, and History*, 111–23.
[75] Pearl Jam, "Insignificance," in *Binaural* (2000).

expected *telos* that may hopefully and retrospectively confer meaning to all our plans, efforts, and actions), instead, courageously insisting on the primacy of the present, and trying to derive some meaning and significance precisely from this. If the existence of us, "stupid human beings,"[76] may also appear meaningless in principle—inasmuch as we, as living creatures, don't seem to be a priori more significant than all other finite beings on this planet—according to the "philosophy of Pearl Jam" this does not imply that we should surrender to this fact and embrace nihilism or, more in general, a desperate, idle, passive, and defeatist worldview. Rather, it is precisely from an honest and disenchanted acceptance of our limitedness and even our metaphysical/cosmological insignificance (given that, contrary to the assumptions of philosophical anthropology's belief in a special place of human beings in the cosmos,[77] it is clear that "to the universe [we] don't mean a thing"[78]) that the very possibility of having a meaningful and significant life seems to arise. "Focus on your focusness, don't allow for hopelessness,"[79] as Pearl Jam convincingly sing in a recent song. As has been noted:

> in the position of questioning they exemplify, Vedder and others are facing a completely new sense of time which challenges *Dasein* in a fundamental way. Emancipation in such a situation faces new problems, and new limits, but also new possibilities. Eddie Vedder, it could be said, has charted those limits and possibilities and dangers in song.[80]

This possibility depends, in particular, on another element that we must introduce now in the constellation of philosophical aspects and implications that are present in Pearl Jam songs: namely, the element of action. In fact, in many Pearl Jam songs the acknowledgment of all the elements gravitating around the primacy of the temporal mode of the present and the radical limitedness and contingency of human life turns out to be something like an invitation to action. An invitation to action, furthermore, that is fueled by a strong component of anger against misery and human oppression (expressed

---

[76] Pearl Jam, "Love Boat Captain."
[77] See Max Scheler, *The Human Place in the Cosmos* (Evanston: Northwestern University Press, 2009).
[78] Pearl Jam, "Love Boat Captain."
[79] Pearl Jam, "Superblood Wolfmoon."
[80] I allow myself to quote here Colin J. Campbell's fitting observations, which emerged during our email exchange about *Pearl Jam and Philosophy*, in an email dated February 3, 2021. I would like to sincerely thank Colin for this and still other stimulating remarks that he offered in our conversations about this topic, and also for being kind enough to read a first version of my essay and polish my rough English.

masterfully in songs throughout their career, including "Why Go," "W.M.A.," "Leash," "Not For You," "Whipping," "World Wide Suicide," or entire albums like *Riot Act*) and that, especially in certain more politically committed songs, explicitly assumes the physiognomy of an act of resistance to the social contradictions and injustice that permeate the existing reality. The famous line from "Corduroy" that critically and courageously claims "[p]ush me and I will resist,"[81] and also the lyrics of a song like "Down" (with emphatic contrast between "down" in the first verse and "rise" in the second verse, and with the crypto-reference to Howard Zinn's memoir book *You Can't Be Neutral on a Moving Train*),[82] are surely fitting examples in this context: "if hope could grow from dirt like me / It can be done / Won't let the light escape from me / Won't let the darkness swallow me."[83]

"To and fro the pendulum throws"[84]: conceptually oscillating between anger and *phronesis* (the Aristotelian virtue of wisdom[85]) as brilliantly exemplified by the image of a pendulum, what I call the "philosophy of Pearl Jam" invites us to understand that it is only through an active intervention in and resistance to the course of the world (freely quoting here Hegel's well-known concept of *Weltlauf*) that insignificance may dialectically generate its very opposite, i.e., meaning and significance in life. If viewed from this perspective, the fact of being metaphysically/cosmologically purposeless, meaningless, and devoid of any pre-given and ontologically guaranteed *telos* does not prevent human beings from becoming meaningful creatures, i.e., from developing by themselves a life rich in value and meaning, with their strength, their courage and their actions. Although probably referring to current political situations and particular events in the USA, the following lines from Pearl Jam's recent song "Seven O'Clock" also seem to fit perfectly with the general interpretive picture or, say, the conceptual constellation that I have tried to construe until now: "this is no time for depression or self-indulgent hesitance / This fucked up situation calls for all hands, hands on deck . . . / Much to be done . . ."[86]

By the way, what I have previously defined as the pendulum-like nature of the "philosophy of Pearl Jam," oscillating between anger and wisdom, also seems to

---

[81] Pearl Jam, "Corduroy," in *Vitalogy* (1994).
[82] I am grateful to Andrea Schembari for having explained to me this detail about the song "Down."
[83] Pearl Jam, "Down," in *Lost Dogs* (2003).
[84] Pearl Jam, "Pendulum," in *Lightning Bolt* (2013).
[85] Aristotle, *Eth. Nic.* VI, 5 (see *The Complete Works of Aristotle. Vol. 2*, 86–99).
[86] Pearl Jam, "Seven O'Clock."

find a reflection in Pearl Jam's particular relation to the culture industry and music business. The latter is indeed metaphorically describable as a sort of unceasing oscillation between a strong drive to aesthetic autonomy and even a genuine "do it yourself" attitude (on the one hand), and an equally powerful impulse and intention not to refuse a priori the mighty means and opportunities offered by the music industry to reach a broader audience (on the other hand). The aim is to use those means and opportunities to achieve musical and/or political aims that otherwise would be hardly achievable; if the control maintained by the music industry becomes too suffocating, the artist's recourse is to step away, to perform some rebellion act and find alternative solutions. Several decisions that have characterized the whole career of Pearl Jam from its very beginning until recent times—such as refusing to make videos of certain songs in spite of strong pressures from their label; limiting the number of their interviews and TV appearances; boycotting the ticket vendor Ticketmaster in the mid-1990s; conceiving of the *Self-Pollution* four-hours-long pirate broadcast out of Seattle available to any radio stations wanting to carry it; leaving Epic Records at the end of their contract and opting to release their last albums through their own label Monkeywrench Records; using their worldwide fame and reputation to promote wider social and political issues; and finally, founding a non-profit organization named Vitalogy Foundation to support other non-profit organizations working in the fields of education, community health, the arts, the environment, and social change—all of these offer perfect exemplifications of what I have described so far in purely conceptual terms.

Following Mark Fisher's penetrating observations about the dramatic antinomies characterizing the post-Cobain musical situation in which "'alternative' and 'independent' [didn't] designate something outside mainstream culture" but had rather become "styles ... within the mainstream,"[87] we might argue that developing a capacity to oscillate between the alternative and the mainstream—thus avoiding being entirely absorbed either by the former or by the latter, but rather learning to dwell in the "in-between" and, in this way, gradually finding their own path—was Pearl Jam's strategy to survive in a world full of annihilating conflicts, neither losing the "'for-real' vulnerability" that

---

[87] Mark Fisher, *Capitalist Realism: Is There No Alternative?* (Winchester-Washington: Zero Books, 2009), 8.

"made [Cobain's] expression so strong"[88] and that has always been present also in Vedder's voice, nor being swallowed and overwhelmed by those antinomies, as sadly happened to Cobain and other leading figures of the grunge scene.[89] Indeed, in his now famous book *Capitalist Realism* Fisher invited the reader to witness

> the establishment of settled "alternative" or "independent" cultural zones, which endlessly repeat older gestures of rebellion and contestation as if for the first time. "Alternative" and "independent" don't designate something outside mainstream culture; rather, they are styles, in fact *the* dominant styles, within the mainstream. No one embodied (and struggled with) this deadlock more than Kurt Cobain and Nirvana. In his dreadful lassitude and objectless rage, Cobain seemed to give wearied voice to the despondency of the generation that had come after history, whose every move was anticipated, tracked, bought and sold before it had even happened. Cobain knew that he was just another piece of spectacle, that nothing runs better on MTV than a protest against MTV; knew that his every move was a cliché scripted in advance, knew that even realizing it is a cliché. Here, even success meant failure, since to succeed would only mean that you were the new meat on which the system could feed.... Cobain's death confirmed the defeat and incorporation of rock's utopian and promethean ambitions.[90]

In a sense, we may interpret what has been described above as Pearl Jam's own attempt (provisional and imperfect as it can be, of course, but nevertheless honest and genuine) to be up to the ambitious task once assigned by Robert

---

[88] I borrow these words from Brad Mehldau's fascinating and, in a sense, also moving observations about Nirvana and the reason that led him to offer a piano-solo jazz version of "Smells Like Teen Spirit": "Kurt Cobain, with his lyrics and way of singing, inadvertently become a spokesperson for my generation. That music spoke to the way we all felt lost and untethered in the world. That could be on a directly personal level, but also in a broader sense—for example, the way our political stance was detrimentally apathetic. Kurt Cobain also had that 'for-real' vulnerability, and it seemed he had no choice but to scream it out at us, completely unhinged, like a scared man-child. That's what made his expression so strong" (Brad Mehldau, 'Liner Notes', in *10 Years Solo Live. 4–CD Box* [Nonesuch Records, 2015]).

[89] Of course, this strategy is not "unique," i.e., only specific to the case of Pearl Jam, although it does seem to uniquely characterize the most emphatic popular music of the last thirty years. I would like to thank Colin J. Campbell for his fitting observations on this aspect and also for his stimulating suggestions about some possible associations between my particular interpretation of the "philosophy of Pearl Jam" on how to make sense of living in the present tense (so to speak) and a few scenes from Mike Leigh's film *Naked*: in particular, the conversation between David Thewliss' character and the security guard in which the question of the temporal mode of the future strongly arises.

[90] Fisher, *Capitalist Realism*, 8–9.

Fripp to pop-rock musicians with these words: "[operating] in the marketplace but not governed by the values of the marketplace."[91]

Never stop trying to make a difference: The primacy of responsibility and action

Returning now, after this brief excursus on the music industry and its contradictions, to the fundamental philosophical dimension of our discourse, on the basis of what has been said before about the primacy of the temporal mode of the future and the search for something necessary and transcendent as an escape from our desperately insuperable contingency, immanence, and transience, the philosophical perspectives disclosed by some Pearl Jam songs may appear quite unusual and even problematic to our *sensus communis metaphysicus*: that is, to the categories coined by Western metaphysics through which we often unconsciously and commonsensically interpret the world and relate to it. In fact, all this points definitely in the direction of a post-metaphysical way of thinking and living that does not require any more of those implausible beliefs or metaphysical stratagems devised by human beings for centuries in order to not come to terms with the basic and undeniable fact of their mortality, vulnerability, and contingency. In this context, it thus makes perfect sense to say, both emphatically and ironically: "Self-realized and metaphysically redeemed / May not live another life / May not solve our mystery."[92]

Following Richard Rorty, "[m]etaphysics—in the sense of a search for theories which will get at real essence—tries to make sense of the claim that human beings are something more than centerless webs of beliefs and desires. . . . Such an appeal to real essence is the antithesis of ironism."[93] If so, "a 'post-metaphysical' culture" is one in which "the imperative that is common to religion and metaphysics," namely the imperative "to find an ahistorical, transcultural matrix for one's thinking . . . has dried up and blown away."[94] In my interpretation, what

---

[91] Robert Fripp's liner notes to *God Save the Queen*; quoted in Eric Tamm, *Robert Fripp: From King Crimson to Guitar Craft* (London: Faber & Faber, 1990), 92.
[92] Pearl Jam, "Mind Your Manners," in *Lightning Bolt* (2013).
[93] Richard Rorty, *Contingency, Irony, and Solidarity* (Cambridge: Cambridge University Press, 1989), 88.
[94] Eduardo Mendieta (ed.), *Take Care of Freedom and Truth Will Take Care of Itself. Interviews with Richard Rorty* (Stanford, CA: Stanford University Press, 2006), 46. On the concept of "post-metaphysical thinking," although from a different perspective than Rorty's, see also Habermas, *Postmetaphysical Thinking* (Cambridge, MA: The MIT Press, 1992), 28–53.

the abovementioned lines from Pearl Jam's song "Mind Your Manners" powerfully express is the idea that, once the need for absolute but untrue certainties, for fraudulently guaranteed future expectations, and for dubious metaphysical foundations is gone, human beings can finally consider themselves free from the need to wait for the meaning of their life to arrive from the unlikely fulfillment of all their desires in a future time, and they can profitably dedicate their time and energy to "rise up / Turning mistakes into gold"[95] in the present, trying to find their direction "magnetically," as it were.

If this is true, then the question concerning the meaning of life logically undergoes a radical transformation. At this point, for example, the abovementioned insurmountable character of certain questions no longer looks as threatening as it used to, because, thanks to a "human, all too human" phenomenon like holding "the hand of love," many theoretical problems and doubts gradually dissolve, and life appears acceptable and tolerable in all its impermanence and transience, i.e., "all [becomes] surmountable."[96] At this point, it also becomes possible to paradoxically argue that "[a]ll the answers" to our questions are to be found in "the mistakes that we have made"[97]—which can be understood, in my interpretation, as a sort of rehabilitation of our fallibility, frailty, and imperfection, not considering them anymore only as obstacles to our realization as human beings but rather suggesting the opportunity to also consider them as conditions of possibility for the amelioration and improvement of our life. After all, as Pearl Jam thought-provokingly claim in one of their most recent songs: "Expecting perfection leaves a lot to ignore."[98]

"Can we help that ... our destinations / Are the ones we've been before"?[99] Without ceding to any form of naïve optimism, Pearl Jam's answer to this dramatic question is a determined "Yes." Freely adapting a famous motto by Antonio Gramsci to the specific purposes of the present essay, we may say that, in the "philosophy of Pearl Jam," a certain intellectual pessimism in the disenchanted grasping of the real problems and conflicts that are present in the

---

[95] Eddie Vedder, "Rise," in *Into the Wild* (2007). I would like to thank Elias Speroni for having opportunely reminded me of the deep philosophical meaning of this song in a long and interesting conversation in a pub in Bologna, after a couple of beers with our friends, sometime in 2016 or 2017. I would also like to thank Caterina Conti for having supported me in the last two years and for having helped me to rise up and find again my direction.
[96] Pearl Jam, "Love Boat Captain."
[97] Pearl Jam, "Who Ever Said," in *Gigaton* (2020).
[98] Pearl Jam, "Dance of the Clairvoyants."
[99] Pearl Jam, "All or None," in *Riot Act* (2002).

world is not at odds with an optimism (critical, not naïve) of the will to act, operate in the reality, and do the right thing.[100] If finally redeemed from metaphysical and ontological needs,[101] human beings may not search anymore for salvation or redemption in any transcendence or future utopian dream, but may be driven instead by the genuine impulse to consciously and courageously take action in the present to change the world and make it a better place, to the extent that it is still possible. A comparison between Benjamin's materialist but still messianic perspective, according to which "the idea of happiness is indissolubly bound up with the idea of redemption,"[102] and Rorty's surely less enthusiastic and fascinating, but also more sober, tenable, and pragmatic acknowledgement of the fact that "[h]uman beings need to be made happier, but they do not need to be redeemed,"[103] may easily show the philosophical change that I am somehow hinting at by means of an interpretation of some songs by Pearl Jam.

Of course, one may legitimately doubt one's power to effectively operate in the world to generate any noteworthy change in a society like the present one, which sadly can be defined—following Horkheimer and Adorno—as "the administered world," or—following the song "Society," covered by Eddie Vedder in the original soundtrack of the film *Into the Wild*—as "a crazy breed." From this point of view, in self-critically reflecting on one's limited capacity and power to change the world instead than limiting oneself to interpreting it,[104] it definitely makes sense to ask oneself: "Does it make any difference?" (this, in fact, being the guiding question of "Indifference," another Pearl Jam song that is particularly rich in philosophical dimensions and implications).

However, notwithstanding these legitimate doubts and perplexities, I think that the "philosophy of Pearl Jam" ultimately remains an invitation to accept the limitedness and fleetingness of the human condition with no resignation, no desperation, no passive acceptation of the existing reality, but rather with the strength to turn the acquired awareness of our inescapable finitude, contingency,

---

[100] Gramsci's exact words, as is well-known, are: "I'm a pessimist because of intelligence, but am an optimist because of will" (Letter from December 19, 1929: in Antonio Gramsci, *Letters from Prison. Vol. 1* [New York: Columbia University Press, 2011], 299).

[101] I borrow the concept of "ontological need" from Adorno, *Negative Dialectics*, 61–96.

[102] Benjamin, "On the Concept of History," 389.

[103] Rorty, *An Ethics for Today* (New York: Columbia University Press, 2011), 13.

[104] In using these words, I implicitly makes reference, as obvious, to Karl Marx's famous motto in the "Theses on Feuerbach," according to which "[t]he philosophers have only *interpreted* the world in various ways; the point is, to *change* it" (Karl Marx, *Selected Writings* [Indianapolis-Cambridge: Hackett Publishing Company, Inc., 1994], 101).

and even ontological insignificance into a principle for action, which would confer significance and meaning to life. Few Pearl Jam songs, in my opinion, coherently and convincingly express these views as "Indifference" is able to do, and so, given that it was precisely an intense and indeed unforgettable version of "Indifference" with which Pearl Jam ended the Bologna concert that I was privileged to hear in September 2006 (much like the particularly dark and captivating version of "Present Tense" that probably remains my most beloved memory of the Milano concert from June 2000), I would like to simply conclude my attempt to offer a philosophical interpretation of some songs of my favorite band by a citation of the following words: "I'll keep takin' punches, until their will grows tired ... / Hey I won't change direction, and I won't change my mind ... / I'll swallow poison, until I grow immune / I will scream my lungs out till it fills this room."[105]

How much difference does a change of philosophical perspective like the abovementioned one make? On the basis of what has been said before, I am tempted to say: "all the difference in the world." Will the failure, frustration, disappointment, and disillusion that may well occur if our struggle for change and transformative action in the world does not succeed lead us to resignation and pessimism? Are we "not trying to make a difference"? Will we "stop trying to make a difference"? Following the "philosophy of Pearl Jam," the only possible answer to this question is: "No way"[106]!

Bibliography

Adorno, Theodor W. *Negative Dialectics*, translated by E.B. Ashton. London-New York: Routledge, 2004.

Aristotle. *The Complete Works of Aristotle. Vol. 2*, edited by Jonathan Barnes. Princeton, NJ: Princeton University Press, 1991.

Augustine. *Confessions*, translated by Francis Joseph Sheed, edited by Michael P. Foley. Indianapolis-Cambridge: Hackett Publishing Company, Inc., 2006.

Bekker, August I. (ed.). *Aristotelis Opera*, ex recensione Immanuelis Bekkeri edidit Academia Regia Borussica (1831–70). 5 Bde., Berolini, apud G. Reimerum, editio altera quam curavit Olof Gigon. Berlin: De Gruyter.

---

[105] Pearl Jam, "Indifference," in *Vs.* (1993).
[106] Pearl Jam, "No Way," in *Yield* (1998).

Benjamin, Walter. *Selected Writings. Volume 4*, edited by Howard Eiland and Michael W. Jennings. Cambridge, MA-London: Harvard University Press, 2006.

Cassirer, Ernst. *Kant's Life and Thought*, translated by James Haden. Yale, NH: Yale University Press, 1981.

Dotto, Simone. *Pearl Jam. Still Alive. Testi commentati*. Roma: Arcana, 2014.

Fisher, Mark. *Capitalist Realism: Is There No Alternative?* Winchester-Washington: Zero Books, 2009.

Gadamer, Hans-Georg. *Philosophical Hermeneutics*, translated and edited by David E. Linge. Berkeley-Los Angeles-London: University of California Press, 1976.

Gadamer, Hans-Georg. *Hans-Georg Gadamer on Education, Poetry, and History: Applied Hermeneutics*, translated by Lawrence Schmidt and Monica Reuss, edited by Dieter Misgeld and Graeme Nicholson. Albany, NY: SUNY Press, 1992.

Gadamer, Hans-Georg. *Truth and Method*, translated by Joel Weinsheimer and Donald G. Marshall. London-New York: Continuum, 2004.

Gadamer, Hans-Georg. *The Gadamer Reader: A Bouquet of the Later Writings*, translated and edited by Richard E. Palmer. Evanston: Northwestern University Press, 2007.

Gramsci, Antonio. *Letters from Prison. Vol. 1*, translated by Raymond Rosenthal, edited by Frank Rosengarten. New York: Columbia University Press, 2011.

Habermas, Jürgen. *Philosophical-political Profiles*, translated by Frederick G. Lawrence. Cambridge, MA: The MIT Press, 1983.

Habermas, Jürgen. *Postmetaphysical Thinking*, translated by William M. Hohengarten. Cambridge, MA: The MIT Press, 1992.

Heidegger, Martin. *Being and Time*, translated by Joan Stambaugh. Albany, NY: SUNY Press, 1996.

Heidegger, Martin. *Contributions to Philosophy (Of the Event)*, translated by Richard Rojcewicz and Daniela Vallega-Neu. Bloomington, IN: Indiana University Press, 2012.

Horkheimer, Max. *Critical Theory: Selected Essays*, translated by Matthew J. O'Connell et al. New York: Continuum, 2002.

Horkheimer, Max and Theodor W. Adorno. *Dialectic of Enlightenment*, translated by Edmund Jephcott. Stanford, CA: Stanford University Press 2002.

Jaspers, Karl. *Von der Wahrheit*. München: Piper, 1947.

Jaspers, Karl. "The Encompassing (English Subtitles)." *YouTube*, 1950. Available online: https://www.youtube.com/watch?v=IuOfaB8bABc (accessed April 3, 2021).

Kant, Immanuel. *Critique of Pure Reason*, translated and edited by Paul Guyer and Allen W. Wood. Cambridge: Cambridge University Press, 1998.

Koselleck, Reinhart. *Futures Past: On the Semantics of Historical Time*, translated by Keith Tribe. New York: Columbia University Press, 2004.

Krüger, Hans-Peter. "Modern Research Procedures and their Conflicts in View of Dignity: Helmuth Plessner's First Transformation of the Kantian *Critique of the*

Power of Judgment." In *Kant's "Critique of Aesthetic Judgment" in the 20th Century: A Companion to Its Main Interpretations*, edited by Stefano Marino and Pietro Terzi, 93–114. Berlin: De Gruyter, 2020.

Löwith, Karl. *Meaning in History*. Chicago-London: The University of Chicago Press, 1949.

Marcuse, Herbert. *The Aesthetic Dimension: Towards a Critique of Marxist Aesthetics*, translated by Herbert Marcuse and Erica Sherover. Boston: Beacon Press, 1978.

Marino, Stefano. *Gadamer and the Limits of the Modern Techno-scientific Civilization*. Bern: Peter Lang, 2011.

Marino, Stefano. *Aesthetics, Metaphysics, Language: Essays on Heidegger and Gadamer*. Newcastle upon Tyne: Cambridge Scholars Publishing, 2015.

Marx, Karl. *Selected Writings*, edited by Lawrence H. Simon. Indianapolis-Cambridge: Hackett Publishing Company, Inc., 1994.

Mehldau, Brad. *10 Years Solo Live. 4-CD Box*. Nonesuch Records, 2015.

Mendieta, Eduardo, edited by. *Take Care of Freedom and Truth Will Take Care of Itself. Interviews with Richard Rorty*. Stanford, CA: Stanford University Press, 2006.

Neri, Ludovica. *Il problema della "logica filosofica" nel* Nachlass *di Karl Jaspers*. Milano-Udine: Mimesis, 2021.

Nozick, Robert. *The Examined Life: Philosophical Meditations*. New York: Simon & Schuster, 1990.

Quinn, Daniel. "Yield." *Ishmael.com*, December 14, 1998. Available online: http://www.ishmael.com/Interaction/QandA/Detail.CFM?Record=373 (accessed April 3, 2021).

Rorty, Richard. *Contingency, Irony, and Solidarity*. Cambridge: Cambridge University Press, 1989.

Rorty, Richard. *An Ethics for Today*. New York: Columbia University Press, 2011.

Scheler, Max. *The Human Place in the Cosmos*, translated by Manfred Frings. Evanston, IL: Northwestern University Press, 2009.

Shusterman, Richard. *Pragmatist Aesthetics: Living Beauty, Rethinking Art*. Lanham-Boulder-New York-Oxford: Rowman & Littlefield, 2000.

Sorensen, Roy. "Nothingness." In *The Stanford Encyclopedia of Philosophy* (Spring 2020 Edition), edited by Edward N. Zalta. Available online: https://plato.stanford.edu/entries/nothingness (accessed March 4, 2021).

Tamm, Eric. *Robert Fripp: From King Crimson to Guitar Craft*. London: Faber & Faber, 1990.

Vedder, Eddie. "Note From Ed on the Passing of Howard Zinn." *Pearljam.com*, January 27, 2010. Available online: https://pearljam.com/news/note-from-ed-on-the-passing-of-howard-zinn (accessed April 3, 2021).

Volpi, Franco. *Il nichilismo*. Roma-Bari: Laterza, 2005.

Wittgenstein, Ludwig. *Philosophical Investigations*, translated by Gertrude Elizabeth Margaret Anscombe. Oxford: Basil Blackwell, 1986.

2

"Just Like Innocence": Pearl Jam and the (Re)Discovery of Hope

Sam Morris

Introduction

The release of *No Code* in 1996 signaled a new direction for Pearl Jam. Hallmarks of the band's early sound remain, to be sure, but *No Code* pivots away from the expressions of trauma that permeated Pearl Jam's first three albums. What Jeff Ament, Stone Gossard, Mike McCready, and Eddie Vedder—along with new drummer Jack Irons—began to move toward is difficult to define at first listen, but it feels different and new. "Sometimes," *No Code*'s leadoff track, alerts listeners to the seismic shift in Pearl Jam's pathos: "Sometimes I reach to myself, dear god."[1] Lyrically, this represents a shift from the outward to the inward, a focus that the band develops further on *Yield*. This inward focus accounts for the musical shift that occurs on *No Code* as well; from this point forward, describing Pearl Jam as "grunge," "90s," or "alt-rock" becomes increasingly misleading and incorrect.

The persona that appears most often on *No Code*, especially during "Sometimes," "In My Tree," "Off He Goes," "Red Mosquito," "Present Tense," and "I'm Open," has entered midlife and is grappling with identity, meaning, and purpose. Instead of relying on a mentor or a muse, though, this persona looks inward for something—something that is actually not new at all: innocence. He claims at the end of "In My Tree" that he has recovered "my innocence... got back my inner sense."[2] Can innocence be more than merely glimpsed? Can it be regained? How? Or, perhaps a better question, can innocence ever truly be lost?

---

[1] Pearl Jam, "Sometimes," in *No Code* (1996).
[2] Pearl Jam, "In My Tree," in *No Code* (1996).

Ament, Gossard, Irons, McCready, and Vedder are certainly not the first people to ask these questions; they are, in fact, participating in a long-standing philosophical and poetic tradition. This chapter examines Pearl Jam's place in that tradition. This examination promises no answers—as Vedder muses in "Love Boat Captain," "Questions rise and answers fall,... / insurmountable."[3] What this chapter will do is guide readers through Pearl Jam's search for innocence as well as its relationship to poets and philosophers who have undergone a similar search. The goal of this search for innocence, in the band's own words, is "[t]o find an approach and a way to live."[4]

I first encountered British Romantic poetry not too long after a friend introduced me to Pearl Jam in 1998. What I noticed as I became more familiar with poets William Blake and William Wordsworth was that they were grappling with some of the same ideas at the end of the eighteenth century that Pearl Jam grappled with at the end of the twentieth century. In fact, poems from Wordsworth's *Lyrical Ballads* (written along with Samuel Taylor Coleridge) and Blake's *Songs of Innocence and of Experience* provide a basis from which to examine Pearl Jam's search for innocence that begins with *No Code* and continues through *Lightning Bolt*. What, though, of *Ten*, *Vs.*, and *Vitalogy*? There are, as I will discuss, some uncanny connections between Wordsworth's and Blake's poems and songs from those three albums as well. This chapter is not simply an exercise, however, in connecting Pearl Jam to a poetic tradition. The British Romantic poetic tradition often includes the Blakean concept of a progression from innocence to experience. U2 notably adopted this concept with its 2014 album *Songs of Innocence* and the 2017 companion *Songs of Experience*. Pearl Jam, meanwhile, diverges significantly from this tradition, dreaming of the possibility of remembered or rediscovered innocence.

This dream of remembered or rediscovered innocence also links Pearl Jam to the long history of utopian theory. Pearl Jam's advocacy for a better world aligns the band with philosopher Ernst Bloch, who defined utopia as a feeling rather than a place. This feeling, most often expressed as hope, is what Vedder's persona finds in his tree; later, in "Given to Fly," he brings hope down from the tree so that he can share it with others. For Pearl Jam, asking questions and searching for answers is a task that may be "insurmountable," but it is a worthy search nonetheless. In *The Principle of Hope*, Bloch writes extensively about the role that

---

[3] Pearl Jam, "Love Boat Captain," in *Riot Act* (2002).
[4] Pearl Jam, "Present Tense," in *No Code* (1996).

art plays in the realization of the utopian impulse; this realization is one of Pearl Jam's greatest contributions to music and to popular culture. From the declaration of openness in *No Code* to the anamnesis of "Given to Fly" to the exhortation of "Save You" to the considerations of death and future generations in songs such as "Love Boat Captain," "The End," and "Future Days," Pearl Jam has mapped a course through the early twenty-first century to guide themselves and listeners to reach into ourselves, find hope that we can recover our innocence, and create a better world.

In this chapter, I divide Pearl Jam's discography into three sections. The first section focuses on the feelings of anger, despair, and hopelessness that pervade *Ten*, *Vs.*, and *Vitalogy*. Though buried under layers of negative emotions, I will show how the impulse to hope is still present. The second section explores the shift I described at the outset of this chapter, which begins to occur on *Vitalogy* but is mostly found on *No Code* and *Yield*. The third section outlines the evolution of the band's search for innocence and a better world from *Binaural* to *Lightning Bolt*.

Shortly after I conceived of this chapter, Pearl Jam announced the release of its eleventh album, *Gigaton*. Little did I know that *Gigaton* would be a radical departure from the way that the band has approached the very ideas that I planned to explore. As a result, I conclude this chapter with a brief discussion of *Gigaton*, an album about apocalypse. How does one continue to have hope at the end of the world? How can one take back their innocence from those who would feed on it? Does any of this work matter? Does it make a difference?

Escape is never the safest path

Discussing Pearl Jam's connection to the British Romantic poetic tradition is from the beginning inherently problematic because the "British Romantic poetic tradition" is itself not easily defined. Michael Ferber attempted a definition for *The Cambridge Introduction to British Romantic Poetry*, which includes "exploring one's self and its relationship to others and to nature, which gave privilege to the imagination as a faculty higher and more inclusive than reason, which sought solace in or reconciliation with the natural world."[5] Other proposed

---

[5] Michael Ferber, *The Cambridge Introduction to British Romantic Poetry* (Cambridge: Cambridge University Press, 2012), 3–4.

tenets of Romanticism are that God is found in nature, art is the "highest human creation," and rebellion against wealth and tradition is vital.[6] Ferber admits, however, that each British Romantic strongly disagreed with at least one of the provisions of this proposed definition.[7] Contradictions aside, for a Pearl Jam fan, reading Ferber's definition might bring to mind "Oceans"—and even images from the song's music video. Trusting that the "currents will shift / Glide me towards you" is precisely the kind of solace-seeking in the natural world in which most (though certainly not all) Romantics believed.[8]

"Oceans" operates as a brief respite from the trauma that dominates *Ten*. The *Mamasan* Trilogy of "Alive," "Once," and (*Ten* B-side) "Footsteps" provides an extended narrative of abuse, incest, alienation, madness, murder, and incarceration—ironically, Vedder came up with the lyrics to these songs while surfing.[9] *Lyrical Ballads*, co-authored by Wordsworth and Coleridge, features poems that are more than coincidentally reminiscent of the songs in the *Mamasan* Trilogy. Aside from Coleridge's most famous poem, "The Rime of the Ancient Mariner," in which the speaker is driven by guilt, not unlike the incarcerated madman in "Footsteps," to tell and retell his story of death and destruction, Wordsworth pens contributions such as "The Mad Mother," "The Convict," and "The Female Vagrant." One could imagine "The Mad Mother" and "The Convict" as alternate titles for "Alive" and "Footsteps"; "The Female Vagrant," meanwhile, could be the "[y]oung virgin from heaven / Visiting" who is victimized in another song from *Ten*, "Deep."[10] Of Wordsworth's poems, Neil Fraistat writes, "[c]haracter after character discovers the inadequacy of a human society based upon sterile preconceptions and close-mindedness and is subsequently cast adrift in a type of death-in-life"; Fraistat goes on to suggest that this kind of alienation appears mostly in either "the cramped near-paralysis of the prisoner or the aimless wandering of the outcast."[11] This description certainly aligns with the man in the *Mamasan* Trilogy who asks "do I deserve to be [alive],"[12] screams "once upon a time I could control myself,"[13] and finally

---

[6] Ibid., 4.
[7] Ibid.
[8] Pearl Jam, "Oceans," in *Ten* (1991).
[9] Jessica Letkemann, "Music for Rhinos. 1990: The Making of Pearl Jam," *TwoFeetThick.com*, 2010, 7–8.
[10] Pearl Jam, "Deep," in *Ten* (1991).
[11] Neil Fraistat, "*From the 'Field' of Lyrical Ballads*," in William Wordsworth, *Wordsworth's Poetry and Prose*, Nicholas Halmi, ed. (New York: Norton, 2014), 606.
[12] Pearl Jam, "Alive," in *Ten* (1991).
[13] Pearl Jam, "Once," in *Ten* (1991).

repeats "it was you" after a brief return to lucidity inevitably fades into a near-catatonic state.[14] From the very beginning, Pearl Jam has been preoccupied with trying to understand the relationship between others and the Self. On *Ten*, this attempt at understanding is solipsistic, full of blame and recrimination of others.

From the first time that I heard "Garden," it struck me as one of the most challenging songs on *Ten*. Though I primarily associate "Garden" with a twentieth-century poet, Sylvia Plath, Blake's poem "The Garden of Love" is perhaps the best poetic connection to Pearl Jam's "garden of stone." In *Songs of Innocence and of Experience*, Blake defines innocence as the state of childlike wonder that exists in the early parts of our lives; he imagines a child wandering through the forest and marveling at the trees and all the other beautiful sights that nature provides. The transition from innocence to experience is the end of childhood; now, one looks at those same trees and is filled with awe rather than wonder. The trees and all the occupants of the forest are still beautiful, yes, but they are also deadly. Experience suffuses beauty with the weight of the constant threats that exist in the world at the hands of nature—and Man. "The Garden of Love" exists in the *Experience* volume; Blake's speaker returns to a place "[w]here I used to play on the green," now "filled with graves, / And tomb-stones where flowers should be."[15] Seeing a place where one once delighted in nature repurposed to house the dead is a prime example of what the transition from innocence to experience signifies. During "Garden," Vedder takes on the persona of someone who interrogates a familial or intimate partner relationship that is/was likely abusive by creating a figurative graveyard. After wandering through that graveyard, she exclaims,

> I don't know...
> I don't care...
> I don't need
> You, for me to live.[16]

She has to continue on, just as the speaker in Blake's poem must. Alicia Ostriker argues Blake's speaker in this poem "has been effectively self-alienated. Repression has worked not merely from without, but from within."[17] On *Ten*, Pearl Jam is not

---

[14] Pearl Jam, "Footsteps," in *Lost Dogs* (2003).
[15] William Blake, "The Garden of Love," in *Blake's Poetry and Designs*, Mary Lynn Johnson and John E. Grant, eds (New York: Norton, 2008), 4, 9–10.
[16] Pearl Jam, "Garden," in *Ten* (1991).
[17] Alicia Ostriker, "*From* Desire Gratified and Ungratified: William Blake and Sexuality," in *Blake's Poetry and Designs*, 562.

quite ready to look within, and so alienation flows from within and without in nearly every song. Of course, in the early 1990s, Pearl Jam was hardly alone in these feelings of alienation—Nirvana and Alice in Chains, among several other bands, were mired in the exploration of similar emotions as well.

If the songs on *Ten* feature a similar message to that which Wordsworth and Blake deploy in their poems—that despite cruel interactions with the world, life goes on in some damaged, irreparable way—*Vs.* heightens the comparison with expressions of anger, despair, and hopelessness. "Go," "Animal," "Daughter," "Dissident," and "Rearviewmirror" all chronicle abuse; "Daughter" and "Rearviewmirror," through their shared imagery of window shades, form a narrative that moves from childhood to adulthood—i.e., the transition from innocence to experience. To help define his conceptions of innocence and experience more clearly, Blake revisits and rewrites some of the poems that appear in *Innocence* for inclusion in *Experience*. For example, *Innocence* features paired poems "The Little Boy Lost" and "The Little Boy Found"; in these poems, a boy is lost in a mist, but his father rescues him. All is well, though tears are shed. In *Experience*, meanwhile, "The Little Girl Lost" features a girl who wanders away from her family and is found, not by her parents, but by "beasts of prey."[18] Lions lead her to a cave and keep her safe—something her own parents could not do. In "The Little Girl Found," the lion leads the parents to their daughter:

> Then they followed,
> Where the vision led:
> And saw their sleeping child,
> Among tygers wild.[19]

Why did the little girl wander away? The speaker suggests that seven-year-old Lyca was tempted away by "wild birds song."[20] Perhaps, though, as Vedder wrote, "can't deny there's something wrong"[21]; her parents were unable to keep her safe, so she escapes only to be found by a predator who can provide safety. But at what cost? As listeners are reminded throughout "Dissident," "Escape is never, the safest path."[22] The lions keep Lyca safe, but with that safety comes isolation, separation from other humans. As described in "Rearviewmirror," the kind of

---

[18] Blake, 'The Little Girl Lost', in *Blake's Poetry and Designs*, 34.
[19] Blake, "The Little Girl Found," in *Blake's Poetry and Designs*, 45-8.
[20] Blake, "The Little Girl Lost," 16.
[21] Pearl Jam, "Daughter," in *Vs.* (1993).
[22] Pearl Jam, "Dissident," in *Vs.* (1993).

safety that requires dependence and isolation results in more abuse, more suffering.

Alongside several songs about relationship violence and abuse, *Vs.* also addresses societal inequities on a larger scale (e.g., "Glorified G," "W.M.A.," and "Rats"), ending with the hopeless "Indifference." Vedder repeatedly questions whether anything he does matters as a reaction to everything that the band has chronicled on the album.[23] Like Vedder, Wordsworth asks at the end of "Lines written in early spring," "Have I not reason to lament / What man has made of man?"[24] Wordsworth's most well-known poem, "Lines written a few miles above Tintern Abbey," also provides a point of comparison for Vedder's indifference. Wordsworth as speaker laments of "weariness" caused by the "din / Of towns and cities"; he attempts to mitigate this world-weariness by bringing his younger sister to a spot in nature that he loves so that she can share the delight that he once felt during his own innocence.[25] Unlike Wordsworth, in the short time between the recording of *Vs.* and the recording of *Vitalogy*, Vedder had not yet found a way to transform his negative feelings into something positive and forward-reaching.

As a result, the anger and hopelessness of *Vs.* bleeds into *Vitalogy*, an album soaked in rage and despair. Vedder fears that these feelings are endless, going so far as to include a comparison of himself to "Sysiphus [sic]" in the liner notes.[26] Even in the seemingly unending catalog of human pain and suffering that is *Vs.* and the despair of *Vitalogy*, though, there is—if one looks hard enough for it—hope. Hope can be found on *Vs.* via "Leash" and on *Vitalogy* via "Not for You." When Vedder pleads to "[d]elight, delight, delight in our youth,"[27] he reminds listeners just as Blake does in the opening line of "The Voice of the Ancient Bard"—"Youth of delight come hither"—that all is not lost.[28] Similarly, during "Not for You," when Vedder claims that "[a]ll that's sacred, comes from youth,"[29] he is all but repeating Wordsworth's message in "Tintern Abbey" about the joys that the young and innocent can take in nature. Buried beneath the trauma on Pearl Jam's first three albums, the impulse to hope is present.

---

[23] Pearl Jam, "Indifference," in *Vs.* (1993).
[24] Wordsworth, "Lines Written in Early Spring," in *Wordsworth's Poetry and Prose*, 23–4.
[25] Wordsworth, "Lines Written a Few Miles Above Tintern Abbey. July 13, 1798," in *Wordsworth's Poetry and Prose*, 26–7.
[26] Pearl Jam, Liner Notes for *Vitalogy* (1994), 8.
[27] Pearl Jam, "Leash," in *Vs.* (1993).
[28] Blake, "The Voice of the Ancient Bard," in *Blake's Poetry and Designs*, 1.
[29] Pearl Jam, "Not For You," in *Vitalogy* (1994).

I still remember, why don't you?

German philosopher Ernst Bloch fled to the United States to escape the horrors of the Third Reich. While in exile, he began *The Principle of Hope*, a massive three-volume catalog of utopian thought filtered through Marxist philosophy; he finished *The Principle of Hope* upon repatriating to Germany after World War II. Of Bloch, Vincent Geoghegan argues, "[n]o major philosopher or social theorist has devoted as much time and space to the phenomenon of utopianism as Ernst Bloch; it is no exaggeration to call him the philosopher of utopia."[30] Bloch's central claim is that utopia is not a place that exists somewhere off in the future; in fact, utopia is not a place at all. Utopia is an energy that lives in all of us—now. Bloch calls this energy the "Not-Yet," which he defines as "a relatively still Unconscious disposed towards its other side, forwards rather than backwards. Towards the side of something new that is dawning up, that has never been conscious before."[31] Utopia, then, is primarily expressed in the form of hope. Another major claim that Bloch makes is that this utopian energy is found in its greatest concentration in youth—just as Pearl Jam claims in "Leash" and "Not for You."[32] During "Not for You," when Vedder accuses and taunts the subject of the song with the question "I still remember, why don't you,"[33] he and the band stake out their position as allies of youth...and hope...and innocence. In the twenty-six years that follow the release of *Vitalogy*, the band's position, though increasingly nuanced, has never wavered.

As I claimed at the beginning of this chapter, *No Code* is the turning point for the band, for it is here that Pearl Jam makes its critical divergence from the British Romantic poetic tradition. Vedder repeats at the end of "Red Mosquito," "If I had known then what I know now";[34] later, this statement is echoed in "I'm Open," a mostly spoken-word track in which the speaker laments, "So this is what it's like to be an adult / If he only knew now what he knew then."[35] Much of *No Code* is an expression of longing for something that eludes both the band and the personas developed throughout the songs on the album. Again, this longing is nearly identical to the desire that Wordsworth expresses in "Tintern

---

[30] Vincent Geoghegan, *Ernst Bloch* (New York: Routledge, 2008), 147–8.
[31] Ernst Bloch, *The Principle of Hope Vol. I* (Cambridge, MA: The MIT Press, 1986), 11.
[32] Ibid., 27, 117, 119, 121–2.
[33] Pearl Jam, "Not for You."
[34] Pearl Jam, "Red Mosquito," in *No Code* (1996).
[35] Pearl Jam, "I'm Open," in *No Code* (1996).

Abbey"—if that feeling of innocence and childhood wonder is gone for him, then perhaps he can convince his sister to appreciate it while she still can. Meanwhile, in "Three years she grew in sun and shower," Wordsworth argues that the only way to truly avoid this longing for lost innocence is by dying young. The speaker takes solace in the knowledge that, Lucy, who he describes as a "lovelier flower / On earth was never sown," dies at the age of three and will therefore never know anything other than "vital feelings of delight."[36] Is growing up so awful?

According to Blake, not necessarily. Biographer and critic Laura Quinney describes Blake's concept of "[v]isionary power" (which sounds a lot like what we call "growing up") as

> not a question of returning to an earlier stage in one's development, of reverting to a purer self as yet undeformed by adulthood or socialization. Instead, you discover something you did not know about your nature and your capabilities. But discovery alone is not enough: you must recast yourself so that you can fulfill the newfound vocation.[37]

Despite their differences, according to both Wordsworth and Blake, one must find a way to move on from remembered feelings of innocence; the temptation to feel nostalgia for a more innocent time is strong but ultimately harmful. Bloch also argues for this forward-moving progression. Nostalgia and memory are concepts that Pearl Jam wrestles with on *No Code*. "Off He Goes" and "Present Tense" offer examples of analyzing one's own memories as a way to forgiveness. Forgiveness is way of recasting, of moving on from past trauma and grief. *No Code* ends with the lullaby "Around the Bend," which again replicates Wordsworth's hope for and message to his sister in "Tintern Abbey." *No Code* represents what Vedder and the other members of the band were unable to do following *Vs.* In recasting feelings of anger and hopelessness toward more positive, forward-looking thoughts, Pearl Jam's mission as a band changes.

Vedder claims to only glimpse his innocence at the end of "In My Tree"; what he reclaims is his "inner sense."[38] While "innocence" and "inner sense" are near-homonyms, not synonyms, knowledge of the Self is generally in line with British Romantic thought. Emma Mason posits that Wordsworth writes poems about

---

[36] Wordsworth, "Three Years She Grew in Sun and Shower," in *Wordsworth's Poetry and Prose*, 2–3, 31.
[37] Laura Quinney, *William Blake on Self and Soul* (Cambridge, MA: Harvard University Press, 2009), 22.
[38] Pearl Jam, "In My Tree."

interacting with nature because he sees it as a way to combat alienation, thus "grant[ing] humans a stable ground on which to redress this alienation by engaging in shared, repeated and 'natural' experience that produces affection."[39] Blake, according to Quinney, believed that "[s]elfhood can never be simply elided; it has to be confronted and transcended."[40] While Blake and Wordsworth believed that these things are accomplished by embracing experience rather than returning to an immature state of innocence, "In My Tree" shows Pearl Jam taking a different path: the search for lost innocence.

Beat poet Allen Ginsberg recalls reading Blake's "Ah, Sun-Flower!" and being struck by a profound realization: "The sky suddenly seemed very *ancient*. And this was the very ancient place that [Blake] was talking about, the sweet golden clime, I suddenly realized that *this* existence was *it*! ... in other words that this was the moment that I was born for."[41] Ginsberg goes on to describe a second realization—that the first realization must never be forgotten.[42] While the first realization is Blakean—awe invoked by experience—the second realization of memory is Platonic. Plato called this kind of memory "anamnesis," the concept that the rediscovery of all that we learned in our pre-birth relationship with the gods is the key to true knowledge. Bloch describes anamnesis as "the doctrine that all knowledge is simply re-remembering."[43] Perhaps the most famous discussion of anamnesis is Plato's "Allegory of the Cave," which, of course, is the inspiration for *Yield*'s first single, "Given to Fly."

In "Given to Fly," the uncertainty of "In My Tree" is removed. The song begins with another man in a tree; this time, however, he discovers the "key to the locks on the chains he saw everywhere."[44] The key is anamnesis, but recall that anamnesis is *not* experience—at least not in the Blakean sense. In the Socratic tradition, true knowledge is not experience; anamnesis, once rediscovered, is true knowledge. Experience is as likely to obscure true knowledge as it is to do anything else. Experience is what causes Plato's and Pearl Jam's heroes to be "stripped and ... stabbed / By faceless men"[45]—prisoners who refuse to see beyond their own perceived reality. Anamnesis is rediscovered knowledge, but it

---

[39] Emma Mason, *The Cambridge Introduction to William Wordsworth* (Cambridge: Cambridge University Press, 2012), 71.
[40] Quinney, *William Blake*, 133.
[41] Allen Ginsberg, "My Vision of Blake," in *Blake's Poetry and Designs*, 520.
[42] Ibid.
[43] Bloch, *The Principle of Hope Vol. I*, 8.
[44] Pearl Jam, "Given to Fly," in *Yield* (1998).
[45] Pearl Jam, "Given to Fly."

is also rediscovered innocence, returning to a state that is close to nature. Wordsworth and Blake warn against nostalgia, a rose-colored remembrance that results in the desire to regress back to childhood innocence, while Plato and Bloch find meaning in the attempt to remember pre-childhood innocence. Nostalgia is backward-looking; anamnesis, ultimately, is forward-looking. Even though Pearl Jam casts off nostalgia in favor of anamnesis on *Yield*, they are still attempting to rediscover innocence. This move puts the band in conflict with the British Romantic poetic tradition, but the band breaks away from Plato as well by altering a crucial detail of his allegory: when the enlightened man returns to the cave, the faceless prisoners murder him because they are unwilling and unable to put away their experience in favor of true knowledge. Pearl Jam refuses that fate, altering the narrative:

> well, fuckers
> He still stands
> And he still gives his love, he just gives it away
> The love he receives is the love that is saved.[46]

Innocence can be rediscovered, and the world can be saved.

Utopias are the things of dreams. Bloch writes extensively about dreams, claiming that the dreams that we have are reflective of our "anticipatory consciousness," the discovery of our "Not-Yet."[47] Pearl Jam takes the daydream of Plato's subverted allegory with its happier ending and imagines an alternative to the duality of innocence and experience. In doing so, Pearl Jam took the time to yield, to rethink, and to forge a new path. Continuing in Blochian tradition, José Esteban Muñoz wrote that utopias are the "hopes of a collective, an emergent group, or even the solitary oddball who is the one who dreams for many."[48] Muñoz is quick to add, however, "Social theory that invokes the concept of utopia has always been vulnerable to charges of naiveté, impracticality, or lack of rigor."[49] "Faithfull," "No Way," "Low Light," "In Hiding," and "All Those Yesterdays" are all concerned with confronting past trauma and embracing anticipatory consciousness. Changing the narrative, however, is risky and has consequences. After *Yield*, Pearl Jam leaves the hit-making trauma of its first three albums

---

[46] Ibid.
[47] Bloch, *The Principle of Hope Vol. I*, 45–338.
[48] José Esteban Muñoz, *Cruising Utopia: The Then and There of Queer Futurity* (New York: New York University Press, 2009), 16.
[49] Ibid., 23.

behind for good, inasmuch as that level of fame mattered in the first place. References to Pearl Jam in popular culture over the last twenty years are as likely to be parodic as anything else. But then, trying to save the world has always been a difficult, risky business.

Won't someone save the world?

Though Pearl Jam's sound has continued to evolve over the past twenty years, yielding to this new expression of utopian energy results in lyrical and thematic consistency that began on *Binaural* and continues through *Riot Act*, *Pearl Jam*, *Backspacer*, and *Lightning Bolt*. Through its lyrics, the band continues to argue that innocence can be remembered and recovered. One way that this argument occurs is through explorations of anxiety and death, which are rife on these five albums. Anxiety comes through loud and clear on *Binaural*—with its "[b]ombs,... dropping down," "Insignificance," a song about the 1999 Seattle protests against the World Trade Organization, is part of a bigger theme of uncertainty.[50] To talk of anxiety and fear might appear to be counterintuitive to the search for utopian energy; indeed, for Bloch, "[h]ope [is the] expectant counter-emotion against anxiety and fear [and] *therefore the most human of all mental feelings* ..."[51] Sometimes, though, anxiety lights the way toward hope. "Grievance," a post-*Yield* song that successfully combines this new outlook with Vedder's signature snarling anger, demonstrates that hope can lie at the end of a journey through fear and anxiety:

> I want to run into the sea
> I only want life.... to be...
> I just want to be...
> I will feel alive... as long as I am free...[52]

Being alive is not trying to escape from fear and anxiety, but rather to embrace the existence of those feelings. Fredric Jameson contends, "[u]topia is not a place in which humanity is freed from violence, but rather one in which it is released from the multiple determinisms (economic, political, social) of history itself."[53]

---

[50] Pearl Jam, "Insignificance," in *Binaural* (2000).
[51] Bloch, *The Principle of Hope Vol. I*, 75.
[52] Pearl Jam, "Grievance," in *Binaural* (2000).
[53] Fredric Jameson, *Archaeologies of the Future: The Desire Called Utopia and Other Science Fictions* (London: Verso, 2005), 275.

Pearl Jam will never lead listeners to discover some fictional Avalon or Shangri-La, but the fight to make the world a better place is a worthy one.

This message grows stronger still on *Riot Act*, particularly during "Save You," a song that exhorts a friend in crisis to come through depression and hopelessness to the other side: "Cause there is but you,. . . and something within you / It's taken control,. . let's beat it, get up let's go!"[54] Once this exhortation begins, the band never lets up. Bloch believed that "hope drowns anxiety"; so does Pearl Jam.[55] "Life Wasted" sees the band pleading with listeners to swim rather than drown (i.e., retreat). "Just Breathe," "Amongst the Waves," and "Unthought Known," meanwhile, are each odes to drowning anxiety so that one never forgets how to experience wonder. This message is in line with Blochian utopianism, but it also reconnects Pearl Jam with the British Romantic poetic tradition. In "'Tis said, that some have died for love," Wordsworth writes of feeling overwhelmed by life and all that surrounds him:

> The clouds pass on; they from the Heavens depart:
> I look—the sky is empty space;
> I know not what I trace;
> But when I cease to look, my hand is on my heart.[56]

Whereas Wordsworth finds comfort in his own heart as a way to negotiate his experiential relationship with nature, Vedder sings of the fantastic world of the innocent: "See the path cut by the moon,. . . For you to walk on,. . . / See the waves on distant shores,. . . Awaiting your arrival."[57]

As for death, Bloch contends that it is "no longer the negation of utopia and its ranks of purpose but the opposite, the negation of that which does not belong to utopia in the world."[58] "Sleight of Hand," "Soon Forget," and "Parting Ways" are significant gestures toward dealing with death. On *Binaural* death is presented as a consequence—past mistakes can define us up to and through death. After 9/11 and Roskilde, though, the band begins to approach death as an eventuality for us all, particularly with "Love Boat Captain" and "Ghost." On *Pearl Jam*, the band finally arrives at Bloch's conclusion that death is not "the negation of utopia"; instead, death is evolution. "I surf in celebration / Of a billion adaptations,"

---

[54] Pearl Jam, "Save You," in *Riot Act* (2002).
[55] Bloch, *The Principle of Hope Vol. I*, 112.
[56] Wordsworth, "'Tis Said, that Some Have Died for Love," in *Wordsworth's Poetry and Prose*, 17–20.
[57] Pearl Jam, "Unthought Known," in *Backspacer* (2009).
[58] Bloch, *The Principle of Hope Vol. III*, 1180.

Vedder claims during "Big Wave."⁵⁹ This evolution continues with the closing tracks on *Backspacer* and *Lightning Bolt*, "The End" and "Future Days," demonstrating a band no longer afraid to contend with issues of death and the meaning of life.

Rather than find a new appreciation for beauty in the world, particularly nature, as the British Romantic poets did, Pearl Jam wants listeners to retain their innocent appreciation of beauty in the world. Songs like "Comatose," "Supersonic," and "Lightning Bolt" provide the listener with models of that appreciation. Again, though, this divergence from the concept of unidirectional progress from innocence toward experience does not signify a departure from the British Romantic poetic tradition altogether. In Blake's "The Angel," the speaker laments that when the angel who protected him earlier in life returned, it was too late, "For the time of youth was fled / And grey hairs were on my head."⁶⁰ While the number of grey hairs on the heads of Ament, Cameron, Gossard, McCready, and Vedder have increased over the years, they refuse to facilitate this one-way melancholy journey. Rather, "Supersonic" reveals that the members of the band may finally be comfortable with their role as guide for their listeners: "I don't need you to live, but I'll never let you go."⁶¹ Over the past thirty years, Pearl Jam initially operated within but then moved beyond the British Romantic poetic tradition; in doing so, the band embraced a philosophy of the utopian that has the potential to enrich the lives of all who listen. "I wanna live my life with the volume full."⁶²

Should've known, so fragile

Etched on the otherwise blank fourth side of the *Gigaton* LP is the phrase, "In The Midst Of The 6th," a reference to the current mass extinction event also known as the "Holocene extinction."⁶³ *Gigaton* is unmistakably the beginning of a new chapter for the band, an admission that we have entered into an apocalyptic epoch.⁶⁴ This shift in focus actually began six years prior on *Lightning Bolt* when

---

⁵⁹ Pearl Jam, "Big Wave," in *Pearl Jam* (2006).
⁶⁰ Blake, "The Angel," in *Blake's Poetry and Designs*, 15–16.
⁶¹ Pearl Jam, "Supersonic," in *Backspacer* (2009).
⁶² Ibid.
⁶³ Pearl Jam, *Gigaton* (2020).
⁶⁴ The band's consideration of this apocalyptic epoch proved to be prescient in light of the Covid-19 pandemic.

Vedder warns the listener during "Infallible," "By thinking we're infallible / We are tempting fate instead."[65] Six years later, the band returns with reality instead of a warning. *Gigaton*'s first single, "Dance of the Clairvoyants," contains the sobering refrain, "When the past is the present and the future's no more / When every tomorrow is the same as before."[66] Time is meaningless at the end. Such a stark message could be the abdication of the fight for a better tomorrow. "Quick Escape" is narrated by a man who has had to flee to Mars after Donald Trump destroyed Earth; he laments "green grass, sky and red wine,"[67] realizing that his own inaction also played a part in the planet's destruction. *Gigaton* could also be a surrender to forces that seem to always be more powerful, to the sorrow and indifference that Pearl Jam has railed against for the last thirty years.

Fortunately, *Gigaton* is none of those things. The album begins with "Who Ever Said," in which Vedder's persona rouses himself from sadness so that he can continue to fight for freedom. "Retrograde" reminds listeners to not let those who seek to erase progress convince us that the lie of the past is better or safer than the promise of the future. Years ago, Vedder asked during "Life Wasted," "Why swim the channel just to get this far? / Halfway there, why would you turn around?"[68] Now, Vedder answers these questions during "Seven O'Clock" by demanding that we should "[s]wim sideways from the undertow and do not be deterred."[69] These are confusing, desperate times; *Gigaton* is a difficult if ultimately rewarding listen because Ament, Cameron, Gossard, McCready, and Vedder refuse to shy away from the truth and from what they have spent their entire career in search of—hope.

Despite the divergence from the unidirectional journey of innocence to experience, the never-ending search for hope is what ultimately situates Pearl Jam in the British Romantic poetic tradition. In "Lines left upon a Seat in a Yew-tree which stands near the Lake of Esthwaite," Wordsworth writes,

> True dignity abides with him alone
> Who, in the silent hour of inward thought,
> Can still suspect, and still revere himself,
> In lowliness of heart.[70]

---

[65] Pearl Jam, "Infallible," in *Lightning Bolt* (2013).
[66] Pearl Jam, "Dance of the Clairvoyants," in *Gigaton* (2020).
[67] Pearl Jam, "Quick Escape," in *Gigaton* (2020).
[68] Pearl Jam, "Life Wasted," in *Pearl Jam* (2006).
[69] Pearl Jam, "Seven O'Clock," in *Gigaton* (2020).
[70] Wordsworth, "Lines Left Upon a Seat in a Yew-tree which Stands Near the Lake of Esthwaite," in *Wordsworth's Poetry and Prose*, 57–60.

Like Wordsworth, Pearl Jam exhorts listeners to look inward to themselves to find the light, the hope, the utopian energy. Only then can that light be turned outward to make the world a better place. Because, of course, there is no time to begin like the end. After thirty years, Pearl Jam has become Blake's ancient bard, who warns youth,

> How many have fallen there!
> They stumble all night over bones of the dead:
> And feel they know not what but care;
> And wish to lead others when they should be led.[71]

Whatever lies in Pearl Jam's future, the band's legacy will be that of five musicians who were not afraid to search for meaning and who constantly strived to make this world the better world that it could be. They looked for and found hope in desolate places, even in the worst of times, and passed on what they found to all who would listen. "Whoever said it's all been said / Gave up on satisfaction."[72]

Bibliography

Blake, William. *Blake's Poetry and Designs*, edited by Mary Lynn Johnson and John E. Grant. New York: Norton, 2008.

Bloch, Ernst. *The Principle of Hope*. 1954–1959. 3 vols., translated by Neville Plaice, Stephen Plaice, and Paul Knight. Cambridge, MA: The MIT Press, 1986.

Ferber, Michael. *The Cambridge Introduction to British Romantic Poetry*. Cambridge: Cambridge University Press, 2012.

Fraistat, Neil. "*From* the 'Field' of *Lyrical Ballads*." In *Wordsworth's Poetry and Prose*, edited by Nicholas Halmi, 601–12. New York: Norton, 2014.

Geoghegan, Vincent. *Ernst Bloch*. New York: Routledge, 2008.

Ginsberg, Allen. "My Vision of Blake." In *Blake's Poetry and Designs*, edited by Mary Lynn Johnson and John E. Grant, 519–23. New York: Norton, 2008.

Jameson, Fredric. *Archaeologies of the Future: The Desire Called Utopia and Other Science Fictions*. London: Verso, 2005.

Letkemann, Jessica. "Music for Rhinos. 1990: The Making of Pearl Jam." *TwoFeetThick.com*, 2010. Available online: http://www.twofeetthick.com/2010/10/18/1990-the-making-of-pearl-jam-a-tft-mini-book (accessed April 3, 2021).

Mason, Emma. *The Cambridge Introduction to William Wordsworth*. Cambridge: Cambridge University Press, 2012.

---

[71] Blake, "The Voice of the Ancient Bard," 8–11.
[72] Pearl Jam, "Who Ever Said," in *Gigaton* (2020).

Muñoz, José Esteban. *Cruising Utopia: The Then and There of Queer Futurity*. New York: New York University Press, 2009.

Ostriker, Alicia. "Desire Gratified and Ungratified: William Blake and Sexuality." In *Blake's Poetry and Designs*, edited by Mary Lynn Johnson and John E. Grant, 560–71. New York: Norton, 2008.

Quinney, Laura. *William Blake on Self and Soul*. Cambridge, MA: Harvard University Press, 2009.

Wordsworth, William. *Wordsworth's Poetry and Prose*, edited by Nicholas Halmi. New York: Norton, 2014.

3

Who's the Elderly Band Behind the Counter in a Small Town?

Radu Uszkai* and Mihail-Valentin Cernea

In 2017, Pearl Jam was finally (and deservedly) inducted into the Rock & Roll Hall of Fame by their longtime friend and die-hard fan David Letterman. After the ceremony, the band performed one of their iconic songs, "Alive," with Dave Krusen, their first full-time drummer, instead of Matt Cameron. Was this the same band as the one which started up in 1990, following the demise of Mother Love Bone and a name change from Mookie Blaylock?

Things were different then, is all different now?

Change is an integral part of our lives. Saying this does not make us exceptional philosophers, albeit Heraclitus might even go so far as to say that you cannot listen to the same Pearl Jam album twice. From a philosophical standpoint—or, more precisely, for metaphysicians—change is interesting because it poses a series of fascinating questions, one of which revolves around identity: how can something remain the same through the passage of time? In the face of unavoidable transformations, is there some underlying principle(s) that allow us to say that an avid concert aficionado who never missed a Pearl Jam concert from 1990 up to 2020 actually witnessed live performances from the same band?

Before sinking the philosophical needle deep, we should note that, among the many reasons that we have to be fans of this band, one of the most overlooked has to do with the fact that Pearl Jam does not have any real identity problems. Sure,

---

* Radu Uszkai's work was supported by a grant of the Romanian Ministry of Education and Research, CNCS-UEFISCDI, project number PN-III-P1-1.1-TE-2019-1765, within PNCDIIII, awarded for the research project Collective moral responsibility: from organizations to artificial systems. Re-assessing the Aristotelian framework, implemented within CCEA & ICUB, University of Bucharest (2021-2022).

they began by naming themselves after the former point guard of the New Jersey Nets, got through a couple of drummers, added Boom Gaspar on keyboards, changed their music style and got—well—significantly older. However, there is virtually no one saying that the band who just recently released *Gigaton* in 2020 isn't Pearl Jam in a metaphysical sense, though some 1990's hardcore nostalgic fans might feel that the band is different (albeit from a purely aesthetic standpoint—more on this later, stay tuned). Maybe with the exception of Mudhoney—who only lost Matt Lukin, the inspiration for the *No Code* song—other Seattle bands have gone through drastic changes. The demise of Green River and Mother Love Bone paved the way for our favorite band. From their starting line-up, Melvins is now left only with (the iconic, though) Buzz Osbourne. Both Nirvana and Soundgarden tragically died after Kurt Cobain's and Chris Cornell's suicides.

The metaphysics of transtemporal identity gets dirtier with Alice in Chains. Layne Staley's death from an overdose in 2002 did not mean—at least formally—the death of Alice in Chains, with Jerry Cantrell upping his vocal output and bringing in William DuVall as a substitute. Stone Temple Pilots (we know we're cheating, they're from San Diego) went through a similar core transformation, but with a twist. They were on hiatus for a couple of years, got back but sacked Scott Weiland and replaced him with Chester Bennington, and then named Jeff Gutt as lead vocalist two years after Scott died, releasing two albums with him.

As the remaining members have no projects to revive Nirvana or Soundgarden, we can safely say that their respective deaths put a dent on any metaphysical analysis of whether they could ever make a comeback as Nirvana and Soundgarden. Melvins, Alice in Chains, and Stone Temple Pilots are in a much more interesting situation. Is it still Melvins if the band only has Buzz from the original line-up? What about Alice in Chains and Stone Temple Pilots? Sure, most of the founding members are still there, but can bands without (at least seemingly essential parts like) Layne or Scott still be called Alice in Chains and Stone Temple Pilots?

Pearl Jam, thankfully, is still alive and kicking out the jams, with no identity problems. Let's explore the reasons for why this is the case, and afterwards complicate things with the philosopher's favorite tool: counterfactuals.

Yield: Metaphysics and social ontology ahead

Philosophers haven't shown a lot of interest in the issue of transtemporal identity of rock bands. One obvious reason might be that, well, for the most part of the history of philosophy rock bands were not a thing, whereas the same cannot be said about objects that were found to be more deserving of philosophical interest like ships. Another reason is that, well, this is actually a really complicated issue. While we are still light years away from claiming that we have a definite theory of the identity of rock bands over time, our account, which dwells on previous work from Brehmer and Cohnitz (2007), Bondarchuk (2013), and Cray (2013), holds that there are five main questions which any exploration of the transtemporal identity of a rock band should answer:

1. Is legal recognition important?
2. Are band names relevant to band identity?
3. What do changes in band membership over time entail with regard to identity?
4. Do significant changes in music style have any impact on the identity of the band?
5. In what way is the identity of a rock band dependent on its social and cultural perception?

Before moving forward, one metaphysical distinction is as important as Dave Abbruzzese drumming on *Vs.*: whose identity are we talking about? Who is the subject matter that raises this philosophical concern? One common misconception that we wish to vanquish is the view that could be summed up as "Band A = member (x) + member (n)." While line-ups do play some part in the identity of a band, they are not the same type of object that bands are. Line-ups (and this applies also to other types of entities like sports teams or governments) regularly change over time, while the same cannot be said about bands. This happens because, as Searle (1995) would put it, rock bands belong to a different realm, namely that of "institutional facts." Governments survive after an election, even if they might have a new Prime Minister with a different political leaning. Ditto in the case of sports teams. Almost no one from the legendary 1990's Chicago Bulls plays/works for the organization anymore, not even Eddie's friend, Dennis Rodman. They completely reshuffled their line-up, changed their playing style, but they are still known and recognized as the Chicago Bulls. So, why are we so certain that both *Ten* and *Gigaton*, while released 29 years apart, belong to the same band? Let's set sail, shall we?

Theseus, the love boat captain

The "Ship of Theseus" is the *Ten* of metaphysical thought experiments concerning transtemporal identity. It's one of the first ever conceived in the history of philosophy, almost everybody knows it, some have entered the field of metaphysics because of its puzzling nature, while others, even though they still find it relevant, tend to think it's at least a bit overrated. Imagine that, while kept in a museum, the ship of the famous Theseus tends to consistently run into a predictable problem: its wooden parts start to rot. Each time this happens, the museum curator replaces a rotten piece of wood with a new one. As time goes by it seems that, in a century or so, all the pieces of the original ship have been replaced. Do we still have the same ship, or is it a new object? What if, to complicate matters even further, someone stored all the original pieces and started building a ship from scratch? Is this the *real* ship of Theseus or is it the previous one?

Our preferred way of solving this puzzle (and yes, there are rival approaches to it) revolves around the "closest continuer" theory, a way out proposed by Robert Nozick. For Nozick, the solution to such puzzles involving transtemporal identity is not particularly hard:

> something at t2 is not the same entity as x at t1, if it is not x's closest continuer. And "closest" means closer than all others; if two things at t2 tie in closeness to x at t1, then neither is the same entity as x [...] how close something must be to x to be x, it appears, depends on the kind of entity x is.[1]

Sounds a bit complicated? Let's make it clearer by applying it, first, to the Theseus puzzle. What happens every time we replace an old piece of rotten wood with another over a span of a century? There is certainly some change at the material level but, from a metaphysical and ontological point of view, nothing of significance changes. We still have continuity of form. Each replacement, plank by plank, ends up producing the closest continuer of the original ship and, as a consequence, it has the only legitimate claim of being the ship of Theseus. With regard to the second scenario, both the altered and the reconstructed ship have a legitimate claim of being the original one and, as such, if they are tied in closeness then we could safely say that neither is the ship of Theseus. It all depends, *pace* Nozick, on what type of object we're talking about and whether

---

[1] Robert Nozick, *Philosophical Explanations* (Cambridge, MA: Harvard University Press, 1981), 34.

there any essential properties that it should have in order for its survival. Long story short, the issue of identity over time is problematic only when there is more than one entity that could have a legitimate claim of being the closest continuer of the original one.

Nozick's own version of the Theseus paradox is closer to our topic. At the beginning of the twentieth century, Vienna was the Seattle of the grunge era, with the Vienna Circle being the hottest band of philosophers there was.[2] Its dissolution was caused by the political instability in Europe caused by the annexation of Austria by Nazi Germany. Let's imagine, says Nozick, that there were twenty members of the Vienna circle and suppose that three of them managed to safely arrive in Istanbul, where they continued to meet and discuss philosophy. In 1943, they heard that all the other members were dead. As a result, they styled themselves as the Vienna Circle (in exile), as they could legitimately claim that they are the closest continuer of the original Circle. In 1945, however, after the war had ended, they received a letter informing them that nine members of the circle managed to flee to safety in the US, where they also continued the philosophical program of the Vienna Circle. Both groups have a *prima facie* right to claim that they are Vienna Circle as both continued the activity of the original group. However, if all members have an equal worth, then the group with the most philosophers wins the metaphysical prize of being the closest continuer and the right to label themselves as the Vienna Circle, whereas the Istanbul group would only be an offshoot.

One key assumption in Nozick's example is that all members are (metaphysically) equal. Things would have been different were we to think that Moritz Schlick would have still been alive and emigrated with the Istanbul group.[3] As the founder of the Vienna Circle, wouldn't Schlick's person vouch for the fact that, even if it had fewer members, the one from Istanbul would have been the closest continuer of the Vienna Circle?

The changes that rock bands go through over time are quite similar to the ones from the previous thought experiments. Various "planks" get changed over time—from the name a band has, to their music style and, more importantly, to band membership. Sometimes, bands split evenly, with members that could be considered essential arguing that their current band line-ups are the closest

---

[2] Depending on how loose we define membership to the Circle, it had some of the biggest figures of contemporary philosophers, from Moritz Schlick, Rudolf Carnap, and Kurt Gödel, to Karl Popper and Ludwig Wittgenstein.
[3] Schlick was tragically assassinated by a former student of his, Johann Nelböck in 1936.

continuer of the original band. Other times, one band member who is considered by some to be essential, like Ozzy Osbourne, leaves the band while another, Tony Iommi, claims that he is still the guitarist of a band titled Black Sabbath, with fans clashing on the issue of whether the band died after the departure of the Ozzman or not.[4]

What "planks" did Pearl Jam lose or have replaced, and were there any changes which would make it problematic to assert that what we currently call Pearl Jam is the closest continuer of the band that Jeff and Stone, following the demise of Green River and Mother Love Bone, established in 1990 alongside Mike, Dave Krusen, and Eddie Vedder, a promising surfer turned vocalist from San Diego, who sang funky tunes with Bad Radio and had just made a cameo on the Temple of the Dog album?

Hear my name, take a good look

"My favorite grunge band is Mookie Blaylock. I really like their drummer, Dave Krusen!" We are willing to make a bet that no one said this in the past thirty years. If anyone did say it, then chances are that she was one of the 299 people present at the Off Ramp Café in Seattle on October 22, 1990, getting a glimpse into the even flow of the future of music.

The name "Mookie Blaylock" did not last for too long. Due to impending legal issues—Mookie's lawyers weren't so enthusiastic about the prospect of a grunge band named after the former NBA star—when the band signed their first professional contract with a label it changed its name to Pearl Jam. Thus, the first "plank" of the original band was replaced.

Searching for the conditions according to which we might say that an entity is the same through the passage of time, one might ponder as to whether the same name would count, in any way, as an essential element and if, once changed, this would signal the death of the original entity.

Is there even a minimal case in favor of this position? In order for something to be the same at different stages in history, should that entity have the same name? As we well know, due to various reasons, people routinely change their names. Be it marriage, an embarrassing first name given by their parents, or in

---

[4] James Bondarchuk, "It's Not Sabbath Unless Ozzy's the Singer (But It's Fine If You Disagree)," in *Black Sabbath and Philosophy: Mastering Reality*, William Irwin, ed. (Oxford: Blackwell, 2013).

order to make a political statement, an individual can have different names but still be the same person. Let's imagine, for the sake of the argument, that both of us change our names to Jeremy. Does this entail that we are different persons? That we are the same person, given that we have the name? Would this generate any significant change in the world, other than confusion when we would go out with our friends?

We are unsure whether Saul Kripke listens to grunge (or even music, for that matter), but he can surely help us in figuring out whether names are integral to someone's identity. Kripke (1980) holds that names do not have any descriptive content whatsoever, as they only function as rigid designators. The only thing that names do is help us in referencing something or someone from the world, nothing less and, certainly, nothing more.

As such, both Mookie Blaylock and Pearl Jam refer to the same object, with the band now called Pearl Jam being the closest continuer of the original band named after Mookie as there was no other band which, by adopting the name "Mookie Blaylock," claimed to be the closest continuer of the original. The band continued on with the same legal status and with the social and cultural recognition of fans and music critics alike.

An additional reason for why name changing is not an issue for the transtemporal identity of bands over time has to do with the fact that, as most readers certainly know, Pearl Jam's case is by no means a singular one. Rock bands routinely change their names (Warsaw became Joy Division, Led Zeppelin could have been known as The New Yardbirds, and "Beatlemania" dodged the bullet after the band changed its name from The Quarry Men) but this does not mean that the respective bands changed in any significant way.

All those yesterdays

If names are not essential for the identity of a band over time, surely things are different when we talk about changes in band membership, right? As we have already alluded in a previous section, not quite.

For Pearl Jam in particular it seems that being their drummer is quite a risky job. That is, if you're not Matt Cameron, the former Soundgarden drummer who joined them in 1998, who has had the longest spell up to date. As we all know, Matt joined the band after Jack Irons decided to retire after drumming with them on the *Vitalogy* tour and being an integral part in *No Code* and in the recording of *Yield*. Jack, who replaced Dave Abbruzzese behind the drum kit after the latter was fired (due to a spat with Eddie after the former's alleged desire to become a grunge rock star), was invited by Stone and Jeff in 1990 to be the drummer of a new band, founded on the demise of Mother Love Bone, originally with Dave Krusen on drums. In between the two Daves, Matt Chamberlain lent them a hand on drums, ending up an integral part of Pearl Jam's history by being their drummer in the "Alive" video. As Bremer and Cohnitz (2007) would put it, replacement was not the only way in which the original line-up of Pearl Jam was affected; budding—adding someone without replacing a current member—also happened when Boom Gaspar joined in 2002, as a touring and session member.

The other ways in which the line-up of a band can change are through fission (a band divides into at least two, like Green River did with Mudhoney and Mother Love Bone), fusion (what happened with Guns N' Roses, with two bands joining into one), and separation (what happened with Nirvana after Kurt died and the remaining members stopped playing together).[5]

The hard problem of the identity of rock bands over time revolves around fission, when two bands who result from the original split both claim that they are the closest continuer of the original band, just like in Nozick's example with the Vienna Circle. Does the replacement of four drummers and the addition of a keyboard player mean anything for the identity of Pearl Jam?

One thing we need to remember is the distinction we made between a band and the line-up: they belong to two distinct ontological realms. First of all, as long as no member who is replaced is deemed to be essential, we need not have any metaphysical worries. Each replacement of a drummer is similar to the replacement of a plank from Theseus' ship, with the new line-up being not only the legitimate one who has a claim of being the closest continuer to the original band but, in our case, the only one.

Things might have gotten a bit complicated if, following his dismissal, Dave Abbruzzese had started a new band with the aim of competing with the line-up that had Jack Irons on drums as the "real" Pearl Jam. Now it is true that Dave did start other musical projects, but at no point in time did he make any claim of being the drummer of the closest continuer of the band that started playing with

---

[5] Manuel Bremer and Daniel Cohnitz, "Is It Still Metallica? On the Identity of Rock Bands Over Time," in *Metallica and Philosophy: A Crash Course in Brain Surgery*, William Irwin, ed. (Oxford: Blackwell, 2007), 184–5.

Dave Krusen in 1990. Remember that the issue of identity over time is complicated in the case of entities like groups according to the closest continuer theory only if there is another group that can have a legitimate claim to continuity. Further complications could arise if competing claims were to find a place in a court of justice. If we are right in saying that bands belong to the Searlian realm of institutional facts, then legal recognition is important for establishing whether an object continues over time or not.[6] Thankfully, this was never the case for Pearl Jam.

A different way to make our claim would be to follow Cray's application of the closest continuer theory for rock bands in relation to the changes in the band's membership. According to him, "a line-up at a time 1 and a line-up at a later time 2 are the same band if and only if they satisfy the *continuity*, *intention*, and *uniqueness* criteria."[7] Since every one of Pearl Jam's line-ups has had significant overlap, the continuity criterion is satisfied (beyond any reasonable doubt, as most of the founding members are still in the band). As each successive line-up always had the intention of being Pearl Jam, then the second criterion is also satisfied.[8] Uniqueness was covered extensively up to this point: each successive line-up following each replacement of a drummer or the addition of Boom was the only one claiming to be the band titled "Pearl Jam" and formerly known as "Mookie Blaylock."

Having said this, we can safely conclude that, even if they had a different line-up when inducted in the Rock & Roll Hall of Fame or when they released *Gigaton* in 2020 in comparison to their membership in 1990, Pearl Jam is the same band that it was more than thirty years ago when they played "Alive" for the first time on stage with Dave Krusen in a club in Seattle.

---

[6] The relevance of legal recognition and continuity should not be exaggerated. First of all, bands can exist outside the realm of formal and commercial activities. Your Friday night garage band you made with your high school friends with a quirky name is still a band, even if it is not a recognized trademark. Secondly, the legal recognition of Pearl Jam as a rock band is relevant only so long as the members of Pearl Jam play their awesome music. If tomorrow they decide to call it quits to music and play basketball after establishing a team named Pearl Jam they would have the legal right to do this, but the resulting group wouldn't be a rock band and, as such, not the closest continuer we have in mind.

[7] Wesley D. Cray, "Fightin' Words: Sabbath Doesn't Need the Ozzman," in *Black Sabbath and Philosophy*, 132.

[8] While it might seem pretty commonsensical, intention is a key criterion because it helps us in adequately distinguishing when a certain line-up plays as Pearl Jam and when it does not. Firstly, all Pearl Jam members had (or still have) side-projects, but none claimed that, in that incarnation, they play as "Pearl Jam." Secondly, even if all Pearl Jam members played with Neil Young on the *Mirror Ball* album, the end product is still credited to the "Godfather of Grunge."

Last exit

Before complicating things a little bit, we need to cover one additional issue regarding the last removable "plank": music style.

We know of no example of a rock band (maybe with the odd exception of Nordic black metal, but this might be because we don't fully get that music) that plays the same thing throughout their musical career. In one way or another, all bands have an evolving music style, due to a wide variety of causes. Maybe one of the band members discovers a lost EP belonging to a 1960s garage band and they try to emulate its style during recording sessions. Maybe your influential guitarist or drummer leaves and the new member, influenced less by funk music and more by metal, changes your sound a bit (just look at Red Hot Chili Peppers when they brought in Dave Navarro). Other times you're the only member from the founding line-up and end up with something as bizarre as *Chinese Democracy*.

Taken at face value, we tend to (at least intuitively) think that aesthetics matters when thinking about the identity of a rock band. At the end of the day, when it's all said and done, we tend to say that Pearl Jam is a grunge band. However, if we were actually to believe this, we would commit a categorical error. In order to clarify this point, let's take a look at the following examples from different fields. Sports teams maintain their identity over time even if they adopt a different playing style. To go back to the Chicago Bulls example, they are the same team as they were back in the 1990s, when they dominated the NBA with their offensive style and robust defense even if, at present, they are no contenders for the Championship. TV series like Seinfeld changed over time, with more complex plots (even for a show about nothing) but remained the same metaphysical object.

In our case, Pearl Jam's style changed due to both changes in the membership (Dave Abbruzzese and Matt Cameron have completely different drumming styles, which influenced the albums they recorded and the live performances) and because Eddie and the gang wanted to experiment a lot. Even if some experimental albums were poorly received (just take a look at the reviews *Binaural* had), saying that Pearl Jam sounds different nowadays (which they do) has almost nothing to do with the survival of the metaphysical identity of the band, but with the aesthetic one. As the style was continuous and it still belongs to the generic "rock" genre, the aesthetic transformations were not dramatic. But even if Pearl Jam were to release an album of Balkan influenced trap music, they would still remain the same band, albeit the clash that would result from this would be fun to watch and read.

Eddie Vedder: Can't find a better man?

If line-ups don't seem to matter for the problem of the transtemporal identity of rock bands, how about individual members? Isn't it the same situation as in the case of line-ups?

To prove it's not, we will summon a terrible metaphysical specter—tremble, dear reader, as Kanye West enters our realm. If you have opened this book, chances are you like Pearl Jam at least a little bit. Now imagine for a second that Eddie Vedder retires, but the band decides to continue and replaces our favorite frontman with Kanye West, the Christian billionaire genius entrepreneur. As Eddie quit, he has no legal claim over the name despite the fact that the Jam we're writing about is his grandmother Pearl's recipe.[9] He can only watch in horror as Pearl Jam's new album has Stone Gossard rapping (though he'd probably be good at it) and more autotune than the entire history of grunge. Is this Vedderless new version truly Pearl Jam?

Legally, the answer is obvious: yeah! Metaphysically, we'll argue that the waters are murkier, even if the closest continuer theory points out to the same answer, and that there is a way to ontologically save Pearl Jam from Kanye. To do this, we'll have to think about what rock bands actually are.

The kind of object we have in mind when we think of a rock band has been hotly debated by philosophers of social ontology and sociologists alike—it's a social group. When philosophers try to provide conceptual frameworks of social groups, they generally accept what has been aptly named the Goldilocks constraint: "An ontology of social groups should include social groups that are common sensical and that figure in explanations and should not overgenerate social groups."[10] This means that if our metaphysical concept of a rock band allows that Eddie Vedder, Eddie van Halen, Jon Bon Jovi, and whatshisname from Nickelback having an implausible beer together is an actual rock band, then it's safe to say we are wrong.

---

[9] This story is not entirely true. In the sense that it is actually false.
[10] Katherine Ritchie, "Social Structures and the Ontology of Social Groups," *Philosophy and Phenomenological Research* 100, no. 2 (2020): 403.

Another thing to note is that we can distinguish between unorganized social groups and organized social groups.[11] Social groups are unorganized when they are formed unintentionally over some feature that the individual members share (think of groupings based on race, gender, economic status, etc.). Organized social groups are defined by an intentionally created structure to the group. Thus, Pearl Jam is an organized social group that often sings about disenfranchised unorganized social groups.

In the history of philosophy, there have been as many approaches to this issue as Pearl Jam's ever-changing drummers. We'll focus here only on two: structuralism and mereology. Structuralists tend to think of social groups as networks in which every individual member is the node. Social structures like these tend to survive individual nodes going through changes. This explains why we can have a Vienna Circle away from Vienna and with fewer members, as in Nozick's example. Unfortunately, it is not so obvious that this type of structuralism can save us from Kanye West. In this philosophical story, Eddie Vedder appears as just a node in a larger social structure—a node that can change in the relevant context. Under this approach, it may well be that the Pearl Jam structure will survive Eddie's departure. As philosophers, we may understand the point of Ritchie's outstanding contribution and its relevance for organized groups like governments, sports teams, or corporations. As Pearl Jam fans though, we cannot agree with this position. Any metaphysical theory that allows a Christian conservative billionaire rapper to be a part of our favorite band cannot be true. Didn't the Goldilocks constraint demand common sense?

On the other hand, mereologists try to approach social groups from the perspective of whole-part relations. Oversimplifying a bit, a social group is a whole while its members are its parts. The mereological approach is usually quite problematic when it comes to the reality of our social world. Classical mereology would look at an impromptu Pearl Jam acoustic concert where only Eddie and Mike are present as not a Pearl Jam concert because not all members of the group are present. But they would be singing Pearl Jam songs and most probably the other band members would not mind this one-off situation. Recently though, mereology is making a comeback in social ontology. One of the most recent proposals on this account is due to David Strohmeier (2019), who tries to unify other new developments in the field, and it hinges on the

---

[11] Ibid., 408–9.

notion of individual agents as parts appropriately designated to contribute to the group's functioning. Appropriate designation depends on the context of the group. As an example, you become part of a corporation if you are hired according to the appropriate formal processes that particular business requires. In the context of rock bands, though, what would appropriate designation mean exactly? The band members get a say—that is obvious. But do the fans?[12] The most honest thing a philosopher can say here is that it probably depends on the band and, as we're about to argue, its history.

In our case, what we want to say is that Kanye's Pearl Jam cannot actually be Pearl Jam because Eddie Vedder has an essential contribution to Pearl Jam's functioning, thus he cannot be as easily replaced as a drummer. His voice, his lyrics, his on-stage persona are a big part of what we use generally to identify Pearl Jam as a band. That is why we could plausibly argue that Eddie Vedder is an essential part of Pearl Jam, i.e., Pearl Jam would just cease to exist without him, like Nirvana disappeared without Kurt Cobain. There are other examples that could point in the opposite direction—we've already mentioned how Alice in Chains survived without Layne Staley. Also, we do admit our Vedder essentialism is a bit offensive to the amazing talent of the rest of the members of the band. If Cantrell managed to bring Alice in Chains back to life, maybe Gossard and McCready could do the same, given the unfortunate chance.

Here is where we think that the cultural recognition of bands comes in as an appropriate designator. In more postmodern terms, the work of art lives somewhere between the author's intent and the public perception of it. A Vedderless Pearl Jam could only survive in the actual world if a significant portion of the fans accept it as such according to their own individual and collective expectations. Pearl Jam as Kanye's new pet musical project would not be met with the kindness that the Alice in Chains revival was met. This being said, we still think that replacing Eddie Vedder is close to impossible for Pearl Jam.

Talking about Black Sabbath, Cray argued that Ozzy is not essential for that band mainly because that is not how essences work in philosophy. If Ozzy was actually essential for Black Sabbath, then the sentence "Ozzy was fired from Black Sabbath" would not make sense in the same way that the sentence

---

[12] To be very clear, this is not a moral question here. We are not asking whether fans should be a part of the process of changing line-ups. Rather, the question is whether fans are, in a metaphysical sense, part of that process.

"Water isn't H2O" doesn't. In that very Aristotelian way of understanding essences, no band member is essential unless they appear in the band name. Which means that Eddie Vedder isn't essential and the Kanye monster rears its head again.

What we haven't properly taken into account until this point in our musings is that social groups, like rock bands, have an important historical component that should be taken into account when we think about essential band members.

Let's not forget the following facts: Ozzy is in less than half of Black Sabbath's total number of albums and Alice in Chains has Layne Staley on half of their current discography. Pearl Jam, on the other hand, has Eddie Vedder on all of its eleven albums. Counterfactually, if Eddie would've left, say, after *Yield*, and the band survived, maybe we would not see him today as an essential member. But, in the actual world, Eddie Vedder is a part of the entire thirty-year history of Pearl Jam, he was there for every album, every concert, and every fight with Ticketmaster. If one was to hear Eddie's voice on a new track on the radio, one's first thought would probably be that Pearl Jam has a new album out, which is definitely not the case in bands with more complicated histories. Unlike material objects, social and cultural objects establish themselves in time through complicated social, cultural, and economic processes. While an Aristotelian would rightly balk at the following statement, it just might be that the essences of social objects are not fixed and unchanging, at least not in their early histories, but become so in time, within a cultural context. We can't imagine the First French Empire without Napoleon, but that is only because it began and ended with him. In the same way, rock bands, unlike most governments and other organized social groups, can, in time, develop essential parts that can be of great use to the grunge metaphysician who wants to establish the transtemporal identity of the whole.

The astute reader will notice that almost the same historical arguments could easily apply to the other permanent members of Pearl Jam. Aren't they essential too? We're happy to concede this point. Yes, Stone, Mike, and Jeff are essential members of Pearl Jam. They've been Pearl Jam for so long, one cannot imagine them not being Pearl Jam. Keeping to Strohmeier's framework, we think that the appropriate designation of group membership for rock bands is cultural and historic. Fans and the passing of time have a metaphysical bearing on the identity of a particular band. This would also explain why there is such a rich diversity of puzzling identity cases in the history of rock music—it is generated by the conjunction of musicians' changing desires and kinship, time, and fan perception.

A simple all-encompassing theory of rock band transtemporal identity may just not be possible.

Prance of the clairvoyants

If girls really want to dance and men really want to fix and fire things, then philosophers, no matter where they identify themselves on the gender spectrum, cannot help themselves to conceptually break things before attempting to fix them and usually fail. What follows is exactly that. Until this point in our paper, the concept of Pearl Jam has survived (metaphysically no less) the changing of their name, their music style, drummers coming and going and even Eddie being replaced by Kanye West (well, not really in this case, but that is for the best). Now for the ultimate test: can automation in the far future take their jobs as well as ours? Let's take another walk into the garden of counterfactuals (with our hands bound only by the most basic laws of logic).

Let's imagine a time a couple of centuries from now or maybe more—what is important for this thought experiment is that everyone alive today is dead. The members of Pearl Jam are dead, we are dead and even you, dear reader, are dead. Pearl Jam probably is not, as we think people will be listening to Pearl Jam for the rest of human existence. AI is now commonplace, as are human-like robots. A record label decides to do the evolution by having AI analyze everything ever recorded about Pearl Jam (songs, live performances, interviews, member Google search histories—we mean literally every trace they've ever left in this world), build robots that look exactly like Pearl Jam, act exactly like Pearl Jam, and sing like Pearl Jam. Let's also assume that the experiment is a resounding success and robot Pearl Jam even manages to compose music that the original band and their fans would approve of. Robot-Pearl Jam starts touring and Eddie's voice is heard again in stadiums throughout the solar system. Can we think of robot-Pearl Jam as an actual instance of Pearl Jam?

The closest continuer theory seems to support robot-Pearl Jam as being actually Pearl Jam. There is no one alive to claim to be Pearl Jam and even the cultural community who could have had an answer to that question has long been replaced. If it walks like Pearl Jam, talks like Pearl Jam, and sings like Pearl Jam, it must be Pearl Jam, i.e., the closest continuer that the future could offer.

But can it really be Pearl Jam if all of its essential members are dead? And if robot-Pearl Jam is Pearl Jam, doesn't it throw the whole essential-parts-of-the-whole theory down the positronic drain? We think it doesn't, because the success of robot-Pearl Jam hinges on the robots successfully replicating the original biological band members. The whole robot-Pearl Jam project assumes that there are such things as essential band members and that it can only call itself Pearl Jam if it recreates the living band of the past today. If it didn't, a robot-Pearl Jam built out of robotic Justin Bieber look-alikes would be possible and we really do not want to go there again.

Implications arrive like butterflies

People often complain that metaphysical discussions have no bearing on real-world issues. Even if Kanye West were to join Pearl Jam, we'd still have our favorite albums. In this case, as we've stated, Pearl Jam doesn't really have any truly difficult identity issues with its relatively stable line-up throughout its history. So, what's the point of this paper? Honestly, the point was to say we really like Pearl Jam, but there is actually more.

First, it is clear that the law can get rock band identity very wrong with unethical implications when it comes to ownership of music and the financial benefits of being a rock star. If metaphysicians can be bothered to investigate the actual complicated history of a social entity like a rock band just to make a philosophical point, legal scholars and lawmakers generally aim for more simple solutions. Tying intellectual property to a legal entity without deploying the complex conceptual apparatus developed by social ontologists seems like a missed opportunity to deliver actual real-world justice. Moreover, if our analysis is right, then the cultural community a band is a part of has more relevance to the identity and success of that band than one might be inclined to think. There may be some normative conclusion to be drawn from this discussion implying that a band has some moral obligations to their fans. Pearl Jam fighting Ticketmaster is an instance of a band respecting those obligations, Metallica going against Napster and the fans who download their music may be the exact opposite of that.

Secondly, even if line-ups do change over time without affecting a band identity by much, there arises a problem of moral merit for the cultural praise a certain line-up may receive. When Pearl Jam was inducted in the Rock & Roll Hall of Fame in 2017, Dave Abbruzzese was left out, even if he was part of the line-up that offered what some consider to be the best Pearl Jam albums. While he is not an essential member of the band per our definition, it does not follow that Abbruzzese is to be ignored. The current line-up of Pearl Jam was celebrated also for the achievements of the line-up containing Abbruzzese, thus it could plausibly be argued that he deserved part of the praise despite whatever disagreements he had with the band in the past. He may not be essential for Pearl Jam's identity, but he is still part of its history and it is that whole history being celebrated by the Rock & Roll Hall of Fame.

Bibliography

Bondarchuk, James. "It's Not Sabbath Unless Ozzy's the Singer (But It's Fine If You Disagree)." In *Black Sabbath and Philosophy: Mastering Reality*, edited by William Irwin, 113–26. Oxford: Blackwell, 2013.

Bremer, Manuel and Daniel Cohnitz. "Is It Still Metallica? On the Identity of Rock Bands Over Time." In *Metallica and Philosophy: A Crash Course in Brain Surgery*, edited by William Irwin, 183–95. Oxford: Blackwell, 2007.

Cray, Wesley D. "Fightin' Words: Sabbath Doesn't Need the Ozzman." In *Black Sabbath and Philosophy: Mastering Reality*, edited by William Irwin, 126–40. Oxford: Blackwell, 2013.

Kripke, Saul A. *Naming and Necessity*. Cambridge, MA: Harvard University Press, 1980.

Nozick, Robert. *Philosophical Explanations*. Cambridge, MA: Harvard University Press, 1981.

Ritchie, Katherine. "Social Structures and the Ontology of Social Groups." *Philosophy and Phenomenological Research* 100, no. 2 (2020): 402–24.

Searle, John R. *The Construction of Social Reality*. New York: The Free Press, 1995.

Strohmaier, David. "Group Membership and Parthood." *Journal of Social Ontology* 4, no. 2 (2019): 121–35.

4

Making a Choice When There Is No "Better Man"

Laura M. Bernhardt

Introduction

The woman at the heart of Pearl Jam's "Better Man" is trapped.[1] She has committed herself to a relationship that makes her miserable, but she can't seem to escape it. In Pearl Jam's *oeuvre*, she is in good company, struggling alongside the protagonists of "Leash," "Daughter," or "Rearviewmirror," among many other songs that explore the impossible-feeling challenge of leaving (or staying) in a hard place.

What keeps a person where she so clearly does not want to be?

When "Better Man" was recorded, the band was actively resisting everything that the music industry expected and demanded of them. The form that resistance took included attempts to take more direct control of their artistic work, sometimes exercised in ways that were damaging.

What keeps a band where they so clearly do not want to be?

This chapter offers a loose exploration of some possible answers by examining "Better Man" and the circumstances of its recording by way of an account of compromised moral and artistic agency that is ultimately best viewed through the lens of Simone Weil's account of affliction.

Song and story

"Better Man" is a hit that almost never happened. Eddie Vedder wrote it when he was still in high school, at a time in his life when he found himself struggling in his relationship with his family; he has publicly acknowledged that the lyrics

---

[1] See Pearl Jam, "Better Man," in *Vitalogy* (1994).

may refer (at least obliquely) to his mother and her relationship with his stepfather.[2] While the band started playing the song in live shows in 1993, Vedder resisted including it on *Vs.*, the album the band released that year, and very nearly had it removed from *Vitalogy* right before its scheduled release in November 1994.[3] Brendan O'Brien, who produced and recorded both albums with the band, recognized the song's commercial potential when he first heard it in 1993, but struggled to convince Vedder to record it at all.[4]

Even when "Better Man" was finally recorded for *Vitalogy*, Vedder remained both protective of it and unsatisfied with it. It wasn't until O'Brien and recording engineer Nick Di Dia merged a stripped-down re-recording of the opening with the much more up-beat original master that the version of the track that currently appears on the album finally came together.[5] Once released, it took on a life of its own—audiences routinely sing the song with and to the band in performances, and it's become a signature piece when Vedder plays solo or collaborates with other musicians.[6]

The song's lyrics present a psychological vignette in which a woman contemplates the trap her life has become for her in the context of an abusive relationship.[7] While she waits anxiously for her man to return, she "practices [the] speech" she'll use to leave him, but she never gives it—when he finally comes home, she pretends to sleep instead and avoids confrontation. The chorus is a repeated expression of despair that also hints at a complex set of emotions ranging from the hopeful to the violent (she lies to him about her feelings, even as "she dreams in color, she dreams in red"). Through the bridge and the end of the song, the listener is also informed that she doesn't want to leave because she did love him, and that "she needs him,"[8] which is given as the reason why she'll be back, even if she does leave (hinting at a familiar pattern of codependence).

---

[2] At the first live performance of the song in Atlanta in 1994, Vedder dedicated the song to "the bastard that married my mama" (see: https://www.youtube.com/watch?v=T8mWGUluRWA). The song has also been dedicated to others who might be read as abusers, including the George W. Bush administration.

[3] Jonathan Cohen and Mark Ian Wilkerson (ed.), *Pearl Jam Twenty* (New York: Simon & Schuster, 2011), 134–5, 152.

[4] Ibid., 134–5.

[5] Ibid., 152.

[6] Ibid.

[7] All lyrics referred to here are drawn from the "Better Man" page on Pearl Jam's website, which reproduces the "official" liner notes version of the song (https://pearljam.com/music/song/better-man).

[8] Or feeds him, which is what Vedder actually seems to sing most of the time. The "official" lyrics—not always trustworthy—insist that it's "needs," but... well. Listen to it. "Feeds" is arguably the more interesting lyrical choice, as it paints a picture of someone who stays in a bad situation for complex reasons—sometimes, what a person wants or needs most is to feel needed, and this is not always a healthy thing.

Musically, after its instrumentally simple opening, the song bounds into an energetic, up-tempo rocker that ends in a playfully extended jam.[9] While the bouncy ending might seem to be at odds with the story the lyrics tell, the sheer joy of it speaks to the possibility of a dangerous sort of hope. It's as if the song, too, dreams in color, and at the end the music moves to the tantalizing possibility of a world beyond waiting and watching the clock. The lyrics tell the story of someone who is trapped, but the music is the sound of the trap opening, with all of the hope and fear that might entail. Even if that hope is still only a dream, it's a powerful one, to which audiences actively respond by singing along. In this respect, "Better Man" is musically akin to "Alive" (in *Ten*, 1991), another Vedder-penned song that gets the sort of ecstatic response from live audiences that transforms a very dark lyrical story into something transcendent.[10]

More importantly, "Better Man" both belongs to and tells one part of a larger story. The tale to which this song belongs is embedded in a cultural moment—the post-punk and grunge scene in Seattle in the late 1980s and early 1990s—and framed by the struggles and histories of its creators and *dramatis personae*. It is a story neatly bookended in the music media by two different *Spin* cover articles about Vedder that stand as representative of his press presence in the early 1990s—he is given a voice, but only in the context of a particular representation of him and what he might mean to the music scene he occupies.

Both Jim Greer's 1993 piece on the release of *Vs.* and Craig Marks' 1995 return to Vedder in the wake of the *Vitalogy* release hit a set of common themes: they are particularly interested in offering a picture of the Pearl Jam frontman as a moody counter-cultural figure, most remarkable for (a) his aggressive sincerity and rejection of cynicism, (b) the personal vulnerability that is the consequence of his sincerity, and (c) his commitment to the transformative power of music for players and audiences alike.[11] For Greer and Marks, much of the story of Pearl Jam is about honesty and authenticity in the face of the pressures of commodification, as filtered through Vedder's unhappy observations about the

---

[9] They frequently jam on The English Beat's 1982 tune "Save It For Later," which has a similar chord progression, as in this medley from a show in Philadelphia (https://youtube/tPTyffpytJQ; accessed April 2, 2021).
[10] Cameron Crowe, "Five Against the World," *Rolling Stone*, October 28, 1993.
[11] See Jim Greer, "The Courtship of Eddie Vedder," *Spin*, December 1993; Craig Marks, "Eddie Vedder Breaks His Silence," *Spin*, January 1995.

effects of those pressures on the band. "Better Man" may have been written while its author was still too young to drink legally, but its incarnation on *Vitalogy* was recorded by a maturing band grappling with the fallout of its own success, and the entire album includes gestures both overt and subversive in that direction.[12]

The period from 1993 to 1995 saw Pearl Jam engaged in acts of resistance ranging from pointedly bizarre public behavior to offstage business choices meant to break the conventional arrangements that would otherwise have bound the band to the priorities of the music industry (most notably their refusal to do videos for *Vs.* and *Vitalogy* and their legal battle with Ticketmaster).[13] In his 1995 interview with Marks, Vedder frames some of Pearl Jam's response to the unrelenting pressure of its own success in terms of two different ways of dealing with it. "You either give people what they want, or you become cynical and that protects you," he tells Marks, and then admits that on *Vitalogy*, they didn't really buy the dichotomy: "I'm not good at either. We're still just being brutally honest and giving it our best."[14] Interestingly, he further confesses that he doesn't actually know why he puts the songs out there, although "[in] the old days, it was a dream to maybe not have to work the midnight shift, and somehow pay your rent by getting a check for your art."[15] This is not, in the context of the interview, treated as the admission of an inconsistency in his views; rather, it reads as the expression of someone who is surprised by the fact that other people value something he's created so very highly.

In response to a question about Kurt Cobain's discomfort with performing and feeling as if he were "faking it" (something Cobain talked about in interviews shortly before his death), Vedder identifies a danger posed by commodified musical production for a popular original performer who prefers raw honesty to cynicism:

> If you go out and play three shows, it's great. If you play sixty, somewhere along the line you're going to become an actor, or you're going to have to put yourself on autopilot just to survive it. That pisses me off because it's my fault, because of

---

[12] See Pearl Jam, *Vitalogy* (1994). "Corduroy" addresses the situation overtly, for example; "Bugs" does so subversively (largely by being unmarketable nonsense). Notably, *Vitalogy* is the first album in which the bulk of the writing belongs to Vedder; *Ten* and *Vs.* are more clearly either collaborative or driven by Gossard and Ament (see Cohen and Wilkerson, *Pearl Jam Twenty*, 153).
[13] Cohen and Wilkerson, *Pearl Jam Twenty*, 140–70.
[14] Marks, "Eddie Vedder Breaks His Silence."
[15] Ibid.

the songs. In order to sing them, they have to be felt. And I don't feel right singing them and not getting into the space of the song.¹⁶

What Vedder's comments suggest here is that the thing that makes Pearl Jam's songs so powerful for the band and for the audience—the authentic involvement of the performers and the audience in the shared emotional space of the music— is also what makes the compulsory performance of those songs alienating and unsustainable. With this in mind, *Vitalogy* is clearly conceived and presented as an act of resistance, effectively an attempt to avoid that alienation while also making it possible for them to sustain their art in continued engagement with their audience by exercising a certain kind of control over how their music is created, marketed, sold, and performed.

It is in this attempt that the protagonist of "Better Man" and the song's creators are most clearly seen to be in analogous positions. Neither of them are where they thought they'd end up, and neither of them are happy about their situation. They each got something they wanted (love, the music, to be needed, to be appreciated, to be heard, etc.), but it isn't what they thought it would be, and it ends up hurting them in unexpected ways. The woman in the song is acutely aware of what's gone wrong and what she needs to do. She isn't in love with the man for whom she waits, but she needs him and is needed by him, and this inevitably brings her back again to a terrible relationship. *Vitalogy*, as an act of resistance, doesn't really succeed in solving the band's problems; while the album received favorable reviews and did very well commercially, the *Vitalogy* tour turned into a personal and professional disaster of the band's own making.¹⁷ They aren't in love with the music industry, but participating in it is what allows them to create and share the music that matters to them. If there is one significant difference between the choices made in the song and those made about and around it, it is perhaps found in Pearl Jam's decision to cancel the *Vitalogy* tour and reschedule dates once it became clear that it wasn't working. The woman in the song never gives the speech she practiced, but the band at least finds a way to stop for a moment and regroup.¹⁸

---

[16] Ibid. Note that *Vitalogy* went forward without drummer Dave Abbruzzese, whose attitude toward commercial success was markedly different from Vedder's. One might be forgiven for thinking, as Abbruzzese apparently did at the time, that the rest of the band felt that they'd been given an ultimatum by Vedder and decided that if they had to choose between the singer and the drummer, the drummer was easier to replace (see Marks, "Eddie Vedder Breaks His Silence"; Neely, *Five Against One*, 293–9).

[17] See Craig Marks, "The Road Less Traveled," *Spin*, February 1997; Cohen and Wilkerson, *Pearl Jam Twenty*, 162–70.

[18] Marks, "The Road Less Traveled," 96.

So, to come back to the beginning: why does a person—or a band—stay where they so clearly do not want to be? Is it simply a matter of tradeoffs gone sour, in which one gets what one wants or needs at a price that turns out to be harmful? Is it all a hellish compromise that one cynically chooses to embrace, for good or ill?

Compromises, moral and artistic

One way to talk about how agents make less-than-ideal choices in response to difficult circumstances is to describe their agency itself as compromised, implying that under some set of conditions, the very power to choose is itself impaired or constrained, and that this therefore requires some reconsideration of the moral responsibility assigned to those agents. The sense of "compromise" at work in such a description is one that tends to emphasize damage done to or limitations placed upon the agent's integrity as a moral being. Uncompromised moral agents, when required to choose, are able to pick what they believe to be the good from an appropriate set of available options; compromised agents, when required to choose, may be constrained to select one of many bad possibilities under circumstances that admit no options that they would otherwise regard as good. The key point of treating agency as compromised in this sense is the underlying assumption that the impairment of autonomy represents a deficiency in moral agency as such, and that consideration of this deficiency might merit a different understanding of the degree or manner in which compromised agents are morally responsible for their choices or actions.

Victims of abuse or violence, for example, are sometimes described as compromised moral choosers; they are trapped in situations over which they may believe that they can exercise very little control, and may therefore be treated as if they were not truly autonomous in their choices. One way of describing this compromised condition is to conceive of agency as "autonomy plus options," as Carisa Showden does in *Choices Women Make*.[19] What Showden argues (drawing heavily on Foucault) is that an account of agency that adequately describes the kinds of choices that abuse victims, sex workers, and women in similarly complicated situations make must include not only autonomy

---

[19] Carisa R. Showden, *Choices Women Make: Agency in Domestic Violence, Assisted Reproduction, and Sex Work* (Minneapolis: University of Minnesota Press, 2011).

(understood as "self-governance"), but also "the external impediments to, and resources available for, achieving one's goals," which she refers to as "freedom" in order to distinguish it from autonomy (which is primarily a matter of internal dispositions rather than external constraints).[20] Agency described as compromised occurs, on Showden's account, when autonomy operates alongside and is constrained by the lack of freedom; a compromised agent's autonomy is altered when that agent's circumstances affect its exercise.

Showden's approach to agency answers the question of why (in general) a woman might stay in an abusive relationship with a resounding "it's complicated," largely due to the complexity of the full set of material, social, political, and psychological conditions that might affect how that woman makes her choices.[21] It's not a simple tradeoff of one desirable object or state for another (or a choice between greater or lesser amounts of misery), in which agency is impaired when autonomy is constrained by limitations on one's freedom; for Showden, "agency and victimization are coincident rather than mutually exclusive categories," and women making hard choices in bad situations are no less autonomous than they would be under conditions allowing them greater actual freedom.[22] This picture is further complicated by the discursive relationship between freedom and autonomy, in which circumstances may also affect judgment or alter the psychological conditions under which autonomy is exercised by a given agent.[23]

In the specific case of the protagonist of "Better Man," the song represents a frustrating cycle of behavior in which it's clear that the protagonist will always "be back again," and cannot be persuaded to stay away even when she seems to know herself to have few positive incentives to stick around (she's well aware that she doesn't love him, and she knows her situation is bad). This frustration makes it seem reasonable to think that there is something questionable about a moral agent who makes decisions this way; surely, if her agency were not in some way impaired, this person would be persuadable in the direction of what is manifestly her best interests. If we follow Showden, however, the problem is not that the woman in the song is wrongly or defectively unpersuadable as a chooser whose agency is compromised, it's that her freedom is constrained in such a way as to alter what counts for her as the best available choice. Showden's preferred approach to addressing this problem in the context of domestic abuse is therefore

---

[20] Ibid., 42–3.
[21] Ibid., chaps. 2–3.
[22] Ibid., 552.
[23] Ibid., chaps. 1–2.

worked out in systemic terms rather than at the level of individual choosers, and is aimed primarily at addressing the conditions constraining freedom in order to best facilitate the exercise of autonomy.[24] For Showden, creating a world in which leaving a bad situation is substantially easier to do is a better solution than working harder to find ways to convince someone to leave, precisely because it addresses the limitations on freedom that appear to compromise the exercise of autonomy.

If we accept Showden's approach to the problem, the application of her analysis to "Better Man" suggests that we may be asking the wrong question. Perhaps we should not be asking why someone stays where she does not want to be—we should instead be asking why she wants to be there (knowing full well that it might be because she believes there is nowhere else to go). The danger of asking this question in just this way, however, is that it may lead us to blame the victim for the harm done to her (as if it were something she desired), which is something Showden avoids. Showden wants to recover agency for abused women, but she certainly does not hold that this requires imposing on them some sort of moral responsibility for the abuse they suffer.[25] It's also something that doesn't sit well with the apparent sympathy Vedder has, as a songwriter, for the woman in his song—her situation is frustrating, but one doesn't get the sense from "Better Man" that she is blameworthy for it.

There is a useful parallel to be drawn here between compromised moral agency as Showden describes it and compromised artistic agency, in which artists whose creative integrity is compromised may feel constrained by their circumstances to produce work that they regard as in some way corrupted or adulterated. This form of compromised agency is most obviously visible in discussions of artistic authenticity, particularly in the context of the establishment or maintenance of a rock musician's aesthetic *bona fides* in the face of the corrupting temptation to "sell out."[26] It may also occur in instances in which the sincerity of the artist's expression or truthfulness of the artist's self-representation is called into question due to certain kinds of uses of their work (e.g., a band with

---

[24] Ibid., chap. 2.
[25] Ibid., chap. 3.
[26] This is an example of what Jeanette Bicknell describes as "authenticity as sincerity" for singers, which she treats as distinct from forms of authenticity centered on faithfulness (to a text, to an author's intentions, etc.) or boundary-policing (which addresses membership in a tradition or group to which a song "belongs"). See Jeanette Bicknell, *Philosophy of Song and Singing: An Introduction* (New York: Routledge, 2015), 56–8.

antiestablishment cred permitting the use of their music in commercials for mainstream consumer products or political candidates).[27]

Of course, the very idea of selling out depends on a set of assumptions about how rock music works that ought to raise some concerns about what really constitutes its aesthetic "authenticity," as Theodore Gracyk points out in his rejection of the Romantic version of rock aesthetics promoted by Camile Paglia and others.[28] Where Paglia and the proponents of Romantic aesthetics in rock see authenticity in resisting commercialism (a resistance framed either as the pursuit of high art or as the maintenance of some sort of original folk lineage), Gracyk rightly points out that there has never been a purely noncommercial rock music.[29] The bands Paglia holds up as examples of her Dionysian creative ideal (like The Rolling Stones) are never too far from the marketing department, and even the folk origins of the form are not free from commercial priorities; old blues musicians need to eat regular meals, too.[30] As Gracyk puts it, the upshot of the complex history of rockers in relation to their music and their market(s) is that "rock musicians themselves use Dionysian authenticity as a standard for artistic success. But they also use it as a selling point, and many do so consciously."[31]

This is one of the sore points to which Vedder frequently returns in his 90s interviews when he discusses the cynicism of the music industry and press—he rejects the claim that Pearl Jam's various acts of resistance are actually just a savvy marketing pose, even as the evidence in favor of that claim increases with the band's commercial success.[32] Gracyk's comment about the role of Dionysian authenticity in rock musicians' own understanding of their work suggests that while Vedder may be entirely honest in his rejection of the idea that Pearl Jam's anti-commercial moves are just a marketing pose, that doesn't foreclose the possibility that they are also a marketing pose.

Taking up Showden's language in this context—parsing the discursive relation of artistic autonomy and artistic freedom—reveals a slightly different version of

---

[27] Ibid.
[28] Theodore Gracyk, *Rhythm and Noise: An Aesthetics of Rock* (Durham: Duke University Press, 1996), 175–206.
[29] Ibid., 182–4.
[30] Ibid., 183.
[31] Ibid.
[32] For examples, see: Crowe, "Five Against the World"; Arion Berger, "Can't Find a Better Man," *The Village Voice*, January 31, 1995; Robert Hilburn, "He Didn't Ask for All This," *Los Angeles Times*, May 1, 1994; Marks, "The Road Less Traveled."

artistic agency, which may shade our understanding of authenticity. Given the history of rock music as a largely commercial aesthetic enterprise, rock musicians are always already selling out in the broadest possible sense (i.e., they get paid to play and record, they sell their musical labor). Their agency is compromised from the very beginning on this reading, as their material conditions constrain their freedom and thereby affect the exercise of their artistic autonomy regardless of their particular commitments with regard to the relation of authenticity to commodification. To choose to make a living in rock is to accept a set of limitations on one's freedom that necessarily shape the music one creates. Paglia's suggestion for avoiding this situation is that rock musicians should escape "the Darwinian laws of the marketplace" in favor of the creative haven of academia, which she seems to think would free them to create autonomously (and thus authentically).[33] Gracyk, however, rejects that option as a viable alternative, and for good reason; academia, rather than freeing rock musicians completely, is just as likely to replace the constraints of the marketplace with the constraints of an insular scholarly culture governed by its own norms and priorities.[34] Rock's enshrinement in the academy would be a different compromise, but still a compromise.

The question of why a band with anti-commercial principles might choose to occupy a position in which they are always already selling out, just like the question of why a victim of abuse might choose to stay in her abusive relationship, may also turn out to be the wrong question. Perhaps instead it would be better to ask why someone who loves rock music (playing it, listening to it, creating it) would choose commodification while sincerely believing that selling out kills what they love about the music. There appears to be a sort of cognitive dissonance at work here, in which the compromised agent doesn't merely condition the exercise of autonomy on material constraints, but actually prefers those constraints in a way that gives the lie to every rejection of selling out and undermines any sympathy one might feel for the musician's frustration with being objectified. Yet it seems wrong to reject out of hand a performer's expression of unhappiness about these conditions, just as it also seems wrong to hold up that unhappiness (e.g., Cobain's suicide) as an expression of some Romantic aesthetic ideal.

Once again: why does a person—or a band—stay where they so clearly do not want to be? The available answers suggested by Showden's version of compromised

---

[33] Gracyk, *Rhythm and Noise*, 194.
[34] Ibid., 204–6.

agency and Gracyk's reasons for the rejection of the Romantic aesthetic for rock music are not entirely comfortable if one wants both to preserve moral or artistic agency and to avoid consigning agents to either responsibility for or complicity in their own unhappy condition. It is possible, however, that viewing the question through a slightly different lens—Simone Weil's concept of affliction (*malheur*)—might offer another way to think about the problem.

Comforting the afflicted

"Affliction," Simone Weil claims, "is not a psychological state; it is a pulverization of the soul by the mechanical brutality of circumstances."[35] While physical suffering is typical of affliction in Weil's work, it is not the entirety of the concept; affliction is "a different thing from physical suffering," a thing that "takes possession of the soul and marks it through and through with its own particular mark, the mark of slavery."[36] This is not to say that physical pain or suffering is distinct from affliction, but rather that physical pain is among the things most likely to make "irresistibly present to the soul" a condition in which life itself is uprooted, "a more or less attenuated equivalent of death."[37] The picture she paints of the afflicted is of a person abandoned to misery and isolation who is, as both component and consequence of that abandonment, effectively the slave of circumstance, under the control of others. It is a picture of a person who has been made into a thing by the exercise of power.[38]

As Richard Bell points out, the concept of affliction in Weil's work is the spiritual successor of an earlier materialist analysis of oppression in *Oppression and Liberty*, an analysis that draws heavily on Weil's own experience of the dehumanizing nature of factory work.[39] She comes to understand the physical and social constraints placed on the body and life of the factory laborer as also

---

[35] Simone Weil, "The Love of God and Affliction," in *The Simone Weil Reader*, George A. Panichas, ed. (Wakefield, R.I.: Moyer Bell, 1977), 462.
[36] Ibid., 439.
[37] Ibid., 440.
[38] In the most extreme case, this reduction of persons to things is actual death; for the afflicted, it is a condition of enslavement (in multiple senses) in life. For a much more extensive discussion of how power operates to reduce persons to things, see Simone Weil, "The Iliad; or the Poem of Force," in *Simone Weil: An Anthology*, Siân Miles, ed. (New York: Weidenfeld & Nicolson, 1986), 162–95.
[39] Richard H. Bell, *Simone Weil: The Way of Justice as Compassion* (Lanham: Rowman & Littlefield Publishers, 1998), 26–7. See also Simone Weil, *Oppression and Liberty* (London-New York: Routledge, 2001), 54–79.

constituting constraints on the soul, and further that affliction affects every dimension of a person's life.[40] "There is not real affliction," she says, "unless the event which has gripped and uprooted a life attacks it, directly or indirectly, in all its parts, social, psychological, and physical. There is not really affliction where there is not social degradation or the fear of it in some form or other."[41] To be afflicted is therefore not simply a matter of being uncomfortable, or unhappy, or ill, or alone. It is a condition in which the confluence of these miseries undermines all attempts to escape them by making the soul an accomplice in its own degradation, "[going] so far as to prevent [the afflicted person] from seeking a way of deliverance, sometimes even to the point of preventing him from wishing for deliverance" by cultivating a profound self-hatred "and sense of guilt and defilement."[42] Ultimately, affliction amounts to "a destruction of personality, a lapse into anonymity" from which the afflicted person finds it nearly unthinkable to escape.[43]

To imagine the compromised moral or artistic agent as afflicted in this way seems to run directly counter to Showden's attempt to recover greater agency for the women whose situations most concern her; it almost appears to require the erasure of agency altogether, positing the complete effacement of autonomy by the forces that constrain freedom. At the very least, imagining a woman like the one described in "Better Man" as afflicted seems to involve a dramatic swing from holding her to some degree responsible for her own suffering (as Showden's approach risks doing) to the equally undesirable extreme of erasing her power to be responsible for anything at all. It seems even more absurd to imagine Pearl Jam (or any other successful musical performer) as afflicted; Gracyk's point about the nature of selling out is well taken, and it is strange at best to suggest that a lapse into anonymity is what's happening at the height of a performer's popularity. Kurt Cobain's suicide, when viewed outside of a Romantic aesthetic sensibility, is the tragic consequence of a number of different personal issues that may have been exacerbated by his fame, but that probably would have troubled him even if Nirvana had never played anywhere but a series of Seattle basements.

Nonetheless, the main reason to find the concept of affliction attractive here for understanding "Better Man" and its performers lies in addressing how taking

---

[40] Bell, *Simone Weil*, 27–9.
[41] Weil, "The Love of God and Affliction," 440–1.
[42] Ibid., 442–3.
[43] Ibid., 460.

the ways in which the world may make people into things seriously also clarifies the process whereby constraints on freedom may be insidiously strengthened by their discursive relationship with the exercise of autonomy. It also makes it possible to draw finer-grained distinctions between different ways in which autonomy may be exercised in response to constraints on freedom, making room for a more nuanced picture of the participants in and victims of oppressive situations. Put another way: while conceiving of compromised moral or artistic agents as afflicted may appear to further weaken or erase their agency, it may also have the beneficial effect of revealing the actual complexities of their condition through understanding how they have been deprived of "personality" and made anonymous.

This case is, of course, somewhat easier to make for "Better Man" than for the man who wrote it. The song's protagonist is a textbook case of someone whom power (in this case, the oppressive influence of an abusive partner) has made into a thing. She talks herself out of leaving—a soul turning against itself—and feels her enslaved condition as necessary (she needs and is needed by him). The woman described in the lyrics of "Better Man" is not someone who embraces what her life has become; she is someone who has resigned herself to an unhappiness of which she is entirely aware and against which she feels ultimately helpless, possibly because she feels as if she deserves it. Her situation speaks to Weil's comment about how affliction is felt by the innocent person, not the criminal. The innocent don't believe they deserve to be saved; the wicked do not believe themselves to be in need of salvation.[44] Convincing her to leave or trying to help her to leave, if she is afflicted in this way, needs more from the one who helps her than the creation of favorable material conditions for departure. For Weil, that help needs to take the form of "[projecting] one's being into an afflicted person," thereby taking on her affliction as one's own.[45] This call for a radical empathy shifts the discussion from the woman's agency to a more concrete apprehension of her being in a way that may prompt a clearer understanding of exactly how the systemic solutions Showden prefers would or would not affect her situation, particularly with regard to responsibility.[46]

---

[44] Ibid., 442.
[45] Weil, "The Love of God and Affliction," 460.
[46] Sophie Bourgault, "Beyond the Saint and the Red Virgin: Simone Weil as Feminist Theorist of Care," *Frontiers: A Journal of Women Studies* 35, no. 2 (2014): 1–27. Bourgault's reading of Weil as a proponent of an ethic of care is a good example of what this turn to empathy for the afflicted might mean in practice.

To conceive of a successful musical performer or band as afflicted is a bit more difficult. As is readily visible in Vedder's interviews, one of the enduring difficulties for a performer in the public eye is the way in which participation in the music industry can make a person into a thing. A band's frontman often becomes the locus of attention for everything from news hooks to parasocial relationships with fans, and the experience of being on the receiving end of that kind of attention can be dehumanizing. The afflicted performer does not become anonymous in the trivial sense of being invisible to the public eye—rather, the performer lapses into anonymity behind a public facade that is, at least to some degree, created and controlled by other people.[47]

This isn't simply a matter of selling out—it's a deeper problem arising from the way in which popular music is created and sold, which often necessarily includes packaging the performers themselves as products. The very intimacy and directness of the shared emotional space that a band like Pearl Jam deliberately cultivates with their audience also has the potential to make that space a site of affliction for the performers. The cynical response that Vedder despises is also the only reliable protection any individual performer has against affliction of this kind; the worst features of the commodification of rock dwell in the cynical or detached performer's heart without being felt there, while it is most acutely felt in the hearts of the sincere. Cobain's suicide is readily understandable as the end point of his affliction, born of physical, psychological, and social suffering that flourished in the commodification of his musical work and his public persona. There is nothing romantic (or Romantic) about it.

To overcome this form of affliction poses a structural challenge not unlike the one facing an attempt to put in place the systemic changes that Showden proposes for helping abused women. It requires finding some way to change how rock music is created and shared; Paglia's call to free rock music from the marketplace is right in spirit on this account, even if moving the music to the ivory tower isn't the best alternative. The other possibility—the one Pearl Jam have chosen for themselves—seems to be to acquire and exercise greater control over the conditions under which they are commodified, which addresses some (but not all) of the forces arrayed against their autonomy.

---

[47] Vedder apparently once responded to an audience member's shouted "I love you" with: "You don't love me, if you really knew me, you wouldn't love me. You love who you *think* I am. And *don't* pretend you know me. Because I don't even know myself." See Ch. 8 in Martin Clarke, *Pearl Jam & Eddie Vedder: None Too Fragile* (Plexus Publishing, 2017).

One last time: Why does someone stay where they don't want to be? If the condition of the person who stays is rightly recognized as afflicted, then perhaps it might be best to ask instead: How can we genuinely encounter the afflicted and take on their affliction for ourselves, in such a way as to truly see them?

Bibliography

Bell, Richard H. *Simone Weil: The Way of Justice as Compassion*. Lanham, MD: Rowman & Littlefield Publishers, 1998.
Berger, Arion. "Can't Find a Better Man." *The Village Voice*, January 31, 1995.
Bicknell, Jeanette. *Philosophy of Song and Singing: An Introduction*. New York: Routledge, 2015.
Bourgault, Sophie. "Beyond the Saint and the Red Virgin: Simone Weil as Feminist Theorist of Care." *Frontiers: A Journal of Women Studies* 35, no. 2 (2014): 1–27.
Clarke, Martin. *Pearl Jam & Eddie Vedder: None Too Fragile*. Plexus Publishing, 2017.
Cohen, Jonathan and Mark Wilkerson (eds). *Pearl Jam Twenty*. New York: Simon & Schuster, 2011.
Crowe, Cameron. "Five Against the World." *Rolling Stone*, October 28, 1993. Available online: https://www.rollingstone.com/music/music-news/pearl-jam-five-against-the-world-244637/ (accessed April 3, 2021).
Gracyk, Theodore. *Rhythm and Noise: An Aesthetics of Rock*. Durham: Duke University Press, 1996.
Greer, Jim. "The Courtship of Eddie Vedder." *Spin*, December 1993. Available online: https://www.spin.com/featured/pearl-jam-1993-eddie-vedder-interview-cover-story/ (accessed April 3, 2021).
Hilburn, Robert. "He Didn't Ask for All This." *Los Angeles Times*, May 1, 1994. Available online: http://articles.latimes.com/1994-05-01/entertainment/ca-52475_1_pearl-jam-concert (accessed April 3, 2021).
Marks, Craig. "Eddie Vedder Breaks His Silence." *Spin*, January 1995. Available online: https://www.spin.com/featured/pearl-jam-cover-story-1995/ (accessed April 3, 2021).
Marks, Craig. "The Road Less Traveled." *Spin*, February 1997. Available online: http://www.fivehorizons.com/archive/articles/spin0297.shtml (accessed April 3, 2021).
Neely, Kim. *Five Against One: The Pearl Jam Story*. New York: Penguin Books, 1998.
Showden, Carisa R. *Choices Women Make: Agency in Domestic Violence, Assisted Reproduction, and Sex Work*. Minneapolis: University of Minnesota Press, 2011.
Weil, Simone. "The Love of God and Affliction." In *The Simone Weil Reader*, translated and edited by George A. Panichas, 439–68. Wakefield, R.I.: Moyer Bell, 1977.

Weil, Simone. "The Iliad; or the Poem of Force." In *Simone Weil: An Anthology*, translated by Mary McCarthy, edited by Siân Miles, 162–95. New York: Weidenfeld & Nicolson, 1986.

Weil, Simone. *Oppression and Liberty*, translated by Arthur Wills and John Petrie. London-New York: Routledge, 2001.

That's Where We're Living: Determinism and Free Will in "Unthought Known"

Enrico Terrone

Introduction

FlashForward is a science fiction television series that opened on ABC in September 2009 and was canceled after twenty-two episodes because of the decline of viewers, in spite of generally positive reviews and a pending cliffhanger. The first episode portrays a mysterious event that causes nearly all human beings to simultaneously lose consciousness for about two minutes, during which they have access to what appear to be visions—flashforwards—of their lives six months later. In the following episodes, it becomes evident that those visions always come true, even when people struggle to prevent the foreseen events from happening. It is only at the end of the seventh episode that FBI agent Al Gough succeeds, at the price of his life, in saving a woman, Celia Quinones, who was foreseen to die. Human free will here makes a point against the apparently indisputable tyranny of a predetermined fate.

At the beginning of the eighth episode, the Pearl Jam song "Unthought Known" is deployed as a sort of reflection on the extraordinary story of Al and Celia.[1] The song here becomes a cinematic element which, borrowing Peter Kivy's words on film music, one might describe as "a palpable player in the drama, though heard but not seen by the audience and neither heard nor seen by the characters."[2] Specifically, I will argue that the combination of "Unthought Known"'s music and lyrics with *FlashForward*'s cinematic narrative ends up in a

---

[1] The sequence is visible on YouTube (https://www.youtube.com/watch?v=zFJGx0DYmlo).
[2] Peter Kivy, "Realistic Song in the Movies," *The Journal of Aesthetics and Art Criticism* 71, no. 1 (2013): 79.

peculiar piece of philosophical art, which is worth figuring out. I will thus extract meaning from the dialectic between the song and the images.

The letter from nowhere

The first images of *Playing Cards with Coyote*—*FlashForward*'s eighth episode—show, in a slight slow motion, a postman delivering a letter to Celia. This is the letter from Al, the man who gave his life to save her. The instrumental intro of "Unthought Known" accompanies the scene but the entering of Eddie Vedder's voice is postponed with respect to the original version of the song included in Pearl Jam's album *Backspacer*. In the edited version deployed in *FlashForward*, the musical module of the intro keeps being repeated on the slow motion images of Celia reading the letter, and in the meanwhile we hear Al's voice saying: "Dear Celia, I don't know your last name, and I don't know where you live, but I know you've two young boys, twins, probably. And I know you didn't have a flashforward."

Vedder's voice enters the song just after Al pronounced the keyword "flashforward," in correspondence with an editing cut that symbolically connects Celia's glance to a traveling shot of the ocean. The song here functions as a sort of imaginary continuation of the letter that makes abstraction from the particular case of Celia, thereby connecting this case to the vicissitudes of the other characters, and capturing its universal meaning. It is as if, through Vedder's voice, we could keep listening to the series of thought and feelings constituting Al's subjectivity. While the words of Al's letter to Celia give us access to Al's mental states just before his death, the lyrics of the song seems to give us access to a possible post-mortem experience of Al, who is now a sort of disembodied subject constituted by nothing but the series of his visual perspectives, which we can share through the images, and the series of his thought and feelings, which we can share through the song.

In previous works, I have argued films can provide us with an imaginary disembodied experience of outer fictional events,[3] just as songs can provide us with an imaginary disembodied experience of inner states of fictional characters.[4]

---

[3] See Enrico Terrone, "Imagination and Perception in Film Experience," *Ergo* 7, no. 5 (2020a): 161–90.
[4] See Enrico Terrone, "Listening to Other Minds. A Phenomenology of Pop Songs," *British Journal of Aesthetics* 60, no. 4 (2020b): 435–53.

Here, I am drawing on those works to show that the combination of motion pictures and songs can enable a complex imaginary experience whereby we can perceive outer fictional events from a disembodied perspective while, at the same time, sharing the thoughts and feelings of a fictional character on those events. Specifically, the combination of *FlashForward*'s images with "Unthought Known" provides us with a sort of imaginary access to the disembodied point of view of a dead fictional character, agent Al Gough. It is as if we were sharing his perspective when, after his death, he is observing, from without, the world within which he had spent his life. We thus see existing things from the imaginary perspective of a subject who no longer exists.

Ordinary thought and scientific knowledge

The original version of "Unthought Known" is a heartfelt song about the human condition, whose title is inspired by Christopher Bollas' *The Shadow of the Object: Psychoanalysis of the Unthought Known* (1987), a book in turn inspired by Freud's idea that one can know things about which one is unable to think. *FlashForward* deploys an edited version of the song whose duration is around two minutes instead of the four of the original version. In this context, the dialectic between thinking and knowing that characterizes "Unthought Known" acquires a peculiar connotation, which is especially interesting from a philosophical perspective. Specifically, the warm spirituality of the song fruitfully interacts with a narrative universe that appears to be governed by a cold determinism since the flashforwards have put human beings in the tragic paradoxical condition of being capable of seeing their future but unable to change it. One can thus interpret the combination of the song with the narrative as a reflection on the human condition in the age of the scientific image of the world, which provides human beings not only with an unprecedented knowledge of the universe they live in, but also with a growing awareness of their impotence and irrelevance in it.

According to metaphysicians such as Wilfred Sellars (1962), Hugh Mellor (1981), Willard Quine (1987), John Smart (1989), and Laurie Paul (2010), science encourages a conception of the universe as a block of space-time strictly governed by the laws of nature, which leaves no room for human initiative. Even if those laws are formulated, following quantum mechanics, in statistical terms, nothing changes at the level that is relevant to human experience and action. In such a world, as pointed out by philosophers of mind such as Daniel Dennett (1992) and Jaegwon Kim (1998), consciousness is nothing but an epiphenomenon, that is, a causally inert side effect of underlying physical and biochemical processes that occur in the brain. Consequently, free will boils down to a representational device, namely, the way in which the brain represents the outputs it sends to the periphery of body, just as perception is the way in which the brain represents the inputs it receives from the periphery of the body. We feel that our actions occur because we have freely chosen them, but the right order of explanation is the other way around: we have the impression of having freely chosen our actions because they occur, and they do so just in virtue of physical and biochemical processes in the brain.

All of this is something we know, at least in the sense that those are plausible conclusions that we can draw for the best scientific theories at our disposal. Yet this is something we find extremely hard to think. That is because, as effectively explained by Peter Strawson (1974; 1983), free will is so entrenched in the most basic emotional responses and moral judgments on which we constantly rely in everyday life that we cannot give it up.

That being the case, the very title of Pearl Jam's song acquires a new connotation in the narrative context of *FlashForward*. The "unthought known" is what could be known through science but cannot be thought in everyday life, since the latter cannot give up the presupposition of free will. The whole narrative of *FlashForward* rests upon this tension. On the one hand, the characters know—not only through science, as we do, but also through their visions—that their future is determined and their free will is illusory. On the other hand, they cannot help but think that they are free to change the predetermined course of action—and since *FlashForward* is a fiction, after all, they can even succeed in doing so, as happens in the story of Al and Celia.

Just as Steven Spielberg's film *Minority Report* (2002), *FlashForward* is an inconsistent narrative from a scientific perspective. Such inconsistency depends on the way in which both *Minority Report* and *FlashForward* deploy science fiction mechanisms that provide characters with mental states of clairvoyance.

While perception allows us to experience the present, and memory allows us to experience the past, we lack an analogous mental state that would allow us to experience the future. Of course, we can make conjectures or predictions on the future, imagine or suppose how it would be, and we can even form intentions concerning our future actions as well as expectations concerning the actions of other subjects. Nevertheless, we cannot experience future actions and events in the direct way in which we experience present actions and events through perception, and past actions and events through memory. The future remains somehow opaque to us in a way in which the past and the present are not.

In *Minority Report* and *FlashForward*, clairvoyance overcomes this limitation by enabling characters to experience the future in the same direct way in which they experience the present through perception and the past through memory. So far so good. Clairvoyance, as such, does not involve inconsistency. Yet, direct experiences such as perception and memory are factive, that is, they entail the reality of what is experienced. If one perceives an event, that event must be real; otherwise one would not be in a state of perception but rather in a state of hallucination.[5] Likewise, if one remembers an event, that event must be real; otherwise one would not be in as state of memory but rather in a state of deceptive imagination.[6] The same holds true for clairvoyance. If the events foreseen will not happen, the putative state of clairvoyance would come down to a wrong prediction. The inconsistency of science fiction narratives such as *Minority Report* and *FlashForward* derives from the fact that they insist that the characters are in a state of clairvoyance, and yet the development of these stories ends up in contradicting what those characters have foreseen.

On the one hand, *Minority Report* and *FlashForward* portray a world that complies with the scientific conception of the world as a block of space-time in which the future already exists and thus, in principle, might be directly experienced. On the other hand, those narratives make room for changes in the future, thereby violating the basic principle according to which the whole universe as a block of space-time is determined once and for all. Given this principle, it makes no sense, from a scientific perspective, to state that the future can be changed.[7] Narratives such as *Minority Report* and *FlashForward* are thus inconsistent, since they portray a future that can be not only seen but also changed.

In spite of their inconsistency, however, these narratives remain interesting from a philosophical perspective since they express a clash between scientific

---

[5] See Michael G.F. Martin, "The Transparency of Experience," *Mind & Language* 17, no. 4 (2002): 376–425.
[6] See Alexander Byrne, "Recollection, Perception, Imagination," *Philosophical Studies* 148, no. 1 (2010): 15–26.
[7] See Damian Cox and Michael P. Levine, *Thinking Through Film: Doing Philosophy, Watching Movies* (Oxford: John Wiley & Sons, 2011); Andrea Iacona, *L'enigma del futuro* (Bologna: il Mulino, 2019).

knowledge and everyday thought. Such a clash depends on the human innate tendency to think of the future as depending on free will in such a way that, even if one saw the future, one still could deploy one's free will in order to make the future different from how one had seen it.

The future can be changed

In the narrative context of *FlashForward*, "Unthought Known" becomes a song on the human condition within a universe that seems to have no room for consciousness and free will. The first verse starts in correspondence with a traveling shot of the ocean, and ends up in the images of worker Aaron Stark who observes his daughter Tracy sleeping. This verse highlights a hidden dimension of the human mind that lies in the brain but is out of the reach of consciousness. The images of the vast expanses of water followed by those of Tracy sleeping nicely match these lines of the song, which concern what lies beneath the realm of conscious thought.

The second verse accompanies the images of FBI agent Demetri Noh, who is studying the post-it notes that he has put on a wall with the aim of making sense of the flashforwards, and then leads us back to Celia who is now meeting the journalists who are crowded in front of her house. The combination of these images with the song's lyrics raises the issue of choosing and acting in a world that seems to be devoid of meaning.

At this point, a close-up shows the newspaper headline "The future can be changed," and then another traveling shot of the ocean begins. Here the edited version of the song skips a verse of the original version, thereby directly jumping to the next one. The lyrics of this verse, emphasized by the crescendo of the instrumental accompaniment, and perfectly matched by the beauty of the California coast, celebrate the irreducible richness of human perceptions, feelings, and emotions. The possibility of changing the future, announced by the newspaper, seems to have brought enthusiasm into the music, the lyrics, and the images.

The traveling shot of the ocean ends up in a hotel on the shore where FBI agent Mark Benford and his wife Olivia are making love in spite of knowing, from Olivia's flashforward, that their marriage is destined to break as she will cheat on him. Here, another part of the song's original version is skipped in order to jump to the verse that occupies the position that in songs is usually occupied by the chorus (but which lacks the auditory specificity that usually distinguishes the chorus from the verses; that is why I prefer to cast it as a verse). Interestingly, this verse matches, and somehow solves, the paradoxical situation that Mark and Olivia are living as a couple. By making love with Olivia, Mark is somehow "dreaming the dream" of the man who will become Olivia's lover, but that man is not really "a rival" of him since the notion of a rival makes sense only against a background of free options and choices, not in a universe where everything is already determined.

The crescendo culminates in the bridge that, in the edited version of the song, connects the main section to the last verse. While we see other characters struggling with their fate, the lyrics of the bridge, which are dramatized by the musical dominance of drums, compensate the previous enthusiastic emphasis on human feelings and wishes with a quite bleak description of the universe, whose nihilism, in the narrative context of *FlashForward*, tends to match the scientific image of the world: "Nothing left, . . . / Nothing there."[8]

Scientific nihilism is not absolute nihilism, it is not the claim that nothing exists. Rather, as pointed out by John Smart, it is the claim that "there is nothing in the world over and above the entities of physics, and . . . everything operates according to the laws of physics."[9] However, from the human perspective, scientific nihilism and absolute nihilism have the same upshot, namely, they both make human existence completely irrelevant and pointless. If there is nothing in the world over and above the entities of physics, and everything operates according to the laws of physics, human beings are nothing but physical mechanisms that operate according to the laws of physics. Surely, human beings are very complicated mechanisms, perhaps the most complicated mechanisms in the universe. Yet one should not mistake quantitative complication with qualitative difference. In fact, these complicated mechanisms, in virtue of their very complication, tend to think of themselves as qualitatively special, but when their thought has reached the level of scientific knowledge, such putative qualitative specificity reveals itself to be nothing but quantitative complication. Here is the ultimate unthought known, what we know but we are not disposed

---

[8] Pearl Jam, "Unthought Known."
[9] J.J.C. Smart, *Our Place in the Universe: A Metaphysical Discussion* (Oxford: Blackwell, 1989), 79.

to think, namely, that there is nothing over and above the cold mechanism of the universe: "Nothing left, . . . / Nothing there."

So what you giving?

The musical bridge leads us to the last verse, which provides the song, as well as the cinematic sequence, with a circular closure. The sound of the drums fades and Vedder's voice is just accompanied by the simple musical module that we already have heard in the intro. The slow motion of the images provides a visual analogue of the slowing down of the rhythm of the song, whose lyrics keep describing a spatiotemporal universe whose immense distances seem to make human life irrelevant: "A distant time, . . . A distant space, . . . That's where we're living."[10]

These lines of the song raise the philosophical issue of our place in the universe. According to Smart (1989), the expression "our place in the universe" can be read in three different ways. First, a "literal" reading according to which the universe is a system of expanding galaxies such that, as Smart puts it, "it can be seen that our location in the universe is in no way an important looking or central one. Indeed there is no central place."[11] Then, a "semi-literal" reading according to which we occupy the highest place in the hierarchy of the entities of the universe. Yet, from a scientific perspective, this makes sense only if we consider the hierarchy in terms of quantitative complication, not in terms of qualitative difference. We are perhaps the most complicated mechanisms in the universe, and yet we remain mechanisms. This claim is questioned by what Smart calls the "metaphorical" reading of the expression "our place in the universe." According to this reading, one can wonder whether the human mind is just a complicated piece of the universe or it is rather the universe that depends on the mind. While the former option leads to realism, the latter rather leads to idealism.

The lines "[a] distant time, . . . a distant space, . . . That's where we're living" in the narrative context of *FlashForward* surely favor the realist option. "To be is to have a place in space and time, regardless of whether this place is occupied by a lifeless thing or by a subject of experience. The latter just has the capacity to represent the

---

[10] Pearl Jam, "Unthought Known."
[11] J.J.C. Smart, *Our Place in the Universe*, 2–3.

spatiotemporal universe in addition to having a place in it. But this capacity does not mean that space and time are a product of the mind, as a transcendental idealist in the Kantian tradition would be inclined to claim. This capacity rather means, from a Darwinian perspective, that the primary function of the mind is to provide the living body with an approximately objective representation of its surrounding environment, thereby improving its adaptation and its capacity of survival and reproduction.[12] It is not that we have a special meaningful place in the universe, it is just that we are capable of representing our meaningless place in it, as the lines "[a] distant time, ... A distant space, ... That's where we're living" remind us.

Drawing on Kant's third antinomy in the *Critique of Pure Reason*,[13] one might say that the scientific image of the world, in which everything has its place in space-time and is determined by the laws of nature, is contradicted by the introspective evidence of free will and spontaneity. Kant notoriously overcomes the contradiction by stating that scientific determinism only concerns the superficial domain of phenomena whereas free will and spontaneity belong to the deeper domain of things in themselves. Yet, from a Darwinian perspective, one might reject Kant's way of drawing the distinction between phenomena and things in themselves. One might state, instead, that phenomena are subjective spatiotemporal representations of an objective spatiotemporal environment that natural selection has endowed us with. Hence, the domain of things in themselves is not something beyond space-time but rather space-time as revealed by science, while the domain of phenomena is rather space-time as represented in everyday experience. If this is right, free will and spontaneity do not belong to the domain of things in themselves but rather to that of phenomena; they are a sort of side-effect, noise, distortion, of our subjective way of representing an objective spatiotemporal order.

Although the song's lines "[a] distant time, ... a distant space, ... That's where we're living" seem to summarize and endorse such a bleak view, the images that accompany them have positive valence. FBI Special Agent Janis Hawk, who was critically injured in Episode 6, is back at the Los Angeles field office, where her colleagues celebrate her return. The FBI team has regained its unity and is ready to address new challenges, as emphasized by the images of Janis kissed and

---

[12] See Robert Nozick, *Invariances: The Structure of the Objective World* (Cambridge, MA: Harvard University Press, 2001).
[13] See Immanuel Kant, *Critique of Pure Reason* (Cambridge: Cambridge University Press, 1999).

hugged by Stanford Wedeck, the head of the office. Finally, a last cut leads us back to the newspaper headline stating: "The future can be changed." The positive valence of these images is matched by the last line of the song, which asks a question that seems to reaffirm the role of human consciousness and free will in the predetermined indifferent universe: "So what you giving?"[14]

The point is that the mind does more than just representing what is going on in the spatiotemporal surroundings of the living body. The mind also assesses events and actions through feelings and emotions. Things are not just represented as far or close, big or small, soft or hard. Things are represented also as pleasant or unpleasant, good or bad, beautiful or ugly. In other words, things are not just perceived but also evaluated. Perception and evaluation are inextricably intertwined in experience. This fact has a crucial consequence. Even if the universe, as such, is irredeemably meaningless, the way in which we represent it makes it meaningful, that is, imbued with values that provide us with goals and purposes in our lives. We thus represent a meaningless universe as if it were meaningful. From a scientific perspective this is just a fiction, but this fiction cannot be given up in the way we give up fictions when we end reading novels or watching films. Engaging with such fiction is what constitutes our existence, is the basic framework of our life as conscious subjects. We cannot help but thinking of such fiction as paramount even though we know that it is just a fiction. From this perspective, "[s]o what you giving?" becomes the question that makes our lives worth living. We are to play a game of values, goals, purposes, and meanings, a game in which the future is up to us, and thus "the future can be changed," in spite of our place in a meaningless universe in which the future is determined once and for all. We are to take such fiction seriously, thinking of if as worthwhile, and give our contribution to it—"So what you giving?"—in spite of knowing its ultimate fictional nature.

The ontology of "Unthought Known"

So far, I have articulated the ontological view that is expressed by "Unthought Known" in the narrative context of *FlashForward*. Specifically, I have pointed out what human beings are and what is their place in the universe according to that conception of the world. Still, something remains to be said on the ontology of

---

[14] Pearl Jam, "Unthought Known."

the song itself. What is "Unthought Known"? In the first instance, one might answer that this is a song written and composed by Eddie Vedder, and released in 2009 as a track of Pearl Jam's album *Backspacer*. Songs, however, are complicated entities from an ontological perspective, since things like songs or films, unlike concrete things like rocks or animals, do not have a single place in space and time. There is no single place in the world where one can find "Unthought Known." Thus, songs, just like films, are better cast as abstract objects, namely types, whose instances or tokens are those particular events called playbacks.[15] From this ontological perspective, "Unthought Known" is a sort of norm that prescribes how its instances should be: they should last four minutes and nine seconds, exhibit peculiar auditory qualities, and have lyrics organized in a structure involving an initial series of five verses, then a bridge ("Nothing left..."), and finally a series of three verses.

The song that we hear in *FlashForward*'s episode *Playing Cards with Coyote*, however, does not abide by this norm since it lasts only two minutes and sixteen seconds, and has lyrics organized in a slightly different structure. So, one can wonder, is that song "Unthought Known"? Well, yes and no. One might answer: "Yes, it is," because there is a proper causal chain that allows us to trace that song back to the original creation by Eddie Vedder (and this also explains why *FlashForward* producers had to pay copyright fees for their use of the song). However, one might also answer: "No, it is not," because what that song does is to establish a new norm rather than following the original one.

In order to solve this tension, one might say that the song we hear in "Playing Cards with Coyote" is a variant of "Unthought Known," namely, as Nemesio García-Carril Puy (2019) puts it, a type "nested into" "Unthought Known"'s type. If this is right, songs such as "Unthought Known" are abstract objects that make room not only for proper instances but also for improper ones. A proper instance of "Unthought Known" lasts exactly four minutes and nine seconds, and exhibits all the features specified by the original type. Improper instances, on the other hand, can have a different duration, a different organization of the lyrics, and different auditory features, and yet they remain instances of the song in virtue of an appropriate causal connection to its creation. For example, the live version of "Unthought Known" recorded in Berlin in 2010 lasts only three minutes and fifty

---

[15] See Theodore Gracyk, *Rhythm and Noise: An Aesthetics of Rock* (Durham: Duke University Press, 1996); Andrew Kania, "Making Tracks: The Ontology of Rock Music," *The Journal of Aesthetics and Art Criticism* 64, no. 4 (2006): 401–14; Julian Dodd, *Works of Music: An Essay in Ontology* (Oxford: Oxford University Press, 2007).

seconds.[16] Eddie Vedder's cover performed at the 2016 Ohana Festival, on the other hand, preserves the original duration but exhibits different auditory features due to its acoustic guitar solo arrangement.[17] In another acoustic cover, which one can hear in the 2011 documentary *Water on the Road*, Vedder also modifies the structure of the lyrics, thereby reducing the duration to one minute and forty-five seconds.[18]

The *FlashForward* version of "Unthought Known" can also be seen as a variant, so understood. In this case, the auditory features of the original version are preserved, and yet the song is edited, thereby changing the organization of its lyrics and reducing its duration, so to adapt it to the narrative context of the TV show. Interestingly, an analogous operation can be found in another TV show, *Castle*, aired on ABC for a total of eight seasons from 2009 to 2016. In each episode of *Castle*, novelist Richard Castle and detective Kate Beckett of New York Police Department cooperate to solve a crime. In particular, "Den of Thieves," the twenty-first episode of the second season, is about a crime involving double-crossing and betrayal in Beckett's team. "Unthought Known" shows up in the finale of this episode, which was aired in 2010, just a few months after the airing of "Playing Cards with Coyote."[19]

The *Castle* editing of "Unthought Known" lasts around two minutes and organizes the lyrics by directly connecting the initial five verses to the last one, thereby skipping the bridge, which was instead crucial to the *FlashForward* editing. The bridge's lines "[n]othing left, . . . / Nothing there," indeed, supplied the ultimate nihilist truth, which was somehow known and yet could not be thought in the narrative context of *FlashForward*. In the narrative context of *Castle*, instead, the emphasis is rather on the hidden psychological dimension that underlies social relations. The investigation carried out by Castle and Beckett in this episode has revealed truths that were somehow known to the other members of the police team, who nevertheless were unable to think of them. And Castle and Beckett, in turn, find it hard to think of their deep sentimental bond in spite of ultimately knowing it. All this does not involve the sort of nihilism that is at stake in *FlashForward* but rather a firm confidence in the capacity of human beings to succeed in thinking what has remained so far

[16] See https://www.youtube.com/watch?v=JFRQIEv6mC0.
[17] See https://www.youtube.com/watch?v=y36BgBb1Rw8.
[18] See https://www.youtube.com/watch?v=CJre7ZGFJm8.
[19] See https://www.youtube.com/watch?v=5i7aft9O3XM.

unthought in their social lives. The key lines of the *Castle* version of "Unthought Known," in this sense, are the optimistic ones stating "[l]ook for love..."[20] which were instead dropped in the bleaker *FlashForward* version of the song.

To sum up, a song like "Unthought Known" does not only express the feelings and ideas that are embodied in its original version, but also constitutes a potential for further versions that can express slightly different feelings and ideas. In this paper I have argued that, in *FlashForward*, "Unthought Known" expresses feelings and ideas concerning the clash between determinism and free will. The song, as it is deployed in the *FlashForward* episode "Playing Cards with Coyote," not only makes us aware that knowledge of the deterministic laws of nature leaves no room for free will but also makes us feel that we cannot give up free will in our practical thought.

Bibliography

Bollas, Christopher. *The Shadow of the Object: Psychoanalysis of the Unthought Known*. New York: Columbia University Press, 1987.

Byrne, Alexander. "Recollection, Perception, Imagination." *Philosophical Studies* 148, no. 1 (2010): 15–26.

Cox, Damian and Michael P. Levine. *Thinking Through Film: Doing Philosophy, Watching Movies*. Oxford: John Wiley & Sons, 2011.

Dennett, Daniel C. *Consciousness Explained*. Boston: Little, Brown and Co., 1992.

Dodd, Julian. *Works of Music: An Essay in Ontology*. Oxford: Oxford University Press, 2007.

García-Carril Puy, Nemesio. "The Ontology of Musical Versions: Introducing the Hypothesis of Nested Types." *The Journal of Aesthetics and Art Criticism* 77, no. 3 (2019): 241–54.

Gracyk Theodore. *Rhythm and Noise: An Aesthetics of Rock*. Durham: Duke University Press, 1996.

Iacona, Andrea. *L'enigma del futuro*. Bologna: il Mulino, 2019.

Kania, Andrew. "Making Tracks: The Ontology of Rock Music." *The Journal of Aesthetics and Art Criticism* 64, no. 4 (2006): 401–14.

Kant, Immanuel. *Critique of Pure Reason*, translated and edited by Paul Guyer and Allen W. Wood. Cambridge: Cambridge University Press, 1999.

Kim, Jaegwon. *Mind in a Physical World: An Essay on the Mind-body Problem and Mental Causation*. Cambridge, MA: The MIT Press, 1998.

---

[20] Pearl Jam, "Unthought Known."

Kivy, Peter. "Realistic Song in the Movies." *The Journal of Aesthetics and Art Criticism* 71, no. 1 (2013): 75–80.

Martin, Michael G.F. "The Transparency of Experience." *Mind & Language* 17, no. 4 (2002): 376–425.

Mellor, David H. *Real Time*. Cambridge: Cambridge University Press, 1981.

Nozick, Robert. *Invariances: The Structure of the Objective World*. Cambridge, MA: Harvard University Press, 2001.

Paul, Laurie A. "Temporal Experience." *The Journal of Philosophy* 107, no. 7 (2010): 333–59.

Quine, Willard Van Orman. *Quiddities: An Intermittently Philosophical Dictionary*. Cambridge, MA: Harvard University Press, 1987.

Sellars, Wilfrid. "Philosophy and the Scientific Image of Man." In *Frontiers of Science and Philosophy*, edited by Robert G. Colodny, 35–78. Pittsburgh: The University of Pittsburgh Press, 1962.

Smart, J.J.C. *Our Place in the Universe: A Metaphysical Discussion*. Oxford: Blackwell, 1989.

Strawson, Peter F. "Freedom and Resentment." In *Freedom and Resentment and Other Essays*, 1–28. London: Methuen, 1974.

Strawson, Peter F. "Liberty and Necessity." In *Spinoza: His Thought and Work*, edited by Nathan Rotenstreich and Norma Schneider, 120–9. Jerusalem: Israel Academy of Sciences and Humanities, 1983.

Terrone, Enrico. "Imagination and Perception in Film Experience." *Ergo* 7, no. 5 (2020a): 161–90.

Terrone Enrico. "Listening to Other Minds: A Phenomenology of Pop Songs." *British Journal of Aesthetics* 60, no. 4 (2020b): 435–53.

No Code Aesthetics

Alberto L. Siani

Introduction[1]

No Code, Pearl Jam's fourth album (1996), is usually not considered to be among the band's most successful ones, both in artistic and in commercial terms. Despite this, or maybe, as I will argue, just for this reason, *No Code* offers some stimulating philosophical starting points, both in its general concept and in the songs it contains. My interpretation of the album focuses exactly on its apparent inconsistency and lack of organic unity, and on the general atmosphere of dissolution, contingency, and heterogeneity pervading it. I read these features not as a sign of a temporary artistic loss on the side of the band, but on the contrary, in terms of a paradoxical project, suspended between the bold rejection of codes and the risk of this very rejection becoming a new code. In doing so, I establish a connection between the intention structuring the album and one of the most famous and controversial concepts in philosophical aesthetics, namely the so-called "end of art" thesis. Given the nature and aims of this contribution, I will of course not attempt to offer a full-fledged, original discussion of this thesis. Instead, I will argue that *No Code* can be read as an illuminating, concrete instance of the thesis, and that, vice versa, employing the end of art thesis as an interpretive framework can have a therapeutic effect, helping us to deal with the feeling of bewilderment the album can generate in us, probably more so than other works by Pearl Jam.

My argument will be structured as follows. First, I will sketch the meaning and content of the end of art thesis (Section 2). Second, I will offer a reading of *No Code*, which, considering together the title, the lyrics, and the musical

---

[1] I wish to thank Çiğdem Oğuz and Burak Özkök for their insightful readings and precious comments.

execution, attempts to interpret the peculiarities of the album in a philosophical perspective (Sections 3.1/3.3). Finally, I will reconnect this reading of the album to the end of art thesis and pursue a mutual clarification of these two and the development of the main threads and implications of what I will call a "no code aesthetics" (Sections 4.1/4.2).

The end of art: Starting remarks

With its many senses, the thesis of the end of art, or the rejection thereof, characterizes a substantial part of the discourse on modernity starting with Hegel and up to our days.[2] Let me clarify straightaway that the thesis does not designate the end of art's existence or reason to exist, but rather the past character of art's highest function. Simplifying a bit, this highest function was, for example, that of classical Greek or medieval Christian art. In those contexts, art was not so much the object of aesthetic appreciation, a cultural or leisure activity, a museum or auditorium item, but rather a powerful medium of expression and transmission of metaphysical, religious, ethical, and political contents. Artworks or artistic events were therefore forms of collective identification and participation in the life of a community, for which they played a central, indispensable role. Their raison d'être shaped their formal attributes and the receivers' expectations accordingly: what we see today as the beautiful harmony of classical or Christian artworks is the reflection of a harmonic view of the universe (or *kosmos*)[3] as a tidy, unified system of elements, each having its precise, preordained position and function. Individual life and collective organizations alike were called to correspond to this universal harmony, and artworks acted as powerful instances and media of this correspondence, rather than as free products of individual creativity aimed at other individuals' aesthetic experience and pleasure.

The end of art thesis designates the idea that art, in modern times, is no longer able to fulfill this highest role. This general idea can be, and has been, specified

---

[2] For a first overview see Alberto L. Siani, "End of Art," *International Lexicon of Aesthetics*, Autumn 2018.
[3] The word meant "order" or "adornment" in ancient Greek, and was also employed to refer, more specifically, to "the universe considered as a system with an order and pattern" (from the Cambridge Dictionary). The contemporary English words "cosmology" and "cosmetics" have this same etymology.

in different ways. Accordingly, art is no longer an adequate vehicle for the truth, nor for the presentation of the divine, nor for the embedment of moral and political principles and values; or art has become irrelevant in a largely disenchanted, prosaic, technological world; or artworks can no longer be beautiful or even distinguishable from common objects; or they are no longer autonomous insofar as they require a non-artistic perspective for their interpretation. For the sake of simplicity, one can identify three main dimensions of the thesis of art's past character. The first dimension is the metaphysical-epistemological one: art, despite it progressively becoming dematerialized and conceptual, is because of its structural materiality no longer able to adequately embody and communicate the truth, i.e., divine, or spiritual, or fully conceptual contents. Thus, art always implies a reference to a less immediate, more discursive (or even philosophical) framework. The second is a practical dimension: art is no longer an autonomous, adequate vehicle for the configuration, presentation, and communication of the highest religious, ethical, and political contents and values innervating modern ethical life. Finally, there is the aesthetic dimension: art has become the more and more fragmented, arbitrary product of the individual artist, thus giving up its claim to universal meaning and relevance, but at the same time becoming a freer, secularized depiction of the human world.

It is important to stress that the idea of an end of art also implies the idea of a new beginning: new possibilities and new functions open up for art with the end of art. Accordingly, here I will insist on two "constructive," emancipatory aspects of the thesis. First, the end of art also implies the liberation of the individual subject with his particularity and contingency, no longer required to harmonically fit in a given, substantial ethical whole. Art no longer expresses a unified worldview to which the individual can adhere through its fruition. The foundation and orientation of the public sphere requires more complex and reflective practices than the ones any artwork can provide. This, however, does not mean that art has become irrelevant: rather, art itself now calls for a more mediated, discursive approach for its interpretation. This further implies the centrality of the right of the individual subject to freely interpret, question, or even ignore the messages proposed by any given artwork. Second, and conversely, art, having been released from its absolute divine-expressing or truth-bearing task, can now be fully human, and freely express all the possible particular and contingent facets of humanity without being bound to specific forms and contents. Art's boundless expressive freedom is a result of the weakening of its highest claims, and reflects the plural character of the modern public sphere.

This brief characterization of the end of art thesis may sound too abstract to be applied to a philosophical investigation of Pearl Jam's *No Code*. It will be the task of section three to offer a correspondingly focused reading of the album, and then of section four to flesh out more concretely how the philosophical thesis and the album can help illuminate each other. Already here, however, I want to point out that the end of art thesis seems to hint toward a "no code aesthetics."

Ambiguities of *No Code*

Immanence, instability, and the possibility of nihilism

Let me move on to a focused discussion of some main traits of *No Code*. My aim will be to link the title with the album's concept and execution in the songs, highlighting thereby its central, paradoxical intention. "No code" is a polysemic expression, even more so in the elliptic context of a music album's title. It is, first of all, a programmatic existential declaration, marking the lack or rejection of preordained rules and boundaries for the declaring individual, in this case Pearl Jam. Accordingly, every individual existence and action is unique, contingent, and incommensurable with others. In the same way, it is an artistic reclamation of freedom and independence from genres and expectations. This reclamation is then linked to a rejection of mainstream commercial discographic labels and practices.[4] But "no code" also points to a survival strategy: changing skin and shape and becoming unrecognizable in order to avoid being overwhelmed by the collapse of a certain kind of music and culture, most notably of the original grunge movement.[5] At the same time, finally, "no code" is also used as a synonymous for the medical "do not resuscitate" code,[6] which in this context can be read as an invitation to let the past (of the band, and of that specific music and culture) go, but also as an ironic blow to hardline purist fans. The openness and ambiguity of the message sent by the title is, of course, one of the components of the fascination exercised by the album itself. The ambiguity, however, seems to

---

[4] Here belongs of course the famous 1994 Ticketmaster fight, on which see Eric Boehlert, "Pearl Jam: Taking on Ticketmaster," *Rolling Stone*, December 28, 1995.
[5] Also from the point of view of the context of its elaboration and release, hence, *No Code* can be read as a perhaps unique opportunity of freedom, experimentation, and autonomy in the band's path.
[6] Eddie Vedder himself hinted to this possibility: see Bart Blasengame, "Trampled Moss and Sitars: Pearl Jam's Tricky, Transformational *No Code*," AvClub.com, August 26, 2016.

run even deeper, as all the dimensions of the title's meaning can be read as trail signs toward new codes: the rejection of all codes can, as a matter of fact, be read as a code. This deeper ambiguity is the main interpretive key of the reading I suggest.[7]

The multidimensionality of the "no code" statement can be tracked all across the album's lyrics. A general implication is the rejection of all dimensions of sense and purpose transcending the very present moment. "Who You Are" tackles the issue of the part the individual subject plays in the great scheme of things, collapsing the nature and purpose of existence into what the individual immediately is. Our part is simply who we are, undercutting any reference to a further level of signification transcending this immediate identification. If individual existence and identity are conceived in this way, then also the possibility of transcending the immediate self through knowledge is ironically dismissed and brought back to naturalistic patterns and immanence in "In My Tree," where knowledge is likened to a growing tree. Not only am I identified with my present existence, but my very knowledge—traditionally, a distinctive human trait—cannot project me above it: in fact, knowledge is seen as just another process of nature, and the subject of that knowledge as just another object in nature, resulting in an exhilarating lightness.

Time itself, this core constituent of our self-feeling, self-consciousness, and personal identity, becomes volatile and elusive, as temporal references and personal identities get mixed up and neutralized in a crossing of verses from different songs, from "Red Mosquito" ("If I had known then what I know now")[8] to "I'm Open" ("If he only knew now what he knew then").[9] All of this eventually leads to an implosion of the self, this only apparently steady groundwork and substance of individual existence. The self as such is no longer the secure, self-evident groundwork for existence and action, but, in a reversion of the Cartesian argument, it is made of the stuff of dreams, on which, however, the subject seems to have an odd decisional power, being able to dream up his new self ("I'm Open"). Dream is no longer the omnipresent illusion threatening the stability of identity, knowledge, and action, but the very source of the self, which consequently shrinks to an inanimate, infinitesimal, unnoticeable serial object, like an anonymous book among many on a shelf ("Sometimes").

---

[7] Again, Eddie Vedder suggested that the reason the album is called *No Code* is that it is full of codes, which fans have obviously tried to uncover. See: http://nocodepage.tripod.com/Pearljamcodebreak.html (accessed April 3, 2021).
[8] Pearl Jam, "Red Mosquito," in *No Code* (1996).
[9] Pearl Jam, "I'm Open," in *No Code* (1996).

The power of dreams and illusions remains, however, limited, hence the suspension of the self has dark, disturbing implications. Without transcendence, purposiveness, and an identifiable self, the only remaining horizon is that of finitude and the always-lurking possibility of annihilation, a theme pervading the album from "Red Mosquito," written by a severely food-poisoned Eddie Vedder, for whom the mosquito becomes a threatening devil visiting him, to "Lukin," inspired by the danger of an obsessive armed stalker. Dreamt or not, the individual self put forward here is just as much vulnerable and finite as the real one it aims to replace, and the presence of death remains inescapable. Even love, often conceived as an eternal bond transcending finitude and death, gets bitterly and sarcastically scaled down to a socially inflated, yet largely insignificant achievement: all our bonds are made out of obligation, and love is just a matter of luck for the few ("Hail, Hail"). Like love, the confidence and the long established rituals of an old friendship are also predictably, structurally marked by an existential before material strain of transitoriness and instability in "Off He Goes." Eventually, the strain creeps from the inside to the outside, pervading the whole world and humankind like a universal pattern of absent-minded fakeness and fabrication ("Mankind").

Openness, care, and new life

However, the pervasiveness of finitude and precariousness does not only lead to pessimistic or even nihilistic conclusions. Even the suffocating enclosure of illusion and universal meaninglessness can, once acknowledged and deciphered, open an inner door restituting sense to the universe and the self. Paraphrasing the Kantian correspondence of starry sky above and moral law within, the blankness inside and the blankness of the ceiling of a closed room (a permanent cell?) can lead one to a statement of openness ("I'm Open"). Despite, or maybe because of, the irreparable ("no tradebacks") discovery of universal illusion and the feeling of loss of all sense, being authentically open (without the obligations, patterns, and fakes seen in the previous paragraph) is still possible for humans. Hence, the precarious openness of finitude contains the flipside to the universal meaninglessness and nothingness, i.e., an equally important element of emancipation, releasement, and hope, giving voice among others to songs such as "Present Tense" and "Around the Bend." "Present Tense" is an anthem to immanence and self-determination, a *memento mori* and a *carpe diem* in the same breath. The tree, here, is not the metamorphic shape of the self, but its source of wisdom and inspiration for dealing with constitutive and inescapable finitude, teaching us to catch the sun's rays, i.e., to "get something out" of the perilous, demanding life's trip ("Present Tense"). The lesson we can learn is expressed through a radical dichotomy of orientation, with a pretty clear-cut choice between past regrets and present tense. When every other approach is deemed to fail, we just need to realize that we can forgive ourselves and that we do not need a justification for our decision to embrace full immanence.

This heartfelt call for immanence may look like a cover for self-indulgence and boundless egoism, which is, however, balanced by a sense of fragility and openness, and the need to take care of it. We see this, for example, in the sweet, moving care for the vulnerability of new life and the profound desire to protect it inspiring "Around the Bend," where the still-lying father sings a lullaby for the moving baby and his future walk of life. In the presence of the fragility of this new life, self-forgiveness is no longer enough and the caring father needs an impossible forgiving and validating word and light to come from the innocent, silent new-born.

Even the elliptic, sharply metallic refrain of "Smile" contains a message of openness and hope of reconnection and happiness, as the title itself makes evident. Thus, the acknowledgment of finitude and precariousness goes hand in hand with the rejection of codes and the affirmation of the free, incommensurable, irreducible character of individual existence.[10] This affirmation, in turn, opens the door both to the possibility of egoism, permanent dread, and nihilism, and to that of care, love, and hope. In this sense, we can already witness a similarity between the intention of the album and that of the end of art thesis: both of them, in concomitance with an "end" and a "no," announce a new "beginning" and a "yes."[11]

Is "no code" a code?

The lyrics of *No Code* thus stay true to the album's overall intention, in that they confirm the infinite possibilities of a life lived beyond prefixed codes. The same can be said of the musical choices giving body and expression to that intention. As already mentioned, both the admirers and the (more numerous) critics of *No*

---

[10] This is, of course, a theme pervading Pearl Jam's production also beyond *No Code*: just think of "I am Mine" from the album *Riot Act* (2002).
[11] In the last section I will further qualify and develop this analogy.

Code have pointed out its heterogeneous, disharmonic musical composition. This is indubitably true even at a superficial listening. We go from the soft, detached intro tunes of "Sometimes" to the loud, aggressive smashing of "Hail, Hail" and "Habit," from the more classic rock of "Red Mosquito" to the alternative percussions and exotic sitar of "Who You Are," from the dazed "I'm Open" to the Neil Young-esque "Smile," up to the pensive, moving ballad tunes in "Off He Goes" and "Around the Bend," the furious, howling "Lukin," the drumming exhilaration of "In My Tree," the slow yet powerful "Present Tense," and the easygoing, singable "Mankind." No doubt, the album constitutes a break from previous Pearl Jam material, a break that made several fans and critics turn up their noses.

All, or at least several facets, of what it means to be human are well displayed through the words as well as through a kaleidoscopic variety of musical choices. While this shows a profound sensibility and maturity on the side of the band, from a philosophical point of view it may seem a rather non-exciting, or even trivial conclusion. It gets more exciting, however, when we realize that this sensible and appealing conclusion is in fact problematic, as it risks contradicting the very programmatic intention motivating it. Briefly, the "no code" statement risks becoming a code itself, and the programmatic declaration of the liberated, incommensurable nature of individual existence risks becoming a codified, normalized platitude, if not just yet another imprisoning 'habit' pretending to be our friend ("Habit"). Would this reversal nullify the "no code" statement, or would it be its utmost, consequential application? In other words: does the "no code" motto call for its own consequential application, at the risk of creating a new code, and hence of contradicting itself, or does it call for a self-violation, and hence, again, for a self-contradiction and nullification? We seem to have come to a sort of variation of the classical, well-known "liar's paradox": any attempt to assign a truth value to the sentence "I am lying" seems to result in contradiction. Analogously, if "no code" becomes a new code, we have a contradiction; if we want to avoid this result and hence violate the "no code" statement, we will need to put forward a code, resulting again in contradiction. Similar paradoxes have been extensively debated in the history of logic.[12] Here, however, we should keep in mind that *No Code* is an artwork, not a logical investigation. Therefore, we need to consider the very artistic means in which

---

[12] For a first overview, see Jc Beall, Michael Glanzberg, and David Ripley, 'Liar Paradox', in *The Stanford Encyclopaedia of Philosophy* (Winter 2019 Edition), Edward N. Zalta, ed.

that statement, and the contradiction it apparently leads to, are embedded. To this aim, the next section will connect the reading of the album offered here to the issue of the end of art introduced in the first section.

Codes for after the end of art

In search of a non-harmonic paradigm

I argue that, while *No Code*'s overall impression of chaos and disharmony persists also on a deeper level of listening, it is possible to trace a pattern and an intention behind the apparent chaos. This is in fact already evident from the album cover, consisting of an apparently random collage of photographs, which, when opening the cover, act like tiles of a geometrical mosaic. While one may dismiss *No Code* on the ground of a lack of harmony and consistence, I suggest that such lack reflects the intention (whether conscious or unconscious, it does not matter here) to create a nonharmonic paradigm. This paradigm, in turn, is motivated by the difficulty raised at the end of the previous section: it is an aesthetic response to an apparently unsolvable existential (and logical) antinomy.

The unpredictable, even bewildering mood, tune, and style shifts in *No Code* can be read as a consistent rejection of codes and rules not only in life in general, but also in art in particular. This "unmusical" musical choice is of particular importance as it also reminds us that art as a human practice has the capacity, and one might even say the "call," to operate this rejection, unlike most other practices in human life, which are for good or bad regulated by stringent networks of codes, conventions, rules, and so on. In this sense, *No Code* aesthetically acts as a nonharmonic, emancipatory paradigm, and as a bold statement of independence. This independence statement stops short of nothing and no one, not even when faced with the dangerous stalker from "Lukin." Finally, independence is also reclaimed as an attitude of personal consistency and capacity to keep moving despite the growing misery (or "bullshit") all around ("Off He Goes").

But how exactly is art able to perform a statement of independence without falling prey to a new codification? Or, we may also ask, which kind of art is able to do so? I want to suggest that the successful aesthetic strategy advanced in *No Code* can be read as an instance of art after the end of art. Certain forms of art do of course respond to a need for codification, not only in aesthetic, but also in cognitive, ethical, political, and religious terms: again, let us think of classical Greek or medieval Christian art. A Greek tragedy or statue, a Medieval cathedral or altarpiece were expressions of a relatively unified worldview, structured around beliefs, norms, customs, traditions, and so on, which constituted the content, the formal principle, and the raison d'être of the artwork.[13] The artwork was, in short, a medium of transmission of normative contents, of collective and cultural identification, and of ethical and religious orientation.

This is clearly not the case for a work such as *No Code*, not only for obvious content and style differences, but also because of a structural difference in the role art is called to interpret, and hence in the very formal principle regulating artistic messages. *No Code* does not (and cannot) transmit binding principles, it neither requires nor calls for identification for its fruition, and it does not provide ethical or religious orientation. While this may be true of most modern artworks, at least in Western culture, a work such as *No Code* embeds this proposition in its very conception and execution, more so than Pearl Jam's previous works. The sense of bewilderment and disorientation it provokes in the listener is, accordingly, not the result of a moment of artistic confusion or random experimentation, but, on the contrary, the consequential result of its inner principle of organization, namely the "no code" proposition. To be sure, one could argue that in this way the codification of the proposition is just moved to a different level, but in no way is it dispelled. However, I would like to resist this objection by pointing out in more detail the strategy displayed in the album and its connection with the end of art thesis.

For a no code aesthetics

Clearly, as we saw, there is a paradoxical dimension to the whole *No Code* project. Of course, there is also a paradoxical dimension to the idea of art after the end of art. While the two topics should be treated in their specificity, one common trait is that in both cases we witness the attempt to transmit a message, without being caught in the web of codifications traditionally associated with that message. This attempt results in a structural dialectic, which, in my reading, should be taken as the very core of such artistic enterprises. First of all, as already mentioned, there is a dialectic of "no" and "yes," of "end" and "beginning." As a matter of fact, one can easily consider *No Code* as both a termination and a

---

[13] Once again, this is obviously a general depiction, which does not apply to each and every artwork.

beginning point in the band's career. This not only in a "biographical" sense, but also as far as Pearl Jam's poetics is concerned: the renouncement of their previous style became in itself a new aesthetic statement.

Second, consistently with the end of art thesis, *No Code* displays a strong dialectical tension between unity and dispersion: there is of course a leading, unifying idea, which is however refracted in a plurality of very different, apparently unrelated fragments, i.e., the single songs. Admittedly, unity of multiplicity or multiplicity in unity is a classic characterization of beauty and artworks. Traditionally, however, this characterization points toward an idea of harmony: a beautiful artwork is the result of the harmonic, unified composition of its several constituents, reflecting and embedding an equally harmonic and unified worldview.[14] This is not the case for *No Code*, where the different constituents, namely the songs, can hardly be said to concur to build a beautiful harmony: in fact, the album, considered as the sum total of the songs, rather creates an effect of utter heterogeneity and disharmony. Neither can it be said that the unifying idea of the album, i.e., the "no code" proposition, is fully represented or interpreted by any of its single songs. The album rather acts as a disharmonic mosaic and draws our attention to the tension between the single songs, as well as between the songs and the whole concept.

This brings us to a third, deeper level of analysis. While we can (and should) of course enjoy the songs and be aesthetically struck with the rich diversity of their styles and techniques, the album's heterogeneity and tension can lead us to go a step further and question its motives (as I am trying to do with this paper). A more harmonic, unified artistic composition, as we may find in previous Pearl Jam albums, would rather invite us to pure, immediate enjoyment, appreciation of the technique and the lyrics, and so on. In other words, it would invite us to a more unreflected contemplation of and identification with the artistic material. On the contrary, a disharmonic work, provided it is not just the result of poor technique, conception, or execution, challenges us to abandon this immediate, unreflected level of enjoyment, and to ask for the reasons of apparently counterintuitive choices. In other words, it invites us to adopt a more reflective, problematic approach. While this does not necessarily result in a comprehensive philosophical approach, it shows us that such artworks are so to speak

---

[14] This is what Władysław Tatarkiewicz famously called "the great theory of beauty," in "The Great Theory of Beauty and Its Decline," *The Journal of Aesthetics and Art Criticism* 31, no. 2. (1972): 165–80.

"incomplete" or "partial," in that they require something else than an immediate aesthetic response. This structural reference to a higher, or at any rate different, philosophical, or reflective approach is, as we saw, a characteristic of art after the end of art.[15] *No Code* hence displays not only a tension between unity and difference, but also one between engagement and detachment. Accordingly, an "appropriate" listening of the album's tension between unity and difference calls for a continuous movement between engaged, immersive fruition and detached, reflective interrogation. This restless tension between different registers is the very creative core of the album, the aesthetic strategy employed to address the logical and existential difficulties we saw arising from its very proposition. In short, this is the main point of a no code aesthetics.

To conclude, I want to sketch some implications of a no code aesthetics. First of all, "no code" in the sense of "do not resuscitate" can apply to art itself, if by "art" we mean art before its end. Art as the harmonic code and expression of a more or less unified worldview is gone because it no longer reflects our needs. Attempts to reanimate it can either result in kitsch, as the surrogate of the search for ideal beauty in a context no longer accepting its grounds,[16] or, worse, in a reactionary longing for a community marked by compactness and strong unifying values, in which the right of the subject's particularity can be seen as a luxury, or even a threat.[17] The very disharmonic, plural, and open nature of art after the end of art, powerfully instanced in *No Code*, calls for a more participative fruition on the side of the receiving subject, hence enhancing his reflective and critical capacities and substantially contributing to the formation of the modern individual. However, while the rejection of codes calls for a questioning of objective forms and contents, it does not mean the triumph of arbitrary, solipsistic subjectivity. We saw this with regard to some of the topics addressed in *No Code*, but this also applies to the issue of the "value" of the artwork itself. In short, it is possible to put a price on the artwork, which means that a value can be negotiated even for such recalcitrant material. This is, to be sure, part of Pearl Jam's "bet" with the album: "And they're not so self-righteous as to deny that, yes, success has its privileges. For example, if you can't put out a glorious, guiltless, mad-blend

---

[15] This point, already present in Hegel, was theorized by Arthur C. Danto in *The Philosophical Disenfranchisement of Art* (New York: Columbia University Press, 1986).
[16] See among others Umberto Eco, "The Structure of Bad Taste," in *The Open Work* (Cambridge, MA: Harvard University Press, 1989), 180–216.
[17] This is e.g. Heidegger's case: see Alberto L. Siani, "Antisubjectivism and the End of Art: Heidegger on Hegel," *British Journal of Aesthetics* 60, no. 3 (2020): 335–49.

mess of tunes and weird tangents like *No Code* when you're at the top, what's the point of swimming through all the sewage to get there?"[18] The artwork's value is no longer an "absolute," inestimable one but, just like any other object for sale, becomes the result of a negotiation following different and even clashing logics. In this sense, while one may certainly disapprove of this "objectification" and "monetarization" of the artwork, we should also be able to acknowledge that the latter does not by any means exclude the possibility of the permanence of the aesthetic element in the cultural industry. The aesthetic dimension is recognized as one of the many elements contributing to the nature and value of an artwork, yet not as the necessarily predominant one. This undermines art's and artists' anachronistic, aestheticist, and elitist claims, contributing to an aesthetic democratization (which, admittedly, often turns out to be massification and consumerism) by instituting an open, even anarchistic dialectic, in which different or contradictory needs and dimensions are bound to find always precarious balances and rest positions, thus enhancing art's possibilities.

Bibliography

Beall, Jc, Michael Glanzberg, and David Ripley. "Liar Paradox." In *The Stanford Encyclopaedia of Philosophy* (Winter 2019 Edition), edited by Edward N. Zalta. Available online: https://plato.stanford.edu/entries/liar-paradox (accessed April 3, 2021).

Blasengame, Bart. "Trampled Moss and Sitars: Pearl Jam's Tricky, Transformational *No Code*." *AvClub.com*, August 26, 2016. Available online: https://music.avclub.com/trampled-moss-and-sitars-pearl-jam-s-tricky-transform1798251103 (accessed April 3, 2021).

Boehlert, Eric. "Pearl Jam: Taking on Ticketmaster." *Rolling Stone*, December 28, 1995. Available online: https://www.rollingstone.com/music/music-news/pearl-jam-taking-on-ticketmaster-67440 (accessed April 3, 2021).

Danto, Arthur C. *The Philosophical Disenfranchisement of Art*. New York: Columbia University Press, 1986.

Eco, Umberto. "The Structure of Bad Taste." In *The Open Work*, 180–216. Cambridge, MA: Harvard University Press, 1989.

Fricke, David. "No Code." *Rolling Stone*, September 5, 1996. Available online: https://www.rollingstone.com/music/music-album-reviews/no-code-204326 (accessed April 3, 2021).

---

[18] David Fricke, "No Code," *Rolling Stone*, September 5, 1996.

Siani, Alberto L. "End of Art." *International Lexicon of Aesthetics*, Autumn 2018. Available online: https://lexicon.mimesisjournals.com/international_lexicon_of_aesthetics_item_detail.php?item_id=37 (accessed April 3, 2021).

Siani, Alberto L. "Antisubjectivism and the End of Art: Heidegger on Hegel." *British Journal of Aesthetics* 60, no. 3 (2020): 335–49.

Tatarkiewicz, Władysław. "The Great Theory of Beauty and Its Decline." *The Journal of Aesthetics and Art Criticism* 31, no. 2 (1972): 165–80.

7

Can Truth Be Found in the Wild?

Paolo Stellino

To my brother, who thirty years ago introduced me to the music of Pearl Jam

In the summer of 1990, after graduating with honors from Emory University, the twenty-two-year-old Christopher Johnson McCandless donated his 24,000 dollars in savings to Oxfam, changed his name to Alexander Supertramp, and set out on a new life as a wanderer.[1] McCandless travelled across North America, and in April 1992 he hitchhiked from South Dakota to Alaska. He arrived in Fairbanks on the 25th, and two days later he sent his friend and former employer Wayne Westerberg a postcard with the following closing line: "If this adventure proves fatal and you don't ever hear from me again I want you to know you're a great man. I now walk into the wild. Alex."[2] On the 28th, McCandless entered the Alaskan bush, following the Stampede Trail. Among other things, he brought with him a big bag of rice, a rifle, a botanical guide to the region's edible plants, and approximately ten books (Thoreau's *Walden*, Tolstoy's *Family Happiness* and a collection of stories that included *The Death of Ivan Ilych* and *The Kreutzer Sonata*, and Pasternak's *Doctor Zhivago*, among other titles). Planning to live off game and wild plants, McCandless used an abandoned bus for shelter, hoping to find refuge from the civilized world in nature. Two months later, he decided to return to civilization. The Teklanika River, which he had safely crossed in April, was now flooded due to melting glaciers, however. He was literally "trapped in the wild," as he noted in one of his last journal entries.[3] On September 6, a group of hunters found his decomposing body inside the bus. Weighing only

---

[1] This chapter was funded by national funds through the FCT—Fundação para a Ciência e a Tecnologia, I.P., under the Norma Transitória—DL 57/2016/CP1453/CT0010.
[2] Jon Krakauer, *Into the Wild* (London: Pan Books, 2011), 3.
[3] Ibid., 195.

sixty-seven pounds, McCandless had died just two and a half weeks prior, from starvation aggravated by accidental poisoning.[4]

Jon Krakauer was one of the first journalists to write about McCandless, publishing an extended article in *Outside* magazine in January 1993. The article was later expanded into a book, published in 1996 with the title *Into the Wild*. As soon as he read the book, Sean Penn decided to adapt McCandless's story to the big screen, but it would be ten years before the family felt ready to give their permission. Penn began filming in 2006, and a year later he asked his friend Eddie Vedder to write the soundtrack for the film, which was released on September 18, 2007. As Penn explained in an interview with Charlie Rose, he intentionally structured his film around Vedder's music and consciously left out narrative in parts so that the songs themselves could make key transitions.[5] In the same interview, Vedder revealed that Penn had given him complete artistic freedom and that he wrote the songs in two or three weeks, in a sort of trance. Penn, Vedder explained, wanted him to be "the interior voice of the character," and this is precisely the impression one gains when listening to the songs, which are all written in the first person, as if by McCandless himself.

In order to understand the meaning of Vedder's poetic, inspiring lyrics, it is useful to recall that the songwriter viewed the McCandless story from a very specific perspective—a perspective filtered through Jon Krakauer's subjective and somewhat idealized portrait of McCandless and through the beautiful and ecstatic images of Penn's film. This is not to say that Vedder's own representation of McCandless's story is not objective—as Edward Said points out in *Orientalism*, following in the footsteps of Nietzsche and Foucault, every interpretation is a reinterpretation, a rebuilding of the object that is interpreted.[6] The question is rather whether and to what extent the McCandless that Vedder came to know through Krakauer and Penn was a romanticized or even ideologized version of the real and true McCandless (if there is such a thing as a real and true person). Krakauer, for instance, has been criticized for the use he made of the literary sources in his book—a use that aimed, so the critique goes, to convey a romanticized picture of McCandless as a kind of "visionary seeker"[7] and modern pilgrim. Caroline Hanssen argues that "Krakauer, as well as McCandless,

---

[4] See Krakauer, "How Chris McCandless Died," *New Yorker*, September 12, 2013; Krakauer, "How Chris McCandless Died: An Update," *New Yorker*, February 11, 2015.
[5] Sean Penn and Eddie Vedder, "Interview by Charlie Rose," *Charlie Rose*, PBS, September 9, 2007.
[6] Edward W. Said, *Orientalism* (London: Penguin Books, 2003), 158.
[7] Matthew Power, "The Cult of Chris McCandless," *Men's Journal*, September 2007, 155.

may have missed the point of London's realism,"[8] highlighting "the irony of McCandless' apparent appreciation of an author whose works for at least a century have warned against man's hubris in nature in general and an accidental death in the subarctic wilderness in particular."[9] José Sánchez Vera points out that "the figure of Thoreau that Krakauer draws upon marks at best a partial and rather romantic interpretation of the actual views held by the great transcendentalist."[10]

On a more general note, it should be pointed out that, from the very beginning, McCandless's life and death sparked a lively debate divided roughly into two camps: on the one hand, McCandless is perceived as a tragic hero who dared to free himself from the oppressive and senseless rules and norms of modern capitalistic society and who died as the result of a tragic mistake, trying to live in communion with nature; on the other hand, he is seen (particularly by many Alaskans) as a greenhorn who, in his naivety and arrogance, misjudged the wilderness and was met with a well-deserved death, which he had probably, more or less consciously, wished for. As is often the case, the truth of McCandless's story likely lies somewhere in the middle. There is indeed no denying that McCandless probably could have avoided his tragic fate had he been better prepared or equipped. When he decided to return to civilization but was held back by the Teklanika river in the beginning of July, having no topographic map of the region, he did not know that a gauging station was located a mere half mile downstream, where a steel cable spanning the gorge supported an aluminum basket used for crossing the river. On the other hand, it is also true that beyond the personal reasons that may have led McCandless to change his name and live the life of a wanderer (in the summer of 1986, he discovered that, at the time of his birth, his father Walt had been living a double life, maintaining a relationship with both Marcia, his then wife, and Billie, Chris's mother), his story has profound symbolic meaning that transcends the specific question of who Chris McCandless really was.

Underlying many of the critiques that have been directed against Krakauer's and Penn's idealized portrayal of McCandless, there is a similar concern: the worry that by romanticizing his story, they are encouraging readers and viewers

---

[8] Caroline Hanssen, "'You Were Right, Old Hoss: You Were Right': Jack London in Jon Krakauer's *Into the Wild*," *American Literary Realism* 43, no. 3 (2011): 193.
[9] Ibid., 191.
[10] José Sánchez Vera, "Thoreau as an Oblique Mirror: Jon Krakauer's *Into the Wild*," *American Studies in Scandinavia* 47, no. 1 (2015): 41.

to model their own lives on McCandless's example. Thus, for instance, Stephen Cook ends his article dedicated to *Into the Wild* by reminding the audience that:

> rational viewers must disengage from the movie's rhetoric and mentally dismiss the highly embellished ending of the movie. Instead, let us consider the *reality* of a 23 year old man reduced to 67 pounds; let us also imagine his final moments trapped and utterly alone in the "Magic Bus"; and finally, let us reflect on the cryptic epiphany Chris McCandless left behind: "Happiness only real when shared."[11]

A legitimate question is whether and to what extent Vedder's lyrics contribute to the idealization of McCandless. Before considering this question, however, it must be noted that the general concern about idealization is justified in part by the fact that McCandless's story "has assumed near mythic status,"[12] to the point that the bus he used for shelter in the last months of his life became a pilgrimage destination for hikers, some of whom had to be rescued (and a few of whom even died), leading the authorities to remove it. There is undoubtedly a certain irony in the fact that McCandless, a staunch defender of "unconventional living,"[13] became a conventional symbol that was promptly appropriated by the capitalistic society he despised so much (McCandless t-shirts are easily found for purchase on the internet, and, until recently, adventurers could pay good money to take a guided trip out to the bus).

Beyond its capitalistic implications, however, the transformation of McCandless's final resting place into a sanctuary and a pilgrimage site can be seen as a paradigmatic expression of what Nietzsche considered the human—all too human—spiritual need for faith or belief—faith or belief that, in this concrete case, acts as a substitute for one's inability or lack of courage to follow McCandless's example (put plainly: it is certainly easier to go on a pilgrimage to the "Magic Bus" than to donate all of one's savings to charity in order to start a new, more authentic life, as McCandless did). The German psychologist and philosopher Erich Fromm describes precisely this psychological mechanism in the following passage from his well-known work *To Have or to Be?*:

> In spite of the security of having, people admire those with a vision of the new, those who break a new path, who have the courage to move forward. In

---

[11] Stephen Cook, "*Into the Wild*: Chris McCandless and His Search for a 'Yonder,'" in *New Wests and Post-Wests. Literature and Film of the American West*, Paul Varner, ed. (Newcastle upon Tyne: Cambridge Scholars Publishing, 2013), 57.
[12] Power, "The Cult of Chris McCandless," 155.
[13] Krakauer, *Into the Wild*, 59.

mythology this mode of existence is represented symbolically by the *hero*. Heroes are those with the courage to leave what they have ... We admire these heroes because we deeply feel their way is the way we would want to be—if we could. But being afraid, we believe that we cannot be that way, that only the heroes can. The heroes become idols; we transfer to them our own capacity to move, and then stay where we are—"because we are not heroes."[14]

Besides the hermeneutical and epistemological problems concerning the possibility of discovering the truth about Chris McCandless—or, to borrow an expression from Matthew Power, to solve "the enigma of Chris McCandless"[15]—it could be argued that the most interesting aspect of his story lies not in the specific details of his life and death (whether he had a death wish or not, whether he died by starvation or by accidentally poisoning himself, and so on) but rather in its universal significance. It is precisely this conclusion that Ron Lamothe reaches in his 2007 documentary *The Call of the Wild*, dedicated to Chris McCandless:

> I soon realize I'm becoming too mired in the details surrounding Chris's death, and that what he symbolizes transcends questions of his physical health, or his wilderness acumen, or whether there are more remote places to get lost than Stampede Trail. Just as I care little how far Thoreau lived from the train tracks, or whether he mooched off Emerson on occasion, so too with McCandless. Like Thoreau's experiment at Walden, the greater meaning of Chris' journey is what lives on. Why he didn't walk out, perhaps, is less important in the big scheme of things, than why he walked in. The former is fleeting, and peripheral, whereas the latter is timeless, and profound. It is the idealized McCandless, the seeker, who in the end matters most to me.

By turning McCandless into a symbol, Lamothe seems to contribute to what Matthew Power has described as "the cult of Chris McCandless."[16] On the other hand, the documentarist is certainly right to point out that, notwithstanding the unfortunate conclusion of McCandless's adventure and despite its possible idealization by Krakauer, Penn, and Vedder, McCandless's story inevitably impels us to question our way of life and our relationship with the world. Mediated through the lyrics of Eddie Vedder's songs in particular, a number of philosophical and existential questions emerge: Are real happiness and freedom

---

[14] Erich Fromm, *To Have or to Be?* (London-New York: Continuum, 1976), 88–9.
[15] Power, "The Cult of Chris McCandless," 155.
[16] Ibid.

possible in a consumer society? Have we lost contact with "real life"? If so, what explains this? Where can genuine truth and happiness be found? Is life in the wild a mere utopia, inevitably doomed to disaster? Can we ever know where to put all our faith and how it will grow, to paraphrase a line from Vedder's song "Rise"?[17] In the following, I will consider aspects of these complex questions, specifically paying attention to the way in which Vedder deals with them in his album *Into the Wild*.

To begin with, it should be recalled that Penn's film is divided into five chapters, corresponding to different stages of McCandless's life: birth (Ch. 1), adolescence (Ch. 2), manhood (Ch. 3), family (Ch. 4), and the gaining of wisdom (Ch. 5). The transition from one stage to another is often emphasized by a song played by Vedder: "Hard Sun" (Ch. 1), "Rise" (Ch. 2), "Society" (Ch. 3—although in this case the song does not correspond precisely to the transition), and "Tuolumne" (Ch. 5). In reality, these five different stages of life are metaphorical (McCandless never started a family, nor did he reach old age) and symbolize the fact that McCandless experienced a spiritual rebirth, which led him to live a new life (Ch. 1, "My Own Birth," takes place following his graduation from Emory). In the lyrics of his songs, Vedder emphasizes this spiritual rebirth, as we see in "Rise" ("Gonna rise up / Burning black holes in dark memories / Gonna rise up / Turning mistakes into gold")[18] and "Long Nights" ("I've got this life / I'll be around to grow / Who I was before / I cannot recall").[19] "Rise" can even be seen as an indirect allusion to the resurrection of Lazarus.

Although McCandless did not strictly speaking experience a religious conversion, his new life was characterized by a high level of spirituality—Vedder's line "I feel part of everywhere"[20] clearly alludes to a kind of *unio mystica* with nature and the world. Having cut ties to his past life ("Watch me leave it all behind," as Vedder puts it in "Far Behind"),[21] McCandless strove for "reconciliation with the absolute totality of things,"[22] to quote an expression from William James's *The Varieties of Religious Experience*, searching for the truth of his existence, hoping to find it in the wild. In this context, James's *The Varieties of Religious Experience* may be particularly helpful in understanding what kind of

---

[17] Eddie Vedder, "Rise," in *Into the Wild* (2007).
[18] Ibid.
[19] Eddie Vedder, "Long Nights," in *Into the Wild* (2007).
[20] Eddie Vedder, "Guaranteed," in *Into the Wild* (2007).
[21] Eddie Vedder, "Far Behind," in *Into the Wild* (2007).
[22] William James, *The Varieties of Religious Experience* (London: Penguin Books, 1985), 164.

inner transformation McCandless underwent. One of the central sections of the work is dedicated to the spiritual rebirth often experienced by what James calls "the sick soul." According to James, whereas the healthy-minded tend to see things optimistically and to minimize the evil aspects of human existence, sick souls are persuaded that "evil is an essential part of our being and the key to the interpretation of our life."[23] In some instances, this pessimistic worldview can be so extreme as to lead the person who holds it to fall prey to pathological melancholy. As a consequence, one is led to put into question the meaning and purpose of life. In fortunate cases, the crisis leads to religious conversion, and the sufferer experiences a second birth. As James puts it: "the man must die to an unreal life before he can be born into the real life."[24] In this condition, deepest levels of truth are often attained.

It is interesting to note that in order to provide a concrete example of spiritual rebirth, James mentions the case of Tolstoy, an author who in fact inspired McCandless. As mentioned above, McCandless brought books by Tolstoy with him into the Alaskan bush, underlining certain passages.[25] Before departing from Carthage, McCandless gave his friend Wayne Westerberg a treasured edition of Tolstoy's *War and Peace*, later describing the novel as "a very powerful and highly symbolic book."[26] At about the age of fifty, following the publication of his two masterpieces *War and Peace* (1869) and *Anna Karenina* (1877), Tolstoy underwent a profound moral and spiritual crisis that led him to despair. He was loved, rich, and famous, but life had suddenly become meaningless and purposeless. As he relates in *Confession* (1882), extracts of which are quoted at length by James, Tolstoy thought of committing suicide: he had to hide the rope in order not to hang himself and stopped going hunting so as not to yield to the temptation of shooting himself. Then something unexpected happened. A new consciousness of life drew him out of his despair, and a thirst for God prompted his religious conversion. Tolstoy understood that "he had been living wrongly and must change," as James puts it.[27] A spiritual rebirth thus took place: a false life based on "conventionality, artificiality, and personal ambition"[28] was replaced with a real and true life based on spirituality, asceticism, and faith. This spiritual regeneration is taken by James, among other examples, to be representative of

---

[23] Ibid., 131.
[24] Ibid., 131.
[25] Krakauer, *Into the Wild*, 15 and 168.
[26] Ibid., 19 and 33.
[27] James, *The Varieties of Religious Experience*, 185.
[28] Ibid., 185.

what he calls the twice-born religion: "the personality is changed, the man *is* born anew."[29]

Although departing from it in certain ways, Christopher McCandless's experience recalls the pattern described by James. It can be said that, before his rebirth, McCandless was a kind of "sick soul," suffering from the absurdity and meaninglessness of conventional life in a consumer society (James's evil). The refrain of "Hard Sun" (originally written by Gordon Peterson)—about a big hard sun that beats on the big people in a big hard world[30]—which can be seen as a reformulation of Kohelet's observation that "there is nothing new under the sun,"[31] seems to allude precisely to the fact that no matter how much money, success, or fame you have, the big hard sun will beat down on you just as it beats down on those who have nothing. Having given away nearly all of his savings, McCandless set out on a new life, experiencing a spiritual rebirth, as emphasized both in the film (the title of Chapter 1 is "My Own Birth") and in Vedder's lyrics ("I been wounded / I been healed").[32] The fact that McCandless changed his real name to Alexander Supertramp is illustrative of his need to cut ties with his past life and start a new one. His metamorphosis was eventually completed in the Alaskan wild, as the following note in his journal shows: "I am reborn. This is my dawn. *Real* life has just begun."[33]

The fact that McCandless entered the Alaskan bush with books by Thoreau, Tolstoy, and Gogol is illustrative of the importance of these authors to his spiritual rebirth. As Krakauer points out, "the heaviest item in McCandless's half-full backpack was his library."[34] James's *The Varieties of Religious Experience* and Tolstoy's *The Gospel in Brief* played a similarly key role in the rebirth of another figure: Ludwig Wittgenstein, one of the most important philosophers of the twentieth century, who, in the First World War, had a transformative experience that to a certain extent recalls McCandless's. What is particularly interesting about Wittgenstein's story is the fact that, like McCandless, he felt that his (conspicuous) wealth was a hindrance to his desire for complete regeneration (as Vedder puts it in "Far Behind," a greater sense of wealth is allowed by empty pockets).[35] By the end of the war, Wittgenstein, the son of a successful industrialist,

---

[29] Ibid., 241.
[30] Eddie Vedder, "Hard Sun," in *Into the Wild* (2007).
[31] *Ecclesiastes*, 1:9.
[32] Eddie Vedder, "No Ceiling," in *Into the Wild* (2007).
[33] Krakauer, *Into the Wild*, 167.
[34] Ibid., 161.
[35] Eddie Vedder, "Far Behind."

was one of the wealthiest men in Europe. In the span of a month, he had given his entire inheritance to his sisters, Helene and Hermine, and to his brother, Paul. Wittgenstein's insistence that his inheritance be given to them in its entirety, without any money being put aside for him (in case he later came to regret his decision), precisely recalls James's claim that the desire for regeneration is incomplete and ineffective as long as one does not give up all possessions. As James puts it: "So long as any secular safeguard is retained, so long as any residual prudential guarantee is clung to, so long as the surrender is incomplete, the vital crisis is not passed, fear still stands sentinel, and mistrust of the divine obtains."[36]

It is also noteworthy that, like McCandless, Wittgenstein sought solitude at the age of 24, leaving the renowned University of Cambridge for Skjolden, a tiny village in Norway, in the environs of which he later built a remote wooden hut, which could be reached only by rowing across Lake Eidsvatnet. During his subsequent stays in Norway, Wittgenstein lived and worked in this hut. Without denying the several differences that distinguish Wittgenstein's case from McCandless's, it should nevertheless be pointed out that what essentially led Wittgenstein and McCandless to seek solitude in nature was a similar motivation: the search for truth. Furthermore, as Wittgenstein's biographer Ray Monk points out, although in Norway Wittgenstein was not entirely divorced from human contact, still:

> he was—and perhaps this is most important—away from society, free from the kind of obligations and expectations imposed by bourgeois life, whether that of Cambridge or that of Vienna. His horror of the bourgeois life was based in part on the superficial nature of the relationships it imposed on people, but partly also on the fact that his own nature imposed upon him an almost insufferable conflict when faced with it—the conflict between needing to withstand it, and needing to conform to it.[37]

As Krakauer's book and Penn's film abundantly show, the artificiality of social relations is one of the main reasons that led McCandless to the extreme decision to break off all connection to his family. McCandless's critique of modern society and civilization was much more profound, however, fueled not only by his knowledge of the several social injustices caused by capitalism,[38] but also by his awareness that civilization was a poison, acting against the possibility of reaching

---

[36] James, *The Varieties of Religious Experience*, 321.
[37] Ray Monk, *Ludwig Wittgenstein. The Duty of Genius* (London: Vintage Books, 1991), 93-4.
[38] Krakauer, *Into the Wild*, 123.

ultimate freedom and knowledge. In a letter to Ron Franz, McCandless exhorted his friend to change his circumstances and to give up his false life of security, conformity, and conservativism, which, far from giving peace of mind, prevented him from living life in its full meaning.[39] Similarly, in May 1992, McCandless left the following message in the "Magic Bus":

> Two years he walks the earth. No phone, no pool, no pets, no cigarettes. Ultimate freedom. An extremist. An aesthetic voyager whose home is the road ... now after two rambling years comes the final and greatest adventure. The climactic battle to kill the false being within and victoriously conclude the spiritual pilgrimage ... No longer to be poisoned by civilization he flees, and walks alone upon the land to become *lost in the wild*.[40]

Notwithstanding its self-indulgent, triumphant, and exuberant tone, this message gives a clear idea of McCandless's view of society and civilization, as well as his understanding of his spiritual pilgrimage, the goal of which was "to kill the false being within," as he puts it. The lyrics of the song "Society," written by Jerry Hannan, place particular emphasis on the fact that a consumer society, based on the accumulation of superfluous goods, can provide only illusory freedom and happiness: our greediness leads us to desire to have more than we need and to think that we will never be free until we have everything we want.[41] Freedom and happiness in this context are illusory because they depend on how much one possesses; given the way in which capitalist societies function, however, one's possessions are never enough to fulfil one's superimposed and artificial need to possess. The paradoxical result of this situation is that consumers forge the chains that bind them. As Vedder puts it in "Guaranteed:" "On bended knee is no way to be free ... Everyone I come across in cages they bought."[42] Only by becoming self-conscious of his or her situation can the individual hope to break these chains. This is precisely the meaning of McCandless's exhortation to his friend Ron Franz, and this is why, in his song "Society," Hannan emphasizes the relation between thinking—when we want more than we have, we still think we need, whereas when we think more than we have, then our thoughts "begin to bleed"—and civil disobedience (to quote the posthumously given title of

---

[39] Ibid., 58.
[40] Ibid., 162.
[41] Eddie Vedder, "Society," in *Into the Wild* (2007).
[42] Eddie Vedder, "Guaranteed."

Thoreau's famous essay)—"Society / Have mercy on me / Hope you're not angry / If I disagree."[43]

Although radical, McCandless's belief that ultimate freedom can be achieved only by taking leave from civilized society recalls Fromm's distinction (in *To Have or to Be?*) between two fundamental modes of existence: the having mode and the being mode. According to Fromm, the having mode of existence is characterized by a relationship to the world that is one of possession and ownership, whereas the being mode of existence can be defined (in contrast to having) as an "authentic relatedness to the world" and (in contrast to appearing) as referring to "the true nature, the true reality, of a person or a thing in contrast to deceptive appearances."[44] Needless to say, the predominant mode of existence in our society is the having mode—a mode characterized by an alienated relation to the things we own and that, in turn, own us. Far from bringing happiness, this mode of existence fosters greed (recall the beginning of Hannan's song "Society") and leads to dissatisfaction. For this reason, many people seek to rediscover a lost original oneness with nature and to embrace the being mode of existence. There is little doubt that Fromm's portrayal of those who are dissatisfied with their mode of existence fits perfectly with McCandless—or at least with Krakauer's, Penn's, and Vedder's McCandless:

> We find that not a few people, especially younger ones, cannot stand the luxury and selfishness that surround them in their affluent families. Quite against the expectations of their elders, who think that their children "have everything they wish," they rebel against the deadness and isolation of their lives. For the fact is, they do not have everything they wish and they wish for what they do not have.[45]

The analogies between Fromm's being mode of existence and McCandless's own mode of existence after his spiritual rebirth are several in number and cannot all be scrutinized here. It suffices to say that many of the qualities that Fromm ascribes to the new man (the emergence of which is the goal of the new society) are qualities that the reborn McCandless appeared to have had, or at least to have cultivated.[46] There is, however, an aspect in Fromm's analysis that needs to be emphasized, for it can help to explain an aspect of McCandless's psychology about which there has been much debate. As the aforementioned postcard he

---

[43] Eddie Vedder, "Society."
[44] Fromm, *To Have or to Be?*, 21.
[45] Ibid., 84.
[46] See ibid., 139–40.

sent to Wayne Westerberg before entering the Alaskan bush shows, even though McCandless knew that his adventure could prove fatal, he did not abandon his long-awaited journey into the wild. This has been interpreted as signaling that McCandless had a more or less unconscious death wish. Fromm's analysis of the fear of dying, however, suggests the possibility of a different interpretation. According to Fromm, we fear death when we hang onto life, that is, when we conceive of it as a private possession we are afraid of losing. Yet the closer we come to shedding the having mode of existence, the more we lose our fear of dying—since, as Fromm puts it, "there is nothing to lose."[47] McCandless's touching farewell message—"I have had a happy life and thank the lord. Goodbye and may God bless all!"[48]—seems to indicate that when the lights went out, to paraphrase one of the lines of Vedder's "Long Nights," he had achieved this wisdom.

Happiness and wisdom lead us to what can be considered—at least from a philosophical point of view—the most important aspect of McCandless's spiritual pilgrimage: the search for truth. This aspect is variously emphasized by both Penn (Carine, McCandless's sister, explains her brother's decision to cut ties with his previous life by saying: "now he was emancipated from that world of abstraction, false security, parents and material excess, the things that cut Chris off from the truth of his existence") and Vedder ("Subtle voices in the wind / Hear the truth they're telling / A world begins where the road ends").[49] McCandless's need to understand, to grasp the truth ("When I try to understand / She just opens up her hands")[50] is not a mere fictional aspect, however, but a concrete urge that emerges from his notes in the books he was reading. As Krakauer points out, McCandless underlined a passage from Thoreau's *Walden* that reads: "Rather than love, than money, than fame, give me truth,"[51] writing at the top of the page, in large block letters, the word "TRUTH."[52]

According to Krakauer, "[u]nlike Muir and Thoreau, McCandless went into the wilderness not primarily to ponder nature or the world at large but, rather, to explore the inner country of his own soul."[53] In a similar way, in the passage from

---

[47] Ibid., 103.
[48] Krakauer, *Into the Wild*, 199.
[49] Eddie Vedder, "Far Behind."
[50] Eddie Vedder, "Hard Sun."
[51] Henry D. Thoreau, *The Portable Thoreau* (London: Penguin Books, 2012), 465.
[52] Krakauer, *Into the Wild*, 117.
[53] Ibid., 182.

Penn's film quoted above, Carine says that his brother was cut off not from truth in general but from the truth of his existence. According to these interpretations, McCandless began his spiritual pilgrimage and later entered the Alaskan bush not to find a universal truth but to discover who he really was—following, in other words, the ancient philosophical imperative *gnothi seauton*, "know thyself." What is interesting about McCandless's story, however, is that even if we admit that he set out in the wilderness in search of his true self—there is no denying that his adventure can be seen as a rite of passage, a need to test himself—he eventually discovered a truth that can be said to transcend the specific context of his individual life, namely that happiness is real only when shared with those we love and care about. McCandless found this universal truth expressed in the following passage from Boris Pasternak's *Doctor Zhivago*: "And so it turned out that only a life similar to the life of those around us, merging with it without a ripple, is genuine life, and that an unshared happiness is not happiness."[54] It is possible, however, that McCandless reached this truth through his own experience and that Pasternak's novel only helped him to become conscious of it. In other words, this was a lived, embodied truth for him—a truth that he found by going into the wild. Indeed, before his Alaska trip, in early April 1992, McCandless wrote the following to Ron Franz: "You are wrong if you think Joy emanates only or principally from human relationships. God has placed it all around us. It is in everything and anything we might experience."[55] Only a few months later, while reading his last book, *Doctor Zhivago*, likely aware that the end of his life was near, McCandless wrote the following instead: "happiness only real when shared."[56] Although it is not possible to know whether his pilgrimage made him a better man (recall the beginning of "Hard Sun": "When I walk beside her / I am the Better Man"),[57] there is no doubt that the wild made him a wiser man.

The story of Chris McCandless has often been compared to that of the environmentalist Timothy Treadwell, who for thirteen summers lived among grizzly bears in an Alaskan national park without any weapons whatsoever. In October 2003, Treadwell and his girlfriend, Amie Huguenard, were killed and almost fully eaten by a brown bear. Like McCandless, not only did Treadwell

---

[54] Boris Pasternak, *Doctor Zhivago* (New York: Pantheon Books, 1958), 147.
[55] Krakauer, *Into the Wild*, 58.
[56] Ibid., 188.
[57] Eddie Vedder, "Hard Sun."

have a romanticized and idealized vision of nature, but he also came from a solid middle-class family and had changed his real name, lying about his origins to his friends. According to Werner Herzog, who made a documentary film about Treadwell in 2005 (the acclaimed *Grizzly Man*), what drove Treadwell into the wild was "an urge to escape the safety of his protected environment." Yet for him, the Alaskan adventure became something more: an occasion to search for his real self. As Herzog puts it: "Beyond his posings, the camera was his only present companion. It was his instrument to explore the wilderness around him, but increasingly it became more. He started to scrutinize his innermost being, his demons, his exhilarations."

Also like McCandless, Treadwell has been the subject of several critiques, and Sam Egli, the helicopter pilot who was called out to assist in the recovery of Treadwell's and his girlfriend's remains, expresses a shared view when, interviewed by Herzog, he observes that Treadwell "got what he deserved." Unlike Penn, Herzog does not present a romanticized version of nature. In *Grizzly Man*, he clearly points out his divergence from Treadwell: "what haunts me, is that in all the faces of all the bears that Treadwell ever filmed, I discover no kinship, no understanding, no mercy. I see only the overwhelming indifference of nature." Like Penn, however (and Krakauer and Vedder), Herzog, far from passing judgment on Treadwell, is able to go beyond his exuberant personality and the mesmerizing beauty of the images he shot, drawing attention to the fact that the meaning of his adventure among the bears transcends the boundaries of his private life:

> Treadwell is gone. The argument how wrong or how right he was disappears into a distance, into a fog. What remains is his footage. And while we watch the animals in their joys of being, in their grace and ferociousness, a thought becomes more and more clear. That it is not so much a look at wild nature as it is an insight into ourselves, our nature. And that, for me, beyond his mission, gives meaning to his life and to his death.

Like Treadwell, Chris McCandless is gone. Even in his case, the argument about whether he was mistaken to enter the Alaskan bush, whether he was unprepared and ill-equipped, or whether he had a death wish, loses its importance. There is little doubt that he overestimated his ability to survive in the wilderness. As long as we judge him for the mistakes he made, however, and as long as we show more interest in solving the enigma of who he really was rather than trying to understand his motivations—motives that Vedder prompts us to consider in his songs—we will likely be unable to grasp the profound meaning of his radical life choice. This choice began when he decided to disagree with society and to prefer a life of wandering in nature and the company of outcasts to the possibility of getting into Harvard Law School and securing a brilliant professional future. I cannot but admire this courageous and brave choice. Although I am not sure whether truth can be found by going into the wild, as an academic philosopher I am firmly convinced that the more our universities are structured according to capitalistic models of production, following the absurd logic of "publish or perish," the more we move away from truth. And if we should perish after all, this time for real and not metaphorically—for, as Vedder sings, such is "the way of the world"[58]—let us remember, with Schopenhauer, that transience is part of human nature and that death is nothing but "a return to the womb of nature."[59] As Vedder puts it in "End of the Road":

Won't be the last
Won't be the first
Find a way to where
The sky meets the earth.[60]

Bibliography

Cook, Stephen. "*Into the Wild*: Chris McCandless and His Search for a 'Yonder.'" In *New Wests and Post-Wests. Literature and Film of the American West*, edited by Paul Varner, 44–58. Newcastle upon Tyne: Cambridge Scholars Publishing, 2013.
Fromm, Erich. *To Have or to Be?* London-New York: Continuum, 1976.
Grizzly Man [Film]. Dir. Werner Herzog. USA: Lions Gate Films, Discovery Docs, 2005.
Hanssen, Caroline. "'You Were Right, Old Hoss: You Were Right': Jack London in Jon Kracauer's *Into the Wild*." *American Literary Realism* 43, no. 3 (2011): 191–7.
Into the Wild [Film]. Dir. Sean Penn. USA: Paramount Vantage et al., 2007.
James, William. *The Varieties of Religious Experience*. London: Penguin Books, 1985.
Krakauer, Jon. *Into the Wild*. London: Pan Books, 2011.
Krakauer, Jon. "How Chris McCandless Died." *New Yorker*, September 12, 2013. Available online: https://www.newyorker.com/books/page-turner/how-chris-mccandless-died (accessed June 29, 2020).

---

[58] Eddie Vedder, "Rise."
[59] Arthur Schopenhauer, *The World as Will and Representation*. Vol. 2 (Cambridge: Cambridge University Press, 2018), 486.
[60] Eddie Vedder, "End of the Road," in *Into the Wild* (2007).

Krakauer, Jon. "How Chris McCandless Died: An Update." *New Yorker*, February 11, 2015. Available online: https://www.newyorker.com/books/page-turner/chris-mccandless-died-update (accessed June 29, 2020).

Monk, Ray. *Ludwig Wittgenstein. The Duty of Genius*. London: Vintage Books, 1991.

Pasternak, Boris. *Doctor Zhivago*, translated by Max Hayward and Manya Harari. New York: Pantheon Books, 1958.

Penn, Sean and Eddie Vedder. "Interview by Charlie Rose." *Charlie Rose*, PBS, September 9, 2007. Available online: https://charlierose.com/videos/18453 (accessed June 29, 2020).

Power, Matthew. "The Cult of Chris McCandless." *Men's Journal*, September 2007, 154–60.

Said, Edward W. *Orientalism*. London: Penguin Books, 2003.

Sánchez Vera, José. "Thoreau as an Oblique Mirror: Jon Kracauer's *Into the Wild*." *American Studies in Scandinavia* 47, no. 1 (2015): 40–60.

Schopenhauer, Arthur. *The World as Will and Representation. Vol. 2*, translated and edited by Judith Norman, Alistair Welchman, Christopher Janaway. Cambridge: Cambridge University Press, 2018.

The Call of the Wild [Film]. Dir. Ron Lamothe. USA: Terra Incognita Films, 2007.

Thoreau, Henry D. *The Portable Thoreau*, edited by Jeffrey S. Cramer. London: Penguin Books, 2012.

8

"They Can Buy, But Can't Put On My Clothes": Pearl Jam, Grunge, and Subcultural Authenticity in a Postmodern Fashion Climate

Stephanie Kramer

On November 15, 1992, the *New York Times* published "Grunge: A Success Story," an attempt to encapsulate the recent explosion of the "subcultural phenomenon" known as grunge and its accompanying fashion aesthetic:

> By last summer the glossy magazines began tracking grunge looks, the threadbare flannel shirts, knobby wool sweaters and cracked leatherette coats of the Pacific North West's thrift shop esthetic. Hollywood weighed in, too, with a grunge-scene movie, *Singles*. Then two weeks ago—all in the blink of a flashbulb—the fashion designer Marc Jacobs, who has never even been to Seattle, was hailed as "guru of grunge."[1]

Seemingly a quintessential characterization of the from-subculture-to-mass-culture machine that had come to be understood as a chief feature of postmodern cultural production, writer Rick Marin correctly traced the story of grunge's underground emergence, subsequent corporate exploitation, and ultimate dissemination amongst the masses, asserting that "the trend timeline gets shorter and faster all the time . . . pop will eat itself, the axiom goes."[2]

The cycle, as Marin pointed out, was by no means a new one. From the mods of the late 1950s–60s to the punks of the 1970s, alternative styles—or "oppositional dress," as dubbed by fashion historian Elizabeth Wilson—had long been a reflection of the desire for individuality within an increasingly fragmented industrial world where the commodification of choice had proven overwhelming.[3]

---

[1] Rick Marin, "Grunge: A Success Story," *The New York Times*, November 15, 1992.
[2] Ibid.
[3] Elizabeth Wilson, *Adorned in Dreams: Fashion and Modernity* (London: Virago Press, Ltd, 1985), 179.

Just as new fashion forms were the reaction to this overpowering presence of a postmodern capitalist machine, so to, they would eventually fall prey to it, ultimately providing a direct source of commodification by the very system that was the impetus of their original oppositional thinking. Articulating this process specifically within the context of youth subcultures, sociologist Dick Hebdige described the "commodity form" or "the conversion of subcultural signs (dress, music, etc.) into mass-produced objects":

> [the subculture] communicates through commodities even if the meanings attached to those commodities are purposefully distorted or overthrown. It is therefore difficult in this case to maintain any absolute distinction between commercial exploitation on the one hand and creativity/originality on the other, even though these categories are emphatically opposed in the value systems of most subcultures. Indeed, the creation and diffusion of new styles is inextricably bound up with the process of production, publicity and packaging which must inevitably lead to the of the subculture's subversive power—both mod and punk innovations fed back directly into high fashion and mainstream fashion. Each new subculture establishes new trends, generates new looks and sounds which feed back into the appropriate industries.[4]

However, with its roots in the mid-1980s and eventual peak in the mid-1990s, grunge fashion followed a different trajectory. While on the surface it seemed yet another manifestation of the postmodern from-subculture-to-mass-culture phenomenon, in reality, the scene's participants were far savvier than their predecessors of oppositional dress's past. Unlike the deliberately cultivated anti-fashion of their subcultural forerunners, who sought to disrupt fashionable standards as a symbol of ideological resistance, members of Pearl Jam—along with their fellow grunge scene mates—simply did not participate in the dynamic of fashion altogether. "I wore shorts year round," Pearl Jam's bassist Jeff Ament noted years later:

> I rode bikes everywhere, didn't have a car, and if I was going to practice I had to carry my bass on my bicycle, so I couldn't wear jeans. I'm not sure what defined what grunge was or wasn't. I never ever wore a flannel shirt. I had a few hats, for sure. That started off when I was in Green River and had a girlfriend who made hats. At the time, I don't think I looked like a rocker, I looked like a dumbass. I was partly function and partly what was laying around.[5]

---

[4] Dick Hebdige, *Subculture: The Meaning of Style* (New York: Routledge, 1979), 95.
[5] Mark Yarm (ed.), *Everybody Loves Our Town: An Oral History of Grunge* (New York: Three Rivers Press, 2012), 349.

This chapter will demonstrate that Pearl Jam—in consciously opting out of participation in oppositional dress, or "spectacular styles," as analogously termed by Hebdige—outsmarted the subculture-to-consumer-culture machine, and in so doing, readapted its subcultural lineage for a postmodern climate. It will look at the concepts of bricolage and pastiche—the former applied by Hebdige to the process of subcultural style formation and the latter set forth by philosopher Fredric Jameson as a framework for postmodern stylistic innovation—and reveal that Pearl Jam's sartorial development did not conform to either of these processes. It will also explore the ways in which Pearl Jam confronted within its creative output its own exploitation at the hands of consumer culture, thereby demonstrating a keen understanding of a Jameson-identified postmodern creative climate that was inextricably tied to capitalism. While the band—and grunge at large—are oft-criticized for not espousing an overt ideological grievance, such as their punk predecessors' challenging of British social class structure, in actuality Pearl Jam demonstrated a resistance to the system of artistic commodification itself, and in so doing, helped to solidify grunge's subcultural output into a category all its own.

While the notion of alternative, oppositional, or "anti-" fashion is typically associated with the subversive and the avant-garde, the possibility of dressing against the fashionable standard has existed since the dawn of fashion itself. In his seminal 1904 essay, "Fashion," George Simmel addresses the duality of differentiation and imitation as a driving process within the system of fashion:

> Just as soon as the lower classes begin to copy their style, thereby crossing the line of demarcation the upper classes have drawn and destroying the uniformity of their coherence, the upper classes turn away from this style and adopt a new one, which in its turn, differentiates them from the masses; and thus the game goes merrily on.... The same process is at work as between the different sets within the upper classes.... Indeed, we may often observe that the more nearly one set has approached another, the more frantic becomes the desire for imitation from below and the seeking for the new from above.[6]

Though Simmel's conceptualization is primarily focused on fashion as an expression of social class, his cyclical model of differentiation and imitation nonetheless applies to all forms of fashionable expression. In his account of fashion's role as a communicator of subcultural resistance, Dick Hebdige echoes Simmel's paradigm:

---

[6] Georg Simmel, "Fashion," *The American Journal of Sociology* 62, no. 6 (1957, reprint): 544.

Thus, as soon as the original innovations which signify "subculture" are translated into commodities and made generally available, they become "frozen". Once removed from their private contexts by the small entrepreneurs and big fashion interests who produce them on a mass scale, they become codified, made comprehensible, rendered at once public property and profitable merchandise. In this way, the two forms of incorporation (the semantic/ideological and the "real"/commercial) can be said to converge on the commodity form. Youth cultural styles may begin by issuing symbolic challenges, but they must inevitably end by establishing new sets of conventions; by creating new commodities, new industries or rejuvenating old ones (think of the boost punk must have given haberdashery!). This occurs irrespective of the subculture's political orientation: the macrobiotic restaurants, craft shops and "antique markets" of the hippie era were easily converted into punk boutiques and record shops. It also happens irrespective of the startling content of the style: punk clothing and insignia could be bought mail-order by the summer of 1977, and in September of that year Cosmopolitan ran a review of Zandra Rhodes' latest collection of couture follies which consisted entirely of variations on the punk theme. Models smouldered beneath mountains of safety pins and plastic (the pins were jewelled, the "plastic" wet-look satin) and the accompanying article ended with an aphorism—"To shock is chic"—which presaged the subculture's imminent demise.[7]

From hippies to punks, Hebdige paints the portrait of a subcultural landscape comprising continuous deaths and births of youth movements at the hands of—and in response to—corporate exploitation of their creative and fashionable innovations. While Hebdige's context of 1970s youth rebellion is worlds away from Simmel's class relations of the belle époque, the two nonetheless portray oppositional dress as an intentional pursuit whose purpose is to express a message about the wearer's relationship to others. In the case of Pearl Jam and grunge, however, the semiotic potential of fashion was rarely a consideration (with the exception of a few overtly political examples), and instead it manifested primarily as a function of utility and availability.

The cannon of fashion history maintains a specific picture of grunge fashion, one that boasts a disheveled layering of such staples as plaid flannel shirts, long johns, ripped jeans, nubby cardigans, and Dr. Martens boots, and which often comes qualified with idiosyncratic descriptors like "slacker style." While this

---

[7] Hebdige, *Subculture*, 96.

depiction derives somewhat from the personal styles of certain participants of the Seattle-area scene, perhaps most famously Nirvana lead singer Kurt Cobain, it emerged predominantly as a projection of mainstream media and corporate fashion companies. *Vogue* magazine's 1992 "Grunge and Glory" editorial and designer Marc Jacobs's spring/summer 1993 collection for the fashion brand Perry Ellis are perhaps two of the more infamous examples of grunge fashion hyperbole at the hands of consumer culture. The former, styled by the eminent editor Grace Coddington, featured models in layers of plaids, florals, and knitwear, flannel shirts either wrapped around waists or left open to reveal a band t-shirt, Doc Martens and combat boots in tow, while the latter was similarly replete with layers of plaid shirts, printed dresses, graphic tees, and slouchy knitwear, all seemingly plucked from a thrift shop. Indeed, both representations comprised ironically costly imitations of the subculture's thrifted staples, a phenomenon notoriously underscored by Jacobs's admission to having sent a plaid flannel shirt purchased cheaply on New York City's St. Mark's Place to a factory in Italy to be recreated in expensive silk.

This commercial apex of grunge fashion, however, was a far cry from what the scene actually looked like. In fact, when the musical genre was in its nascent phases in the mid-1980s, fashion influences—like the scene's musical influences—were multifarious. The sonic inspirations of punk rock, heavy metal, and even glam rock saw young people dressing in a range of styles, from studded leather jackets and combat boots, to teased hair and ripped t-shirts, to button-up shirts and tennis shoes (see Figures 8.1–8.3).

As the scene developed and codified towards the late 1980s, remnants of these disparate aesthetics coalesced and were supplemented with functional garments ubiquitously worn by the area's outdoor enthusiasts and logging industry workers alike. Bob Whitaker, manager of Seattle grunge band Mudhoney, has since observed:

> Someone, I think it was [photographer] Charles Peterson, jokingly attributed grunge clothing to my dad, because he was the first full-time employee and later the CEO of REI, Recreational Equipment Inc. At the old shows at Metropolis, you'd see guys in ski jackets. Everyone was wearing their parent's beat-up mountaineering clothing, their crappy down parkas, and flannel and stuff like that.[8]

---

[8] Yarm, *Everybody Loves Our Town*, 349.

Figure 8.1 Boys on the Ave. Seattle, 1983. Courtesy Michael Lavine.

Figure 8.2 Mötley Crew. Seattle, 1983. Courtesy Michael Lavine.

Figure 8.3 Young Pioneers. Olympia, 1984. Courtesy Michael Lavine.

"People were wearing flannel here long before grunge came out," echoed Tad Doyle, front man of the seminal grunge band, *Tad*: "It's cold here. It's a cheap and effective clothing apparatus for living in the Northwest. I don't even associate it with a fashion statement or lack thereof."[9]

Indeed, in 1993, Pearl Jam bassist Jeff Ament encapsulated the dual need for economy and utility in his fashion choices, as well as in those of his colleagues:

> Ever since I've lived here, I've known people who went to thrift shops because they *had* to.... They couldn't afford to buy clothes at Kmart. Even the whole long-johns thing—it was because most people don't have cars. My transportation is a mountain bike, and it has been for seven years. So you couldn't wear jeans or anything restricting. You'd go to a thrift store and buy a pair of baggy old shorts, go to the women's department at Kmart, buy some tights and cut out the feet so you'd have an extra six inches. It was cheap, and it was functional. In the summer, you just took off the tights and wore your shorts. It was year-round wear. Same with the whole flannel thing. And at this point, a lot of people, myself included, won't even wear flannel because it's this total hip thing.[10]

---

[9] Ibid., 350.
[10] "Grunging Acceptance," *Harper's Bazaar*, January 1993, 117.

Interestingly, when Ament and Pearl Jam guitarist Stone Gossard performed together in two earlier Seattle bands, grunge forerunner Green River (1984–87) and alternative metal darling Mother Love Bone (1988–90), the musicians' fashion choices were often markedly flamboyant, demonstrating an intentional approach to their sartorial presentation as integral to performance (see Figures 8.4–8.5).

However, when they formed Pearl Jam out of the ashes of Mother Love Bone due to the untimely death of lead singer Andy Wood in 1990, the new music's more stripped-down aesthetic encouraged a disengagement with calculated performance wear. While Gossard tended towards basic, "normcore" looks comprising jeans, slacks or shorts, t-shirts, knitted tops, or button-up shirts with an occasional vest, Ament, though echoing his bandmate's unadorned approach, injected a sportier flare, often cutting off the sleeves of his t-shirts, layering baggy shorts over spandex shorts, at times wearing sports jerseys (he was an avid

Figure 8.4 Jeff Ament (center) and Stone Gossard (right) with Green River, ca. 1985. Photographer unknown (https://land-of-the-ice-and-snow.tumblr.com/post/144910737926/mother-love-bone).

Figure 8.5 Jeff Ament (right) and Stone Gossard (second from right) with Mother Love Bone, ca. 1989. Photographer unknown (https://www.kerrang.com/features/the-life-and-legacy-of-andrew-wood-the-lost-hero-of-grunge).

basketball player), and topping it all off with his signature flamboyant headwear, relics from a hat-designing girlfriend (see Figures 8.6–8.7).

Both musicians tended towards high-top sneakers with exposed, bunched up socks, with Gossard also opting for boots. Their sartorial choices were comfortable, utilitarian, affordable, and neither accorded with the reigning trends of the day nor stood in opposition to them. Their shift from calculated performance wear to quotidian casual clothing not only demonstrated the aesthetic diversity of the grunge scene, which boasted no prevailing subcultural style, but it also revealed an eventual detachment from the semiotic implications of fashion altogether.

When San Diego native Eddie Vedder joined the group as lead singer, he brought with him an analogous sartorial approach informed by comfort, affordability, and the sporty functionality of his California surfer lifestyle. Vedder favored t-shirts, often blank versions upon which he could scrawl political messages, such as the version he wore during a performance on *Saturday Night Live* in 1992, which boasted a coat hanger on the front (an abortion prochoice symbol), along with the phrase "No Bush 1992" on the back, referencing the impending American presidential election between George H. Bush and Bill Clinton (see Figure 8.8).

Figure 8.6 Pearl Jam, 1992; from left to right: Dave Abbruzzese, Eddie Vedder, Mike McCready, Jeff Ament, Stone Gossard. Courtesy Michael Lavine.

Figure 8.7 Pearl Jam performs on *Saturday Night Live*, April 11, 1992; from left to right: Mike McCready, Jeff Ament, Eddie Vedder, Dave Abbruzzese, Stone Gossard (still from https://www.facebook.com/PearlJam/videos/alive-saturday-night-live-1992/266999990903111/).

Figure 8.8 Eddie Vedder performs in Pearl Jam on *Saturday Night Live*, April 11, 1992 (still from https://vimeo.com/125108141).

Vedder typically layered his t-shirts under jackets, pairing them with jeans, corduroy trousers, or knee-length shorts over spandex shorts, with high-top sneakers or boots over exposed socks (see Figure 8.6). Like Ament, Vedder was an avid basketball player, and would on occasion wear a basketball jersey with shorts and boots (see Figure 8.9).

In fact, Vedder was a sports fan in general and regularly donned a backwards baseball cap over his long wild locks, an accessory favored by other band members as well (see Figure 8.10).

At 1992's Drop In the Park, a free concert held in Seattle's Magnuson Park, Vedder wore a helmet emblazoned with Chicago White Sox baseball player Jack McDowell's number twenty-nine (see Figure 8.11), about which he opined:

> Number twenty-nine is a friend of mine named Jack McDowell. This is my tribute to him here. He was the first pitcher to win twenty games and he gave me one of his caps that I wore all through the European tour and the American tour. It was kind of a good luck thing. I always had a good show with it. And he seemed to be playing well as long as we were playing well.[11]

Figure 8.9 Eddied Vedder (right) and Mike McCready (left) on *MTV*'s "Headbanger's Ball," September 28, 1991 (still from https://www.youtube.com/watch?v=FlD5ZDxDY7c).

---

[11] *MTV News* (TV Program), MTV, September 20, 1992.

Figure 8.10 Pearl Jam, 1992; from left to right: Stone Gossard, Jeff Ament, Eddie Vedder, Dave Abbruzzese, and Mike McCready. Courtesy Michael Lavine.

While sports fandom and the wearing of its associated attire was typical of numerous American males during the 1990s, it was considered anathema to many of the Seattle underground's purists, who viewed sport and its ensuing commercial trappings as reflective of a machismo sensibility that did not accord with their feminist-leanings ("I definitely have a problem with the average macho man," Kurt Cobain famously proclaimed).[12] Pearl Jam's flouting of these interests and clothing staples in spite of a blatant feminist stance conveyed in

---

[12] Michael Azerrad, "Nirvana: Inside the Heart and Mind of Kurt Cobain," *Rolling Stone*, April 16, 1992.

Figure 8.11 Eddie Vedder at "Drop In the Park" festival, Seattle, September 20, 1992 (still from https://www.youtube.com/watch?v=lRq6NKyYSJg).

both their lyrical content and personal politics demonstrated just how little credence they gave to sartorial signifiers. They simply wore what worked from a functional and budgetary perspective and did not overthink the meaning of their fashion choices within the context of their creative output or ideology.

Indeed, guitarist Mike McCready and 1992–4 drummer Dave Abbruzzese followed suit, both tending towards functional, relaxed garb, such as t-shirts, shorts, and loose-fitting pants, though McCready occasionally injected a statement jacket, hat, or head adornment into his look (see Figure 8.12).

While many of the band members did wear button-up shirts, it is notable that plaid flannel versions were not a mainstay (see Figures 8.5 and 8.12); certainly the utilitarian basic was worn on occasion, but contrary to its representation within consumer culture, it did not carry any form of semiotic significance that expressed the Seattle scene's philosophical leanings or subcultural resistance

Figure 8.12 Pearl Jam at the *MTV Video Music Awards*, September 2, 1993. From left to right: Stone Gossard, Jeff Ament, Mike McCready, Eddie Vedder, Dave Abbruzzese (photo by Ron Galella, Ltd./Ron Galella Collection via Getty Images).

against the mainstream. "What we were wearing was never an issue," affirmed Soundgarden guitarist Kim Thayil:

> [a]nd the fact that it's an issue to someone else is strange. It's nice to know that a handful of rock bands can make a bunch of money for people who don't even buy records. There's something creepy about taking the whole Salvation Army sort of aesthetic and marketing it with a designer name.[13]

In this regard, Pearl Jam and grunge stood in stark contrast to youth cultures of the past, perhaps most notably, punk. "My style was deliberately calculated," professed punk pioneer Richard Hell of seminal New York punk bands Television and Richard Hell and the Voidoids:

> I wore pegged black jeans. Before I did that, no one on the street wore anything but blue denim jeans. Black ones were hard to find. I was able to find only one store in the entire city that carried them.... None of the clothing cost very much which was part of the point. It was an alternative to the international stadium

[13] "Grunging Acceptance," 117.

jet-set superstar queens who'd stolen rock and roll and spoiled it. Part of what excited me about rock and roll was all the languages of it, clothes and hair most definitely included. You could subvert certain of its signifying potential while indulging others.... There are some misconceptions about the origins of the hairstyle and torn clothes that have gotten a lot of play in punk journalism.... The other is the weird false anecdote that all my clothes were torn because an angry girlfriend had done that to my wardrobe and I couldn't afford new clothes. That didn't happen. It's the kind of thing punk interviewees like to say to sound "insider savvy." It's obvious from all the publicity pictures I oversaw from 1974 on that I was deliberately proposing torn togs.[14]

Hell, who is often credited for punk's signature torn t-shirt style (before the look was replicated and popularized by London fashion designers Vivienne Westwood and Malcolm McLaren), boasts no pretenses about the calculated nature of his fashion choices, along with the lengths to which he went in order to realize them. Additionally, there was an intention of subversion within his strategy, one that relied upon the embedded symbolism of certain articles of clothing, from the quotidian to the aberrant. This sentiment was echoed by Vivienne Westwood who referred to the aesthetic of the punk clothing that she created out of her London boutique, *Seditionaries*, as "confrontational dressing."[15]

For Pearl Jam, there was nothing confrontational nor oppositional behind the band members' dressing, with their style instead emerging from a combination of indifference and convenience. Having grown up during an era considered widely to be the peak of Postmodernism, the band members were already tuned into the cycle that had contributed to the development of their subcultural predecessors, one that valued newness and shock value in an "it's all been done" climate. For Jameson, this exhausted creative wellspring meant that anything new was the direct result of referencing forms of the past, a process known as pastiche:

> There is another sense in which the writers and artists of the present day will no longer be able to invent new styles and worlds—they've already been invented; only a limited number of combinations are possible; the most unique ones have been thought of already. So the weight of the whole modernist aesthetic tradition—now dead—also "weighs like a nightmare on the brains of the living,"

---

[14] Richard Hell, *I Dreamed I Was A Very Clean Tramp: An Autobiography* (New York: Ecco Press, 2013), 116–19.
[15] Hebdige, *Subculture*, 107.

as Marx said in another context. Hence, once again, pastiche: in a world in which stylistic innovation is no longer possible, all that is left is to imitate dead styles, to speak through the masks and with the voices of the styles in the imaginary museum. But this means that contemporary or postmodernist art is going to be about art itself in a new kind of way; even more, it means that one of its essential messages will involve the necessary failure of art and the aesthetic, the failure of the new, the imprisonment in the past.[16]

Indeed, such thinking was the driving force behind early postmodern subcultures like the Teddy Boys of the 1950s, a group of working-class British youth who resisted their fated caste determination with an escapist vision of the future that manifested in the adoption of symbols of Britain's prosperous past, including fashions (notably suiting) of its thriving early twentieth-century Edwardian era. As expounded by historian Harry Hopkins:

> But most significant perhaps, was the Teddy outfit's function as the badge of a half-formed, inarticulate radicalism. ... A sort of half-conscious thumbing-of-the-nose, it was designed to establish that the lower orders could be as arrogant and as to-the-manor-born as the toffee-nosed ones across the River. ... The uniform's most important features lay, firstly, in the fact that ... it was, in origin, English class-based, secondly in its cost which ... might exceed £100. ... The Teddy costume conquered district after district in those years, making the fortunes of many a little corner tailor—and hairdresser—astute enough to "humour the kids".[17]

Like Richard Hell, the Teds' replication and subversion of sartorial symbols from the past, demonstrated a calculated strategy behind their style as a mode of communication and expression. Echoing Jameson's conceptualization of pastiche, Hebdige readapted the anthropological term, bricolage, as an additional process by which subcultural style is cultivated. Characterized by the combining of disparate elements in order to generate new meanings, bricolage, or "structured improvisations," was the chief mechanism, according to Hebdige, behind the development of punk style:

> Objects borrowed from the most sordid of contexts found a place in the punks' ensembles: lavatory chains were draped in graceful arcs across chests encased in

---

[16] Fredric Jameson, *The Cultural Turn: Selected Writings on the Postmodern. 1983–1998* (New York: Verso Books, 1984), 7.
[17] Harry Hopkins, *The New Look: A Social History of the Forties and Fifties* (London: Secker & Warburg, 1964), 427–8.

plastic bin-liners. Safety pins were taken out of their domestic "utility" context and worn as gruesome ornaments through the cheek, ear or lip. "Cheap" trashy fabrics (PVC, plastic, lurex, etc.) in vulgar designs (e.g. mock leopard skin) and "nasty" colors, long discarded by the quality end of the fashion industry as obsolete kitsch, were salvaged by the punks and turned into garments (fly boy drainpipes, "common" miniskirts) which offered self-conscious commentaries on the notions of modernity and taste. Conventional ideas of prettiness were jettisoned along with the traditional feminine lore of cosmetics. Contrary to the advice of every woman's magazine, make-up for both boys and girls was worn to be seen. Faces became abstract portraits: sharply observed and meticulously executed studies in alienation. Hair was obviously dyed (hay yellow, jet black, or bright orange with tufts of green or bleached in question marks), and T-shirts and trousers told the story of their own construction with multiple zips and outside seams clearly displayed. Similarly, fragments of school uniform (white brinylon shirts, school ties) were symbolically defiled (the shirts covered in graffiti, or fake blood; the ties left undone) and juxtaposed against leather drains or shocking pink mohair tops. The perverse and the abnormal were valued intrinsically. In particular, the illicit iconography of sexual fetishism was used to predictable effect. Rapist masks and rubber wear, leather bodices and fishnet stockings, implausibly pointed stiletto heeled shoes, the whole paraphernalia of bondage—the belts, straps and chains—were exhumed from the boudoir, closet and the pornographic film and placed on the street where they retained their forbidden connotations. Some young punks even donned the dirty raincoat— that most prosaic symbol of sexual "kinkiness"—and hence expressed their deviance in suitably proletarian terms.[18]

Unlike the Teddy boys or punk, Pearl Jam and grunge did not look to the past for sartorial inspiration, nor did they consciously attempt to create new meanings out of seemingly incongruent and eccentric components. "To me the thing about grunge is it's not anti-fashion it's *un*fashion," observed James Truman, former Editor-In-Chief of now-defunct men's magazine *Details* in 1992, "Punk was anti-fashion. It made a statement. Grunge is about not making a statement, which is why it's crazy for it to become a fashion statement."[19] Walter Thomas, then creative director of *J.Crew* took this notion one step further: "By the time you see a trend in [American chain retailer] Kmart, it can be three years after

---

[18] Hebdige, *Subculture*, 107–8.
[19] Marin, "Grunge: A Success Story."

that trend first hit the catwalk. The difference with Grunge is that it was *already* for sale at Kmart, not to mention the Salvation Army."[20]

It was indeed this apathy demonstrated by Pearl Jam towards the manufacture and performance of a fashionable subcultural image that emerged as the most resistant act of all. Unlike the new forms produced during the early twentieth-century's period of modernism that were at first viewed as radical before integrating into the canon, even the most radical cultural production during postmodernism, according to Jameson, was immediately accepted by way of conversion into a commodity:

> If then we suddenly return to the present day, we can measure the immensity of the cultural changes that have taken place. Not only are Joyce and Picasso no longer weird and repulsive, they have become classics and now look rather realistic to us. Meanwhile, there is very little in either the form or the content of contemporary art that contemporary society finds intolerable and scandalous. The most offensive forms of this art—punk rock, say, or what is called sexually explicit material—are all taken in stride by society, and they are commercially successful, unlike the productions of the older high modernism. But this means that even if contemporary art has all the same formal features as the older modernism, it has still shifted its position fundamentally within our culture. For one thing, commodity production and in particular our clothing, furniture, buildings and other artifacts are now intimately tied in with styling changes which derive from artistic experimentation; our advertising, for example, is fed by postmodernism in all the arts and inconceivable without it.[21]

Pearl Jam's opting out of the system that converted subcultural innovation into mass market commodities, in a sense, upended the balance between the innovative and the mainstream. If radical new forms were the commercial norm in the 1990s, then Pearl Jam's utilitarian fashion mainstays were, in effect, subversive and the epitome of subcultural resistance.

The band, moreover, explicitly emphasized this philosophy through direct confrontation of the commercial systems at play. In 1994, Pearl Jam released their third album, *Vitalogy*, which, according to biographer Kim Neely, conveyed "the sound of a band determinedly climbing out of its grunge pigeonhole and exploring its creative future."[22] While the album featured a host of tracks that

---

[20] Charles Cross, *Here We Are Now: The Lasting Impact of Kurt Cobain* (New York: Harper Collins, 2014), 80.
[21] Jameson, *The Cultural Turn*, 18–19.
[22] Kim Neely, *Five Against One: The Pearl Jam Story* (New York: Penguin Books, 1998), 302.

addressed the dangers of fame, as well as the strain of artistic expression under the pressure of corporate profit generation, one song in particular alluded directly to the creative vehicle of fashion. "Corduroy," according to Vedder, was so named for a jacket that the singer wore frequently during the band's ascension:

> Yeah, that song was based on a remake of the brown corduroy jacket that I wore. I think I got mine for 12 bucks, and it was being sold for like $650. [Laughs.] The ultimate one as far as being co-opted was that there was a guy on TV, predictably patterned, I guess, after the way I was looking those days, with long hair and an Army T-shirt. They put this new character on a soap opera, so there was a guy, more handsome than I, parading around on *General Hospital*. And the funny thing is, that guy was Ricky Martin. [Laughs].[23]

Indeed, Vedder wore this jacket recurrently throughout 1992 during regular tour gigs, as well as during more high-profile performances including *MTV*'s *Video Music Awards* and *Unplugged* broadcasts (see Figures 8.13–8.15).

Its namesake song's lyrical content addressed the band's refusal to sell out as a grunge posterchild in the name of corporate greed, and the jacket served as both a literal and metaphorical symbol of this resistance: "I don't want to take what you can give ... / I would rather starve than eat your bread ... / ... / I don't want to hear from those who know ... / They can buy, but can't put on my clothes."[24]

The tale of the jacket was so ubiquitous that it emerged as a hyperbolized theme for the band as its members reasserted their philosophy during the mid-1990s. A 1993 *Rolling Stone* profile written by director and friend Cameron Crowe averred:

> Still, Pearl Jam offer fans a challenge: Bootleg us if you can, take our album, pass the music around, don't glorify us. Vedder long ago traded away the brown thrift-store jacket given him by Gossard, the one remade and marketed by the fashion industry as a $1,000 piece of grunge wear.[25]

By 1994, Pearl Jam's strategy of confronting the corporate marketing machine was at its most intense, epitomized by the band's infamous contesting of ticketing giant Ticketmaster's pricing system. It was during this period when Vedder was shot by Pearl Jam photographer Lance Mercer wearing an evocative "I Heart Grunge" t-shirt while bearing a piece of electrical tape over his mouth, an at once clever and powerful commentary on the corporate marketing of grunge with Vedder as its mouthpiece (see Figure 8.16).

---

[23] Josh Modell, "Interview with Eddie Vedder of Pearl Jam," *The Onion AV Club*, June 11, 2002.
[24] Pearl Jam, "Corduroy," in *Vitalogy* (1994).
[25] Cameron Crowe, "Pearl Jam: Five Against the World," *Rolling Stone*, October 28, 1993.

Figure 8.13 Eddie Vedder performs at Lollapalooza festival, Montage Mountain, Pennsylvania, August 15, 1992 (courtesy Getty Images, photo by Ebet Roberts/Redferns).

Figure 8.14 Eddie Vedder performs at *MTV Video Music Awards*, September 9, 1992 (still from https://www.youtube.com/watch?v=AKqvfGFuKSo).

Figure 8.15 Eddie Vedder performs on *MTV*'s *Unplugged*, March 16, 1992 (still from https://vimeo.com/107992868).

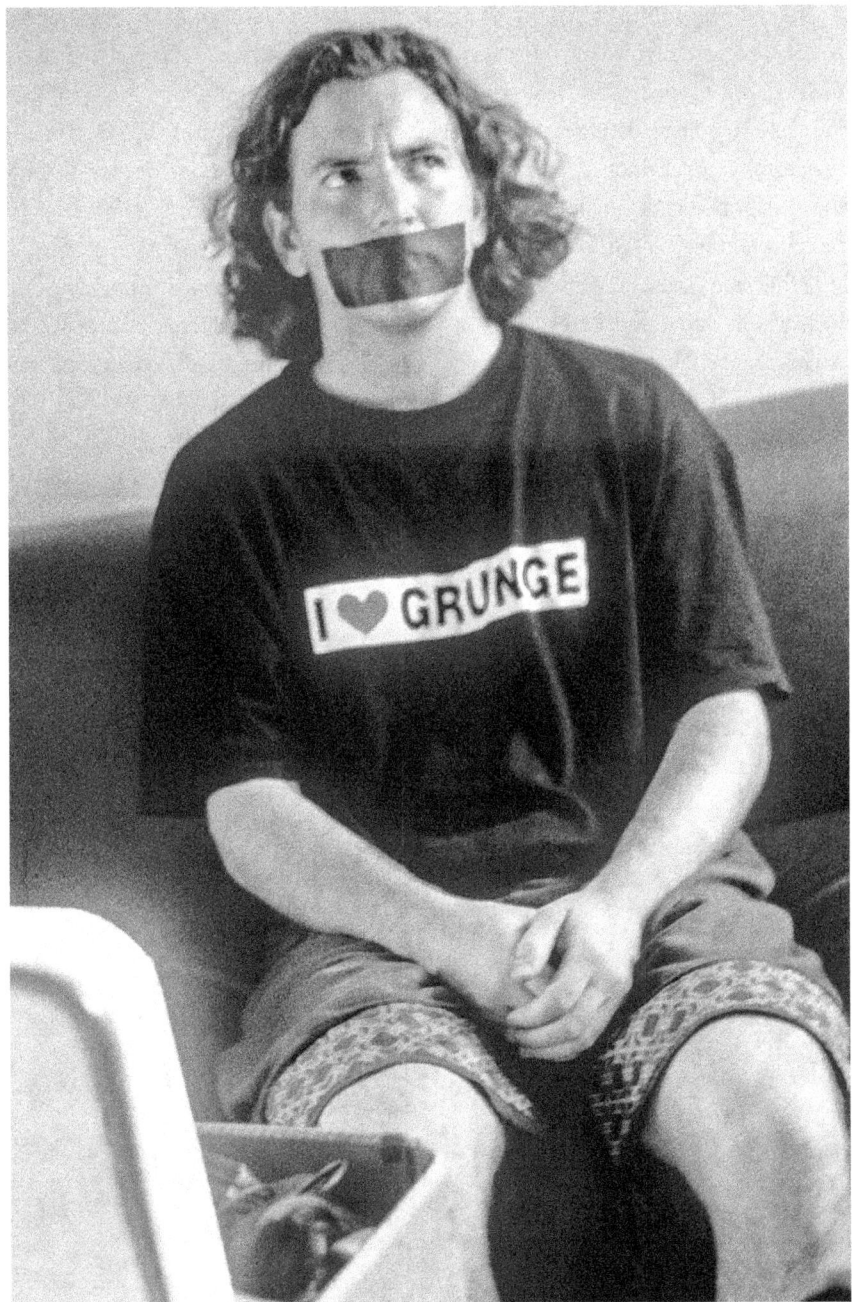

Figure 8.16 Eddie Vedder, Brixton, UK, 1993 (courtesy Lance Mercer).

Indeed, the moniker "grunge," whose origins are still contested today, was never something with which the scene members wanted to be associated; unlike their 1970s predecessors who proudly identified as punks, members of this movement did not distinguish themselves as "grungers." Instead, they understood the term as a product of marketing. "It's so profitable," Vedder opined, "[a]nd they'll just keep taking and taking and taking, and they just don't know how to restrain themselves. You know, they're frothing at the mouth over this."[26]

While the image of Vedder in the "I Heart Grunge" t-shirt did not circulate widely in its day, its recent resurrection as a limited-edition t-shirt print sold by Los Angeles and Seattle-based streetwear brands, *Pleasures* and *Alive & Well*, speaks to an enduring fascination with Pearl Jam, grunge and fashion (see Figure 8.17).

Though grunge as both a scene and a marketing concept disappeared almost as quickly as it ascended (with fashion periodicals like *Vogue* citing it as one of the decade's "worst looks" by 1996), the significance of its subcultural approach

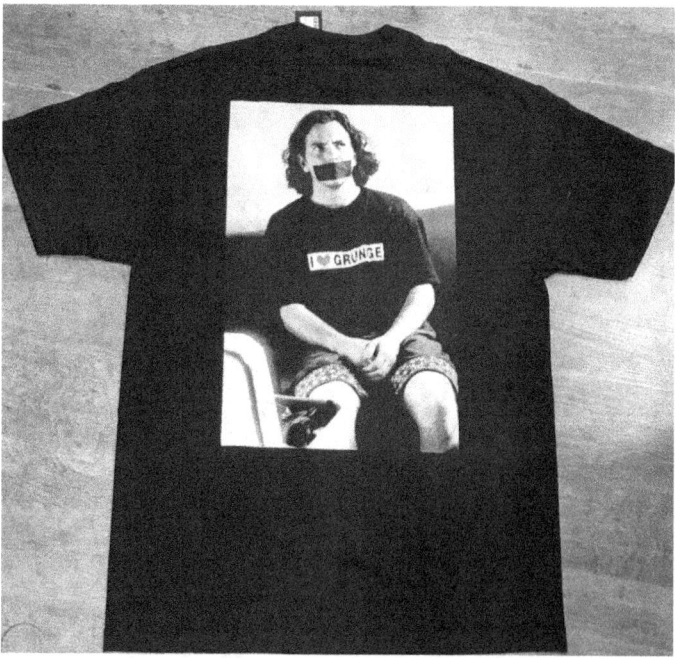

Figure 8.17 Alive and Well X Pleasures X Lance Mercer t-shirt, 2017 (https://www.worthpoint.com/worthopedia/eddie-vedder-love-grunge-shirt-lance-1890959516).

[26] *Hype!* (Film), Dir. Doug Pray, Cinepix Film Properties (1996).

to fashion remains profound.[27] On the surface it might seem that Pearl Jam and their musical counterparts fell victim to a decades-old subcultural plight: corporate exploitation and commodification. But in actuality, they outsmarted the system from the beginning, never maintaining an ideological allegiance to their fashion choices, and instead using the mainstream's appropriation of these choices as fodder for their own resistance of a capitalist machine. While their subcultural predecessors saw their fashion innovations fall prey to the postmodern capitalist machine, and while future generations of Internet Age subcultures have patently sought to be part of the machine, Pearl Jam sits in a category all of its own and has contributed to grunge's inimitable position along the trajectory of subcultural style.

Bibliography

Azerrad, Michael. "Nirvana: Inside the Heart and Mind of Kurt Cobain." *Rolling Stone*, April 16, 1992. Available online: https://www.rollingstone.com/feature/nirvana-inside-the-heart-and-mind-of-kurt-cobain-103770 (accessed July 15, 2020).

Betts, Katherine. "Fashion: The Best and Worst Looks of the '90s." *Vogue*, January 1996, 118–31.

Cross, Charles. *Here We Are Now: The Lasting Impact of Kurt Cobain*. New York: Harper Collins, 2014.

Crowe, Cameron. "Pearl Jam: Five Against the World." *Rolling Stone*, October 28, 1993. Available online: https://www.rollingstone.com/music/music-news/pearl-jam-five-against-the-world-244637 (accessed July 15, 2020).

Harper's Bazaar. "Grunging Acceptance." January 1993, 116–17, 142.

Hebdige, Dick. *Subculture: The Meaning of Style*. New York: Routledge, 1979.

Hell, Richard. *I Dreamed I Was A Very Clean Tramp: An Autobiography*, New York: Ecco Press, 2013.

Hopkins, Harry. *The New Look: A Social History of the Forties and Fifties*. London: Secker & Warburg, 1964.

Hype! [Film]. Dir. Doug Pray. USA: Cinepix Film Properties, 1996.

Jameson, Fredric. *The Cultural Turn: Selected Writings on the Postmodern. 1983–1998*. New York: Verso, 1984.

Marin, Rick. "Grunge: A Success Story." *The New York Times*, November 15, 1992. Available online: https://www.nytimes.com/1992/11/15/style/grunge-a-success-story.html (accessed July 15, 2020).

---

[27] Katherine Betts, "Fashion: The Best and Worst Looks of the '90s," *Vogue*, January 1996, 118.

Modell, Josh. "Interview with Eddie Vedder of Pearl Jam." *The Onion AV Club*, June 11, 2002. Available online: http://www.avclub.com/article/eddie-vedder-of-pearl-jam-13789 (accessed July 15, 2020).

MTV News [TV Program]. MTV, September 20, 1992.

Neely, Kim. *Five Against One: The Pearl Jam Story*. New York: Penguin Books, 1998.

Simmel, Georg. "Fashion." *The American Journal of Sociology* 62, no. 6 (1957, reprint): 541–58.

Wilson, Elizabeth. *Adorned in Dreams: Fashion and Modernity*. London: Virago Press, Ltd., 1985.

Yarm, Mark, edited by. *Everybody Loves Our Town: An Oral History of Grunge*, New York: Three Rivers Press, 2012.

Pearl Jam's Ghosts: The Ethical Claim Made From the Exiled Space(s) of Homelessness and War—An Aesthetic *Response-Ability*

Jacqueline Moulton

Exordium

On two evenings in August 2018, Pearl Jam comes home—is home—using voice, sound, and rhythm to craft the contours of a city, becoming for these evenings a city itself; putting into tonation the cadence of a city's consciousness to create out of a place and space community, intention, song, and story. On these summer nights, Pearl Jam performs *The Home Shows* in Seattle, Washington, it having been five years since they graced a Seattle stage. Dubbed *The Home Shows*, these two performances were crafted and enacted in order to philanthropically raise funds, awareness, and knowledge of the homelessness crisis within the band's home city. A few ballads in, frontman Eddie Vedder speaks into the stadium's open air and initiates the stage, the crowd, and the band with these words: "We're Pearl Jam and we're from Seattle, Washington. So I guess that must mean we're home."[1] The numerical iterations of *The Home Shows* are indeed prodigious: 180,060 people attend, tickets sell out in minutes, 10,839,000 dollars are raised.[2] The resulting data from *The Home Shows* tell one story, but harder to quantify is the deeper question these shows evoke—the ethical question of contemporary dwelling, the question of who is at home and who is not, of who is living exiled. On the eleventh track of the three and a half hour set, Vedder begins by telling a story of a friend, a man who experienced homelessness on Seattle's city streets until the day of his death.

---

[1] Michael Rietmulder, "Review: Pearl Jam, Seattle Fall in Love All over Again at Joyous Home Shows on Night One at Safeco Field," *Seattle Times*, August 8, 2018.
[2] Daniel DeMay, "Pearl Jam Puts Spotlight on Seattle Homelessness with Historic Home Shows," *Seattle Post-Intelligencer*, August 8, 2018.

To evoke the ethical question itself is to conjure forth conceptions, iterations, and practices of home. The word *ethos*, in its original Greek, signifies both dwelling and a way of being, meaning character, habit, and home. The historicity of the word *ethos*/ethics reveals its concern with the individual alongside its complex and interdependent environment. *Ethos*, meaning both home and character, aligns the ideals and practices of being at-home and of identity alongside the positionality of the ethical within an interconnected world. The eleventh track performed at *The Home Shows* was "Even Flow," from Pearl Jam's inaugural album *Ten*, a narrative ballad describing the life of a man living unhoused, who "[f]reezin', rests his head on a pillow made of / concrete, again."[3] "Oh, ceilings" the next verse sings, rendering forth the *ethos* of dwelling; "few and far between all the legal / halls of shame, yeah"[4] the lyric line continues, revealing the integration of the judicial and of the legislative within ethical conceptions and the material praxis of physical dwelling places. Who is at-home in our communities and who has been exiled? To investigate the ethical claim made from the space of exile is to step into the realm of dwelling, its inhabitants, and its environments.

A contemporary question of urgency

Ideologies and discourses of home are often the singular narrative of the center versus its margins, the ideology of inside versus outside The philosopher and feminist scholar Donna J. Haraway disrupts this singular narrative when she writes that "who is at home must be permanently in question."[5] Housing/home/dwelling/(*ethos*)—how we humans take up (inter)relational and ecological space within and upon our world is the space and discourse of the ethical and this question of dwelling is, I believe, the contemporary question and urgency to which our sensibility must be attuned in order to imagine and craft equitable pathways forward. Our conceptual and material implications of home (*ethos*) reveal a contrasting disparity with that of the exile. The space of the exile and the exiled being ask the very question and claim of ethics upon the contrived at-home-ness of the "center." If this is the contemporary question then what is

---

[3] Pearl Jam, "Even Flow," in *Ten* (1991).
[4] Ibid.
[5] Donna J. Haraway, *Manifestly Haraway* (Minneapolis: University of Minnesota Press, 2016), 141.

the contemporary answer? This chapter works toward, not an answer or the answer, but rather imagines the answer to be response, a multiplicity of response(s)—the work, pathway, and experience of the aesthetic. The ethical claim and question precedes not only an ethical response but also an aesthetic one, allowing for the ethical to be transfigured within the aesthetic in order for ethics to be enlivened and resonated toward the troubles facing contemporary time and space upon a troubled earth. This project follows the aesthetic sensibilities, concern, and historicity of Pearl Jam around the proliferating crises of homelessness and war—both of which explore and disrupt the discourses and binaries between home and exile. Pearl Jam's discography and aesthetic practices elucidate the necessity of an aesthetic response to the ethical claim and question of the exile(d) spaces and beings.

The uncanny—Home and war

Home—the embodiment of the relationship between place and identity. Home is composed of matter and psychological experience, of both material space and conceptual orientation of the self, of the other, and of the human in relation. At the date of *The Home Shows*, Seattle's homeless population was more than 12,000 people living outside on city streets.[6] It is a population outcast and exiled, living within the construction and elaboration of the city itself, sleeping on benches, sidewalks, and in doorways. This community intimately knows the city, walks its corridors, makes a home out of the same open-air that fills the stadium as Pearl Jam strikes its first chord and begins their set. The conception of home is haunted by its pervasive other, the uncanny—the sense of being not at-home. For Sigmund Freud, the uncanny was an exploration into the study of the aesthetic, "the theory of the qualities of feeling."[7] These experiences of the uncanny are the feelings of which "undoubtedly belongs to all that is terrible—to all that arouses dread and creeping horror."[8] Yet, for Freud, the uncanny is more than what arouses fear, it is what works in tandem to that which we have known and

---

[6] Kate Walters, "Seattle Homeless Population Is Third Largest in U.S., after LA and NYC," *Kuow.org*, December 18, 2018.
[7] Sigmund Freud, "The 'Uncanny,'" in *The Standard Edition of the Complete Psychological Works of Sigmund Freud. Vol. 17 (1917-1919): An Infantile Neurosis and Other Works*, ed. James Strachey (London: Hogarth Press, 1955), 219.
[8] Ibid.

experienced, something at once both foreign and familiar. The word uncanny is the English translation from the German *unheimlich*, a contrast to the German word of *heimlich*, which means belonging to the home, comfortable, familiar, not strange, having roots.[9] Through Freud's conception of the uncanny, our ideas of home (*ethos*) and its haunting otherness are brought into the realm of the aesthetic, bringing together in deconstruction/construction the threads of dwelling, ethics, and aesthetics. For Jacques Rancière, the aesthetic is the "distribution of the sensible" of the artistic product and of the artistic production. Rancière extends aesthetics outside theory and writes that it "refers to the specific mode of being of whatever falls within the domain of art, to the mode of being of the objects of art."[10] The aesthetic, as the sensible (being of the senses) experience, is the space in which both individual and communal life may be imagined and reimagined. To ask questions of how we dwell within the world is to engage both the ethical and the aesthetic in dynamic epistemological conversation.

As home is haunted by its other (the uncanny), so too can peacetime and wartime be imagined within the configurations of *heimlich/unheimlich*. As the comfort of home is haunted by a resonating terror of exile and of homelessness, so too are the dwellings of peace haunted by the impacts and perpetuations of war. The friend of whom Vedder speaks before launching into "Even Flow" on stage at *The Home Shows* was a man named Eddie, a veteran living unhoused on Seattle's city streets. The haunting of war resides within contemporary dwelling, peace, and our ideas and conceptions of home—of ethics. These hauntings of exile, of homelessness, and of war, come to find themselves put into rhythm and song within the realm of the aesthetic, put to music and ushered out on stage by Pearl Jam, allowing for sensibility to be distributed and the materiality of aesthetics to become important components of communal and individual life. The First Gulf War elicits from Pearl Jam the song "Yellow Ledbetter,"[11] an outtake from Pearl Jam's first album, *Ten*. Vedder explains that this song is an "anti-patriotic song," a song written from the experience of a friend who lost his

---

[9] See ibid., 220.
[10] Jacques Rancière, *Dissensus: On Politics and Aesthetics* (London: Bloomsbury Academic, 2010), 22.
[11] Songs like "Yellow Ledbetter" are not the exception for Pearl Jam but are rather, throughout the historical course of their entire discography, even up until 2020, a pervasive thread. Themes of anti-war ballads and of political participation make strong appearances in Pearl Jam records from the album *Ten* in 1991 up until the 2020 release of *Gigaton*, where America's forty-fifth president is mentioned by name, as are the ways in which Donald Trump and his administration have wreaked environmental disaster across the globe.

brother in the Gulf War.[12] Yellow Ledbetter narrates a story of a letter that arrives announcing a familial death, telling of a brother never coming home, about a body that may come back in either a box or a bag. Later, in 2002, the song "Bu$hleaguer," the twelfth track off of *Riot Act*, takes aim at then-President George W. Bush and his wartime policies.[13] "Uncanny and immutable"[14] lyrically describes the American president and how Bush presented as confident and refined wherein, in contrast, something more horrifying lurked beneath; the *unheimlich* here comes to bear upon the surface and war, in such instances, becomes the "ethical" choice, shattering illusions of peace. The line "[b]lackout waves its way through the cities" is repeated throughout "Bu$hleaguer,"[15] and the resonance of terror felt within the self, which Freud defines as the uncanny, is the liminal space between aesthetics and ethics, between home and exile, between war and peace. The terror of waves of blackout is a fear which comes up from within, a fear which is familiar and therefore impactful, fear which is close. The uncanny is a haunting from within, a haunting from within dwelling, ethics, and aesthetics—prompting us to ask new questions of what the ethical claim and the ethical response can be and how it can come to impact communal and equitable structures of living interdependently upon a shared world. The uncanny allows us to ask new questions and imagine new responses to the dichotomies of both the ideologies and lived practices of being at-home and of homelessness.

How to live—Ethics and ghosts

Theodor W. Adorno writes a decisive statement in his 1951 text *Minima Moralia*: "ethics today means not being at home in one's house."[16] He is speaking to the need of displacement in order to rupture our default relationship of ownership and identity within dominating political and ethical ideologies. The landscape from which Adorno's critical philosophy is written hails from the aftermath of his own exile and of the absolute devastation of violence brought to bear throughout WWII. The singularity of these historical events has passed, and

---

[12] Dick Weissman, *Talkin' 'bout a Revolution: Music and Social Change in America* (Milwaukee: Backbeat Books, 2010), 303.
[13] Pearl Jam has created many more anti-war songs than the few mentioned here, notably such songs as "Army Reserve," "World Wide Suicide," "Cropduster," and "Do the Evolution."
[14] Pearl Jam, "Bu$hleaguer," in *Riot Act* (2002).
[15] Ibid.
[16] Theodor W. Adorno, *Minima Moralia: Reflections on a Damaged Life* (London: Verso, 2005), 34.

yet those living in exile, migrant populations, refugees of war, and homeless communities are increasing. Dwelling, a classical and well-discussed philosophical body of work, is once again on the forefront of contemporary ethics. Dwelling is the way in which we inhabit ethics and the ways in which we interact with the environments we are interconnected with and as such, the question becomes how to address the ethical anew. Perhaps one of many answers is that the epistemological movement and "the sensible distribution" (Rancière) of the aesthetic transforms the ethical within itself. Often what we envision and perform as the ethical response is actually the aesthetic at work and at play.

"We're Pearl Jam and we're from Seattle, Washington. So I guess that must mean we're home."[17] Pearl Jam is home and sings to a sold-out hometown crowd, yet the nature of the gathering of *The Home Shows* (to raise money and awareness around Seattle's homeless crisis) resides within the shadow side of our ideals of home—that of exile, of home*less*ness. Adorno writes, in regards to dwelling, that "things are worst of all, as always, for those who have no choice at all."[18] The band begins the moody and forceful song "Even Flow," a song wherein the evocation of a specific human's experience points toward the larger narrative of homelessness. Vedder tells the crowd the story of Eddie, the man who often took up dwelling in the foyer of the band's Pioneer Square office building in Seattle.[19] After returning home from tour, Vedder learned his friend Eddie had died, never having heard Vedder's homage to him in the song "Even Flow." "I never really told that story before tonight,"[20] Vedder says. The story of Eddie haunts the stadium as rhythm, cadence, word, song, and voice fill in the silence and vacancy he leaves behind. To speak of, to write of, to sing of that which is spectral is, for Jacques Derrida, the very ethical question and pathway itself. For there to be ethical engagement, Derrida writes that there must be the dialogue of the ghost, "it is necessary to speak *of the* ghost, indeed *to the* ghost and with it."[21] Eddie, who made a home in the city of Seattle was also exiled from within it, living in doorways, under an overpass, and in the foyer where Pearl Jam sets down to compose their first record, *Ten*. The beginning bars of "Even Flow" are carried

---

[17] Rietmulder, "Review: Pearl Jam."
[18] Adorno, *Minima Moralia*, 34.
[19] Rietmulder, "Review: Pearl Jam."
[20] Ibid.
[21] Jacques Derrida, *Specters of Marx: The State of the Debt, the Work of Mourning, and the New International* (New York: Routledge, 1994), xviii.

by the band and, before joining in, Vedder, rather quietly, says to the crowd, "this one's for Eddie."[22]

The ethical question is to ask "how to live?"—a question to which Derrida answers in a reversal, "only from the other and by death."[23] Derrida's question of "how to live?" comes from the marginal space of exile in the form of an ethical claim made upon our presupposed cohesion of the ideology of the center against its cast-out otherness of the outside. Both homelessness and war make upon the aspects of individual, political, and communal life an ethical claim, a claim that demands a response. What the pathway of the aesthetic reveals is that this response, if it is actually to meet the cry and call of the exile(d) must and (often already is) the response of the aesthetic, of the ethical transfigured within the aesthetic. We learn to live both from the other and from death, which aligns the ethical question with the aesthetic-ethical question of the ghost—the ghost whose absent-presence fills both the space of the home and of the exile. In telling the story of Eddie's life and death on stage, Vedder conjures forth the spectral presence of Eddie before the crowd and the heart of *The Home Shows* is revealed—that we, communally and aesthetically, must learn how to respond to the ethical claim and question made from the exile(d). If we are to learn "how to live"—which is the question of dwelling (*ethos*), the contemporary ethical question, then we must speak with the other and with death. The ghost is the question, the border between life and death, dwelling within the liminal space between home and exile. As Vedder speaks of Eddie he seems to remember his very face, conjuring up in rhythm and cadence the presence of a specter who is no longer present, a life lost to the cruelty of exile. Pearl Jam brings us, via the aesthetic, into the realm of the ethic, and yet the ethic is reformulated within its relationship with the aesthetic. Whereas the claim, question, and cry from and of the exiled spaces is an ethical one, the response must be (in part) an aesthetic one if it is to gain any traction toward equitable relations upon a troubled planet plagued by proliferating crises of homelessness and war. The aesthetic response is one that illuminates a multiplicity of ways of knowing the world and of ways of navigating relations and knowledge outside of the strict parameters of language. The aesthetic, through the effectuation of "sensible distribution," allows for languages other than the dominant language of *logos*—allowing for the other languages of sound, of song, of poetry, of multiplicities of expression

---

[22] Rietmulder, "Review: Pearl Jam."
[23] Derrida, *Specters of Marx*, xvii.

and experience to be heard. Learning to live evokes the other and death, and so these experiences of the spectral, of mourning, of multiplicity, of response are within the workings and machinery of the aesthetic. To listen and dialogue with the ghost is, for Derrida, a foundational principle of responsibility, a responsibility to who is "beyond all living present."[24] Haraway fissures the word responsibility, building within it a fertile rupture as she contracts the word into response-ability. She defines response-ability as a "cultivation through which we render each other capable, that cultivation of capacity to respond."[25] The imagination required for the capacity to respond to the other and to death (to ethical living) is the pathway of the aesthetic. Despite the massive amount *The Home Shows* raised, Vedder speaks to the heart of the matter, the important work which is, in his words, "to elevate the empathy and understanding for our homeless neighbors."[26] Pearl Jam's response reshapes the question of "who is responsible?" into the communal and aesthetic act of response-ability. As Vedder tells the story of Eddie, he is responding to the other, to death, and to Eddie. Vedder pays homage to a ghost, a homage wherein ethics is rendered alive, transfixed, and extended through the aesthetic pathway.

"Yellow Ledbetter," akin to "Even Flow" invokes a ghost—that of a brother lost whose absence now defines presence. Eddie's ghost is also the ghost of war, the haunting of wartime violence within dwelling, within peace, within ethics. As Hitler rose to power, Adorno himself was exiled from his home country. In 1949, Adorno returned to a devastated and demolished Germany and wrote that "dwelling, in the proper sense, is now impossible."[27] If dwelling is a concatenation of ethics then perhaps Adorno's declaration can be extended imaginatively and experimentally to be read within contemporary time and space as such: ethics, in the proper sense, is now impossible. Rancière writes that "ethics amounts to the dissolution of norm into fact: in other words, the substation of all forms of discourse and practice beneath the same indistinct point of view."[28] Ethics is often not unencumbered enough from the consensus of political identity and ideology in order to think, to imagine, and to practice meeting material and urgent needs from the exiled spaces of homelessness and war. The ethical

---

[24] Ibid., xviii.
[25] Donna J. Haraway, *Staying with the Trouble: Making Kin in the Chthulucene* (Durham: Duke University Press, 2016), 8.
[26] Rietmulder, "Review: Pearl Jam."
[27] Adorno, *Minima Moralia*, 37.
[28] Rancière, *Dissensus: On Politics and Aesthetics*, 192.

response, often caught within political and cultural hegemonies and its judicial machinery, as well as being caught within the apparatus of language, cannot alone be an adequate ideology. The aesthetic is a generative, temporal, and nonlinear pathway, one which moves outward from the debilitation of thought within consensus and of the dominant hegemony in power and is enabled to enliven and reconfigure ethical responses within the pathway of the aesthetic. For Adorno, ethics meant no longer being at-home, meant no longer residing within the exclusionary power structures of the regime. Henceforth, the question becomes how are we to move outward? The aesthetic allows for a (fragmented and in-process) multisensory and multi-material movement, putting traction and galvanization into the ethical. The ethical claim of the exiled space haunts our thinking, our politics, our aesthetics—and (partial/temporal) response-ability puts "who it is at home" into question, the response to which cannot only be an ethical one, but an aesthetic response as well.

War on terror—Consensus and aesthetics

Within both homelessness and war, there are the large-scale conceptual processes and proliferation of crises as well as individual and singular events abiding within. In reflection upon the events of the September 11, 2001 attacks against the United States (9/11), Derrida, in an interview with the philosopher Giovanna Borradori for the text *Philosophy in a Time of Terror*, is asked, "can philosophy help us to understand what has happened?"[29] He responds by claiming that such an event certainly requires a philosophical response, "a response that calls into question, at their most fundamental level, the most deep-seated conceptual presuppositions in philosophical discourse."[30] Derrida's answer reveals the entrenchment of philosophy, politics, of ethics, of human thinking itself within the polarities of the discourse between self versus other, of home versus exile, of good versus evil. 9/11 prompts a philosophical response, one which questions the discourses of the ethical and, in turn, so too do these events prompt an aesthetic response. The question of whether or not art should (or whether it is or is not) political or ethical are questions this project sets aside in order to look at

---

[29] Giovanna Borradori (ed.), *Philosophy in a Time of Terror: Dialogues with Jürgen Habermas and Jacques Derrida* (Chicago: University of Chicago Press, 2003), 100.
[30] Ibid.

the question(s) which prefigure these inquiries—the question which asks, can ethics today even be possible, productive, viable, equitable, and if so, how and in what ways? Products and the production/experience of art (aesthetics) reveal meaningful ways in which ethics may be deconstructed/reconstructed ad infinitum via the aesthetic at work—the aesthetic as response-ability (Haraway). The aesthetic equipped as temporal, situated, as a multi-epistemological forum, invoking a multiplicity of senses, working in a multitude of languages, languages able to be attuned to the uncanny, the ghost, to the voice of the exile.

In 2003, Pearl Jam took the album *Riot Act*, written in the aftermath of 9/11, on the road, embarking on a world tour originating in Australia and eventually returning for a North American leg. Gracing a Melbourne stage on February 18, Vedder wears a blue shirt with the words: "No War No Way."[31] On April 1, performing at the Pepsi Center in Denver Colorado, Pearl Jam's first show since the "war on terror" had started, Vedder appeared on stage wearing a George W. Bush mask.[32] As the band begins the opening chords to the song "Bu$hleaguer," Vedder moonwalks, mimicking playful classic dance moves, then removes the mask to place it atop a microphone stand in order to address the song to the uninhabited and referential mask singing, "[a] confidence man, but why so beleaguered? / He's not a leader, he's a Texas leaguer."[33] A week later in an interview with *Rolling Stone*, Vedder says, "if you can't be critical of a president during time of war, doesn't that encourage him to *be* at war?"[34] On April 30, at the Nassau Coliseum in Uniondale, New York, the song "Bu$hleaguer" is met with an adverse reaction from the crowd. "Boos" are clearly heard throughout the venue all the way through to the start of the second encore at which point Vedder addresses the crowd, "you didn't like that one, I don't understand. Maybe you like him 'cause he's gonna give you a tax cut."[35] As the crowd morphs from "boos" to a successive and interruptive chant of "USA! USA!" Vedder speaks again, his voice calm, steady, sure, and says:

> I'm with you. USA. I just think that all of us in this room should have a voice in how the USA is represented. And he didn't allow us our voice. That's all I'm

---

[31] David Fricke, "Eddie Vedder's Combat Rock," *Rolling Stone*, May 29, 2003.

[32] Less than a month earlier, in March 2003, The Dixie Chicks tell a London concert audience: "We do not want this war, this violence, and we're ashamed that the President of the United States is from Texas."

[33] Pearl Jam, "Bu$hleaguer."

[34] Fricke, "Eddie Vedder's Combat Rock."

[35] Jonathan Cohen and Mark Ian Wilkerson (ed.), *Pearl Jam Twenty* (New York: Simon & Schuster, 2011), 272.

saying. We love America. I am up on a stage in front of a big crowd. I worked in a goddamned drug store. I love America, right? This is good, this is open, honest debate, and that's what it should be. If we keep this back and forth, good things will happen. If you don't say anything, you don't know what will happen. 'Cause we are on the brink of forever. And if we don't participate in where this thing is going, when we are the number one superpower in the world, you want to have a part in and make sure it is a good thing, yeah? Plus or minus, be active. This is a good thing.[36]

Pearl Jam plays two more songs against a backdrop of "boos" until Vedder tosses the microphone down in frustration and walks off the stage.[37] As early as 2003, Vedder seems to envision the ongoing cost of war when he says to the Uniondale crowd "cause we are on the brink of forever," and as such he seems to forecast a world cast into an interminable war. This unending "war on terror" as decreed and named by George W. Bush in a speech delivered to Congress on September 16, is a war which lingers, transforms, and emerges anew all the way into the year 2021.

On September 24, 2001, a Gallup poll declares that George W. Bush's approval rating is the highest in Gallup history; this poll taken on September 21–22 found that "90% of Americans approve of the way Bush is handling his job as president,"[38] an approval rating rolling in after George W. Bush's declared "war on terror." The political response to this attack of terrorism on American soil as a "war on terror" was commonly accepted and heralded as an ethical and patriotic response. Rancière writes that "on the evening of the same day, the president already had the words on hand to capture what had happened: forces of evil had attacked the forces of good."[39] Ethics, morality, and politics reside alongside binary divides, between presupposed clear and distinct divisions of good versus evil that often works to transfigure ethics into an inhibiting consensus, a consensus originating from a hierarchical dichotomy between inside/outside, between inclusion/exclusion, between good/evil. Upon an inquiry into ethics and its impact upon communities, Rancière writes, "consensus

---

[36] Ibid.
[37] Vedder tells Fricke from *Rolling Stone* that after what the media hailed as the impalement of the rubber George W. Bush mask on a mic stand, Pearl Jam's office in Seattle was hit with a wave of threats, "e-mails and phone calls in the hundreds" calling Vedder and the band, "unpatriotic, un-American." Of course, the backlash which Pearl Jam received for their anti-war stances paled in comparison to the backlash which The Dixie Chicks received for their anti-war sentiments.
[38] David W Moore, "Bush Job Approval Highest in Gallup History," *Gallup News*, September 24, 2001.
[39] Rancière, *Dissensus: On Politics and Aesthetics*, 106.

describes the community as an entity that is naturally unified by ethical values."[40] What is often defined as the ethical within political and cultural discourse is an encircling of consensus. "Consensus is not simply an agreement between parties in the name of the national interest. It implies positing an immediate identity between the political constitution of the community and the physical and moral constitution of a population."[41] This effect of consensus is a debilitation of the ability to think, of becoming response-able, of imagining and enacting ways of being able to deconstruct the supposed inherent and sovereign borders of consensus.

These binary divides of consensus are able to be put into question through the aesthetic pathway and experience, which obfuscates clear and structured borders, which is able to live and move within the liminal spaces. Does Pearl Jam's song "Bu$hleaguer" and its performance disrupt the hegemonic dogma of consensus, does it rupture the political binary between good and evil? Yes, but not in a way that is exhaustive and complete—which is precisely the point. There is not one answer to the ethical claim and question, but rather many answers. The sensible distribution (Rancière) of the aesthetic is a multiplicity of pathways, deconstructing the cohesion of the consensus through providing a differing epistemological experience of the world in which we find ourselves, a world plagued by its human impacts of war, of violence, of exclusion, of pervasive and proliferating homelessness. When Pearl Jam performed "Bu$hleaguer" on stage at Uniondale, the consensus and political/ethical ecosystem of that time was a general high approval of both George W. Bush and his corresponding "war on terror." Pearl Jam's response (their response-ability in practice) to both Bush and the war presents an aesthetic reconfiguration of experience, thought, politics, and who it is we believe to be at-home and who we believe are justifiably cast out in exile. The aesthetic pathway/experience represents, in a multisensory way, more than one way to know and to think of the world, ourselves, and others. The aesthetic response to the ethical claim made from the space of exile ruptures the habitual homogeneity of ethics as consensus and renders the aesthetic-ethical response mobile, temporal, partial, and able to expand and step through the borders of consensus. The aesthetic work of the artist puts the notion of ethics to work in poetic and interdependent ways—ways that expand human thinking to be able to contend with the work needed to operate outside (between, through,

---

[40] Ibid., 108.
[41] Ibid.

under) the strict dichotomies between home and exile (between who it is at-home and who is exiled). Ethics must not be at-home within consensus, must not be in service to the hegemonic ideologies of us versus them. Therefore, ethics requires the aesthetic's epistemological reconfiguration in order to be enlivened in response and in response-ability. The aesthetic allows for ghosts, for mourning, for poetics, for rhythm and song—all vehicles from which to disrupt the borders of the consensus.

In denouement—Borders and mourning

Pearl Jam performed on the set of *Saturday Night Live* for the first time in April 1992, about eight months after Pearl Jam's inaugural album *Ten* was released. For the band's second performance of the night, Vedder changes into a t-shirt, on the front of which the image of a coat hanger is depicted (a common prochoice symbol) and on the back, in handwritten letters are the words, "No Bush 92," which Vedder flashes to the camera as the song "Porch" comes to an end.[42] London, July 11, 2014, during a three-hour Pearl Jam set, Vedder, before launching into a cover of the 1970 Edwin Starr song "War," states to the crowd: "So why people at war? Stop the fucking shit, now! Now! Now! We don't want to give them our money. We don't want to give them our taxes to drop bombs on children! Now! No more! Now!"[43] Vedder's impassioned and lively anti-war disquisition was taken as an "anti-Israel diatribe" as reported on by the Jerusalem Post and controversy consequently ensued.[44] Against the backdrop of the band playing, Vedder's impassioned plea asks in angered tones, "how can we be dropping bombs on each other, what the fucking fuck he asks?"[45] The music builds and the band ramps into the song "War"—"War, huh, Yeah! / What is it good for?"; "Sing it again" Vedder shouts and the crowd does, responding loudly, "[a]bsolutely nothing."[46] Vedder's voice breaks and in what sounds like exhaustion alongside a stifled sob, as the band plays the song out he pleads with the crowd, "please, please, please, we beg of you." Vedder raises his hands up, his head

---

[42] John Reynolds et al., "Pearl Jam: Saturday Night Live, 1992," *TwoFeetThick.com*.
[43] Olivia Forman, "Eddie Vedder's Anti-War Rant Outrages Israeli Pearl Jam Fans," *Spin*, July 15, 2014.
[44] Ibid.
[45] Ibid.
[46] See GotsomePearlJam, "Pearl Jam. Daughter. Milton Keynes National Bowl," *YouTube.com*, July 11, 2014. "War" was written by Normal Whitfield and Barrett Strong for Motown Records in 1969.

looking upwards, one hand holding a wine bottle and the other outstretched, clasping them together above his head in a gesture of begging, of prayer. "Please, peace," he says as he drops to his knees. "Please. Please. Please" is heard as Vedder's voice gets softer, his shoulders slumping inward and down.[47] On July 16, 2014, Vedder composes a letter in response to this anti-war speech and its consequent backlash, entitled "Imagine That—I'm Still Anti-War"; he writes: "When attempting to make a plea for more peace in the world at a rock concert, we are reflecting the feeling of all those we have come in contact with so we may all have a better understanding of each other. That's not going to stop anytime soon."[48] Over a decade had passed since Vedder wore the "No Bush 92" shirt to the time he penned the words, "Imagine That—I'm Still Anti-War"; through lyric, mask, shirt, and through tune, rhythm, reverberation, the aesthetic pathway performs its work not only on, in, and through language, but also in sound, in poetics, in communal experience[49]. The aesthetic continues to be one fragment (among many) that does not originate or point to a whole (or consensus), but rather offers other ways of thinking and knowing our worlds, of being able to be equipped to (re)learn them and ourselves in equitable ways.

As Rancière identifies consensus as communities that are unified via ethical values and as a fusing of identity with the political/moral discourse, so too it can be seen that what is deemed the ethical becomes the mechanics that operate in service to hegemonic ideologies. These ideologies often inhibit the ability to think alongside modes of difference, stunting equitable responses to the exiled spaces of homelessness and war. Ethics (without much attendance and care— and the aesthetic attunement) becomes a land of unthinking consensus, as well as a proprietor and executor of borders, of walls, of the boundaries of identity. The us-versus-them, the at-home versus the foreigner are both conceptions of the ideology of the border, of inclusion and exclusion, and as such the ethical imagination often resultantly falls within these binary discourses. On stage in England 2014, Vedder's impassioned anti-war speech addresses these discourses of space: "there are people out there who are looking for a reason to kill! They're looking for a reason to go across borders and take over land that doesn't belong

---

[47] Ibid.
[48] Eddie Vedder, "Pearl Jam. Imagine That—I'm Still Anti-War," *Pearljam.com*, July 16, 2014.
[49] Pearl Jam's critique of war persists from their first album *Ten*, all the way through into *Gigaton*, their 2020 album. The song "Quick Escape" remarks on the crossing of borders and on ecological destruction, calling out the American President by name: "The lengths we had to go to then / To find a place Trump hadn't fucked up yet."

to them."⁵⁰ This irreverent and violent takeover across borders and lands is America's dark and dangerous history, a history which is repetitively born anew in a myriad of avenues and encounters. Can the pathway and experience of the aesthetic be what allows us to think and move and create outside the ethical monolith of the consensus? Can the aesthetic be (in fragment and in part) what may hermeneutically allow us to listen and engage with the voices which call out in different languages from the excluded place of exile? Ethics (*ethos*) resides within the domain of being at-home, of the home itself, of the ideology of the center versus the margins of nation, of state, of identity, whereas what is needed in the face of such a troubled world (troubles of homelessness, global war, climate crisis) is a disruption of how we define who is at-home and who is cast out (exiled), a deconstruction of identity, a learned and sensuous ability to hear the voice of the other, the voice of those living unhoused, of the victims of war, of our very planet. To learn how to listen is to learn how to live (equitably and ethically) and requires, as Derrida argues, "only the other and death."⁵¹ Here, the question (urgency) becomes what is required to listen and to engage with the other and with death? The aesthetic pathway is required, the aesthetic as that which utilizes more than human language—integrating fragments of song, rhythm, poetry, image, and resonance not into a whole but into a multiplicity of pathways. These differing epistemological pathways open up pathways for mourning and joy, the space for the other and for the exiled, for the presence of the ghost, the ghosts of war, the ghost of homelessness, and the ghost of Eddie.

The image of Vedder on his knees pleading for peace, the story of Eddie's life and death told on stage before thousands at *The Home Shows*, the ache of wartime loss resonating throughout "Yellow Ledbetter" are all the rhythms, anthems, and resonances of a deep mourning—a mourning for the other and a mourning for/of death. "It's important to elevate the empathy and understanding for our homeless neighbors," Vedder tells the Seattle crowd, "so this one's for Eddie."⁵² Mourning is a way in which to relearn the world, ourselves, and our inter-relationality upon a shared and in-trouble planet. Mourning is an efficacious reconfiguring epistemological mode of moving outside the restriction of ethics as consensus. Mourning is an aesthetic-ethical way of knowing the world in expansive ways, an attunement to the space and places of the exile, to those cast

---

[50] Vedder as quoted by Ryan Reed, "Eddie Vedder Unleashes Anti-War Rant Onstage in England," *Rolling Stone*, July 16, 2014.
[51] Derrida *Specters of Marx*, xvii.
[52] Vedder as quoted by Rietmulder, "Review: Pearl Jam."

out from the comfort and safety of being at-home. Mourning is the sound of silence, of wailing, of poetic expression—a resonance that is able to reverberate outside of the restricting sphere of human language. "War hurts. It hurts no matter which side the bombs are falling on," Vedder writes.[53] War hurts. Exile hurts. Homelessness hurts. The world is hurting. The planet aches. How shall we respond and in which ways will our responses be effectively response-able? Will we allow ourselves, our identities of individual selves and our communities, and our at-home-ness to be put into question? The pathway of the aesthetic rumbles with song, with ghosts, with mourning, with pleasure, with the voice(s) of the exile(d)—will we learn to dance (and weep) along? This chapter is for those who sleep in doorways, for those who make homes out of the sharp spikes of inhospitality and exile. This one is for a world struggling and dying between our ideologies and politics of home and exile. This one is for the planet that creaks and moans under treading human feet. This one is for those whose lives have been lost to the violence of war. This one is written in order for philosophical thinking to be enabled to be brought to its knees in order to plead for peace. This one is for peace, please. "Please, *peace*." Please. And this one—this one's for Eddie.

Bibliography

Adorno, Theodor W. *Minima Moralia: Reflections on a Damaged Life*, translated by Edmund F.N Jephcott. London-New York: Verso, 2005.

Borradori, Giovanna, edited by. *Philosophy in a Time of Terror: Dialogues with Jürgen Habermas and Jacques Derrida*. Chicago: University of Chicago Press, 2003.

DeMay, Daniel. "Pearl Jam Puts Spotlight on Seattle Homelessness with Historic Home Shows." *Seattle Post-Intelligencer*, August 8, 2018. Available online: https://www.seattlepi.com/homeless_in_seattle/article/Pearl-Jam-puts-spotlight-on-Seattle-homelessness-13142195.php (accessed March 31, 2021).

Derrida, Jacques. *Specters of Marx: The State of the Debt, the Work of Mourning, and the New International*, translated by Peggy Kamuf. New York: Routledge, 1994.

Forman, Olivia. "Eddie Vedder's Anti-War Rant Outrages Israeli Pearl Jam Fans." *Spin*, July 15, 2014. Available online: https://www.spin.com/2014/07/eddie-vedder-anti-war-israel-rant-pearl-jam-video (accessed March 31, 2021).

Freud, Sigmund. "The 'Uncanny.'" In *The Standard Edition of the Complete Psychological Works of Sigmund Freud. Vol. 17 (1917–1919): An Infantile Neurosis and Other Works*, edited by James Strachey, 217–56. London: Hogarth Press, 1955.

---

[53] Vedder, "Pearl Jam. Imagine That—I'm Still Anti-War."

Fricke, David. "Eddie Vedder's Combat Rock." *Rolling Stone*, May 29, 2003. Available online: https://www.rollingstone.com/music/music-news/eddie-vedders-combat-rock-233360 (accessed March 31, 2021).

GotSomePearlJam. "Pearl Jam. Daughter. Milton Keynes National Bowl." *YouTube.com*, July 11, 2014. Available online: https://www.youtube.com/watch?v=X4ukBCCyczA&feature=emb_err_woyt (accessed March 31, 2021).

Haraway, Donna J. *Manifestly Haraway*. Minneapolis: University of Minnesota Press, 2016.

Haraway, Donna J. *Staying with the Trouble: Making Kin in the Chthulucene*. Durham: Duke University Press, 2016.

Moore, David W. "Bush Job Approval Highest in Gallup History." *Gallup News*, September 24, 2001. Available online: https://news.gallup.com/poll/4924/Bush-Job-Approval-Highest-Gallup-History.aspx (accessed March 31, 2021).

Rancière, Jacques. *The Politics of Aesthetics: The Distribution of the Sensible*. London-New York: Continuum, 2004.

Rancière, Jacques. *Dissensus: On Politics and Aesthetics*. London-New York: Bloomsbury, 2010.

Reed, Ryan. "Eddie Vedder Unleashes Anti-War Rant Onstage in England." *Rolling Stone*, July 16, 2014. Available online: https://www.rollingstone.com/music/music-news/eddie-vedder-unleashes-anti-war-rant-onstage-in-england-80108 (accessed March 31, 2021).

Reynolds, John, et al. "Pearl Jam: Saturday Night Live, 1992." *TwoFeetThick.com*. Available online: http://www.twofeetthick.com/2006/05/02/saturday-night-live-1992t (accessed March 31, 2021).

Rietmulder, Michael. "Review: Pearl Jam, Seattle Fall in Love All over Again at Joyous Home Shows on Night One at Safeco Field." *The Seattle Times*, August 8, 2018. Available online: https://www.seattletimes.com/entertainment/music/photos-pearl-jams-home-shows-rock-for-a-cause-on-night-one-at-seattles-safeco-field (accessed March 31, 2021).

Vedder, Eddie. "Pearl Jam. Imagine That—I'm Still Anti-War." *Pearljam.com*, July 16, 2014. Available online: https://pearljam.com/news/imagine-that-i-m-still-anti-war-1467245120 (accessed March 31, 2021).

Walters, Kate. "Seattle Homeless Population Is Third Largest in U.S., after LA and NYC." *KUOW*, December 18, 2018. Available online: https://www.kuow.org/stories/here-s-how-seattle-and-washington-compare-to-national-homeless-trends (accessed March 31 ,2021).

Weissman, Dick. *Talkin' 'bout a Revolution: Music and Social Change in America*. Milwaukee: Backbeat Books, 2010.

Wilkerson, Mark Ian and Jonathan Cohen (eds). *Pearl Jam Twenty*. New York: Simon & Schuster, 2011.

10

Pearl Jam: Responsible Music or the Tragedy of Culture?

Cristina Parapar

Introduction

It is doubtless true that the philosophical work of Theodor W. Adorno has been fundamental to any understanding of how ideology operates within art, the fetishist character of traditional harmony, or the historical dialectic of musical material. Nevertheless, many detractors question his writings *Aesthetic Theory*, "On Jazz," "On the Fetish Character in Music and the Regression of Listening," or *Philosophy of New Music*, with arguments that are at times imprecise, at times simply dishonest.

 A witness of the emergence of mass culture, the rise of totalitarianism, and the development of propaganda, Adorno has been vilely accused of the most ferocious "aesthetic crimes." The shadow of Adorno's elitism or pessimism regularly hovers over his head, and that of his analyses of the future of mass society and *Kulturindustrie*. In response, it should be remembered that the German philosopher lived in the United States between the late 1930s and the 1940s, during which he examined, not without distrust, the refinement of the techniques of reproduction and mass distribution, the development of mass media, the rise of capitalism, and the omnipresence of radio or television in America. At the same time, he suffered from the control and repression of European dictatorships, and the crisis and decline of Western culture. Accordingly, having returned to Germany in the late 1940s upon completion of his writings on popular music, one can easily imagine that certain historical determinations had shaped his judgments on these themes.

 If we understand, therefore, his judgment on popular music in this context, it would seem difficult to deny that the Adornian categories have become reified concepts bound to the dance music and hit tunes of 1930s–40s. In this vein, it is necessary to ask whether Pearl Jam is one of those popular music groups that challenges and impugns the music theory of the German philosopher. Thus, our objective here is to question whether Pearl Jam's music could be considered as a philosophical example that proves the possibility of critical self-reflection within popular music. Can Pearl Jam's music go beyond its commodity character? Can it put subject and object, individual and collective, in tension? Can this music operate dialectically? Can it, as Max Paddison says, neutralize at least some of the effects of the culture industry?[1] *Riot Act*: responsible music or the tragedy of culture?

If this essay aims to reveal the potential of critique within Pearl Jam's music (its critical and self-reflective capacities), it is worth analyzing their work seriously, that is, applying the same method that Adorno employed on high art, modern music, or the Vienna School. We must think dialectically and try to overcome the classic dilemmas: responsible music/musical commodity, progress/regression responsibility/entertainment, critical/uncritical, reflection/pleasure, authenticity/ideology, autonomy and negativity of art/reification, and fetishism of the aesthetic object, or truth content/untruth.

Responsible music versus popular music?

In the philosophy of music, the term "popular music" is plural and often ambiguous. On the one hand, we can use the term popular music as a synonym for folklore, that is, the traditional music of a region or a culture. These musical traditions date back to Ancient Greece. Recall the Greek tonalities: Dorian, Ionic, and Aeolian. In Ancient Greece, these melodic scales already represented the ethos of a people; one which extends across countless peoples and epochs to this very day.

On the other hand, the term "popular music" tends to be used interchangeably with "mass music." This use must nevertheless be limited by a very precise timeframe: the decade of the 1930s, when records were first produced, reproduced, and distributed massively. The journalist Chris Smith thinks that in 1948 "the music industry was at war,"[2] where individual record companies were

---

[1] See Max Paddison, *Adorno, Modernism and Mass Culture: Essays on Critical Theory and Music* (London: Kahn & Averill, 2009).
[2] See Chris Smith, *101 Albums That Changed Popular Music* (Oxford-New York: Oxford University Press, 2009).

vying to win the battle of the record. RCA and Columbia released the LP format, the 78rpm, 10", 12", and so on. According to Smith, *The Voice of Frank Sinatra* (1948) by Frank Sinatra is, for example, the first album released at $33^{1/3}$ speed and, therefore, is the first album that can be considered a "long player," to be marketed and played comfortably. Sinatra himself is followed by a league of other crooners, and the boom of mass music evidently explodes with Elvis Presley (*Elvis Presley*, 1956).

Other scholars reduce the notion of popular music to the "hits"—the songs that are at the top of the music charts. Under this alternative view, popular music would simply refer to the canon of popularity of certain singles or albums.

Therefore, the notion of popular music presents a degree of indetermination, and thus requires us to seriously question its meaning. What are the differences between these three meanings? And what are the similarities? One aspect shared among them seems to be a tripartite stigmatism: low culture, standardization, and a regression in listening. For this reason, discredit and stigmatization have accompanied popular music since it garnered the title of *Leichte Musik*, that is, light popular music.

It could be said that Adorno is primarily responsible for this condemnation, since to the traditional distinction between low and high culture, the German philosopher added another: responsible music and light music. Musical modernism, represented by Schönberg, Webern, or Berg, embodies progress and aesthetic, historical, and political responsibility in the face of the entertaining and distracting character of light music. Against Adorno, we consider that the popular music distributed by the *Kulturindustrie* typically bears little resemblance to the avant-garde, authentic, and responsible works of the Second Viennese School.

Leichte Musik was born as a result of hybridization between folklore, the electrification of instruments, and mass distribution and reproduction. According to Adorno, this new musical phenomenon brings standardization, musical fetishism, simple entertainment, and a regression in listening. The irresponsibility and lack of seriousness of this music explains its function: entertainment or distraction. Therefore, the regression of listening, and regression in types of musical behavior, lead to regression in all areas of the human being. In other words, light music contributes to standardization, uniformity, and one-dimensional thinking generally, in Marcusian terms.

In spite of these strict declarations by Adorno, the purpose of his analysis should not be underestimated. The problem is that Adorno witnessed the birth of the boom of hits, formula radio, and mass music; and the negative aesthetics and dialectic character of this musical material do not chime well with the first jazz standards played on the radio. Let's remember then that the author of *Philosophy of New Music* escapes from Germany to the United States in the 1930s, and later takes refuge in New York to begin a research program at Princeton University. Here he studies the success of American radio hits between 1939 and 1941.

Who sat at the top of the charts at the time? Benny Goodman, Duke Ellington, Dick Jurgens, Shakey Horton, or Frank Sinatra, among others. Thus Adorno selects some thirty-odd swing tunes or crooner ballads from this period, all of which effectively share a common musical form, mode of production, and distribution. His fundamental interest is to study the formal, aesthetic, and ideological construction of these works to explain their popularity and commercial success. However, it seems that Adorno's theoretical limitation lies precisely in the fact that his analyses are essentially based on the popularity and ideological power of these musical commodities. He "strangely" forgets their genealogy and the historical contexts which support their musical form, omitting gospel, European folklore, topical songs, religious chants, etc. Undoubtedly, Adorno's merit is remarkable, as he connects the one-dimensionality and standardization of light music with the ideological repression of totalitarianisms and the rise of capitalism. Unfortunately, as Christhian Béthune points out, the German philosopher seems obsessed with the pleasure that jazz brings and, for this reason, "doesn't read what he plays under the mask of the bouffant where jazz is affluent." Béthune holds that Adorno was unable to grasp the "subtle duality (*la subtile dualité*)" of this music. What might be meant by such a term, and how does it connect to the subversive character of jazz?

In *Adorno et le jazz. Analyse d'un déni esthétique* the French author recalls that the beginning of jazz's success dates back to an historical context rife with racial conflict. In the United States, "music (and its corollary, dance) were, alongside sports, the principal means for a black man to climb the social ladder, and to assert himself as a subject, all while giving the white man, who held the power, the reassuring impression of his still 'knowing his place.'"[3] The subtlety of

---

[3] "la musique (et son corollaire, la danse) fut, avec le sport, le moyen privilégié pour un Noir de s'élever dans l'échelle sociale et s'affirmer comme sujet, tout en donnant aux Blancs, détenteurs du pouvoir, l'impression rassurante de 'rester à sa place'" (Christine Béthune, *Adorno et le jazz. Analyse d'un déni esthétique* [Paris: Klincksieck, 2003], 137: my translation).

jazz, therefore, has two faces: the progressive incursion of black people into the cultural environment from which they were excluded, and the counter-hegemony they constituted for the dominant (white) aesthetic.

In addition, since Adorno's analyses of popular music took place in 1941, the German philosopher does not seem to pay significant attention to later authors and albums, themselves very different from those structures that spearheaded the early days of swing. For all these reasons, Agnès Gayraud redefines popular music. She points out that popular music is neither synonymous with light music nor with folklore or hits. In *Dialectique de la pop*, Gayraud assumes that the Adornian aesthetic categories that refer to popular music are insufficient. They have gradually become obsolete and are currently deficient.

Naturally then, Gayraud revisits the concept of popular music. The first step is to call it "recorded popular music (*musiques populaires enregistrées*)" or "pop." Therefore, in this chapter when we refer to popular music, and more specifically to the work of Pearl Jam, we necessarily speak of *musiques populaires enregistrées*. Why? Firstly, the term denotes a musical category in which a variety of genres, subgenres, and hybrids are brought together and which cannot be reduced to popular music in the Adornian sense. They do not constitute music that is adapted to static musical forms, but rather, are in continuous transformation. Pop music or *musiques populaires enregistrées* is, in Gayraud's mind, the globalized musical phenomenon in which the influences of African-American music, the remnants of European folklore, and many other incorporations from extra-Western musical traditions (such as African percussion or the Indian sitar) take their form from the technical determinations of modernity and postmodernity (electrification, amplification, transformation of sound, which are the characteristics of recorded music).[4]

Secondly, Gayraud explains how pop music is produced: by the method of recording. This method is also the mode of mass production *par excellence*, and is an ontological aspect of modern and postmodern music. In other words, it is a distinctive phenomenon of this music, characteristic of and exceptional to an era, a trace of history in music. For this reason, recording and electrification determine not only the mode of production and reproduction of this musical phenomenon, but also its form and form-content, in terms of Hegelian dialectics.

---

[4] See Agnès Gayraud, *Dialectique de la pop* (Paris: Éditions La Découverte, 2018: my translation).

Thirdly, it is necessary to bear in mind that pop does not necessarily hold musical writing or "musical genius" in high esteem. Formal innovation or complexity can be valued, but on many occasions the listener of *musiques populaires enregistrées* privileges aspects that reveal only a certain degree of "originality." This may be the work of the sound engineer or the richness of an artist's timbre, rather than the compositional elements of the song.

Fourthly, it is important to recall the flexibility and porosity of pop music material. We observe that the sound material of pop can merge different traditions, scales, modulations, and influences from both high and low culture. A hit, to Adorno's surprise, can deviate from the hit scheme. Think of Micah P. Hinson's *A Dream of Her* (2007) which revisits Pachelbel's Canon, or Rick Wakeman's symphonic rock album *Six Wives of Henry VIII* (1973). Throughout the twentieth century, it has become clear that pop is open to any kind of sound material, even noise and shouts. To this end, groups like the Sex Pistols have likely made a significant contribution.

To summarize then, pop can never produce categories *a priori*. Pop is full of contradictions and these contradictions feed its definition: diverse, complex, difficult to ascertain ... and perhaps also responsible. For all these reasons, we propose to reconsider the fact that *musiques populaires enregistrées* are not necessarily a commodity that fulfils a specific psychosocial and ideological function, namely, entertainment in the capitalist system. It is possible that we have borne witness to the formation of a new aesthetic category worthy of being elevated to the status of authentic and responsible music. If the *raison d'être* of popular music is not necessarily to fulfill a psychosocial function, could it be said that *Gigaton* or *Vitalogy* possess a certain aesthetic/political autonomy? Could it constitute popular and responsible music at the same time? In response, we must recognize that in *Philosophy of New Music*, Adorno explains that dissonance speaks to listeners about their own situation. Quite clearly, the material of popular music at least occasionally does speak to its listeners in this way. So Pearl Jam's act of responsibility is precisely his representation of the *Zeitgeist*. It must be conceived, to quote Gayraud, as the hope of reconciliation between immediacy and truth, between rapture and reflection, between entertainment and emancipation.[5]

---

[5] Ibid., 85.

Music and the real content: Popular music as a social cement

When Terry Eagleton rethinks the aesthetic left theories, from Schiller, Marx, Marcuse, Adorno, and Morris, he reminds us that in modernity, art could be negative, which is to say, it offers a negative knowledge of reality. As he explains in *The Ideology of the Aesthetic*, in the postmodern era the foundations of society, the dominant ideology, and the symbolic order are so powerful that art can hardly deny the real. In other words, the symbolic order on which the real is based—or that which art could attack—is difficult to overturn. The critical (or negative) art of the postmodern era can hardly act in our administered world, it can hardly be anything other than a commodity. This is why Eagleton writes:

> You can't bring it to its knees with organic craftsmanship, so you have to try instead the silent scream, the scream which in Munch's famous painting rips open the blank face of the solitary figure and reverberates endlessly around the canvas. The aesthetic becomes the guerrilla tactics of secret subversion, of silent resistance, of stubborn refusal. Art will pulverize traditional form and meaning, because the laws of syntax and grammar are the laws of the police. It will dance on the grave of narrative, semantics and representation, celebrate madness and delirium, speak like a woman, dissolve all social dialectics into the free flow of desire. Its form will become its content—a form which repulses all social semantics and might just allow us a glimpse of what it might conceivably be like to be free.[6]

As we cannot create a negative work of art as was possible in Modernity, the postmodern work of art silently subverts the dominant symbolic order. In order to reveal itself negatively, the postmodern *artifact* does so from a kind of secret resistance.[7] But, what is it rebelling against? What content is revealed negatively? According to Adorno's aesthetic theory, there are two possible answers, or two different moments.

A first type of negative revelation involves the truth content of a work. The truth content of a musical work shows its incompleteness, its indefiniteness, its fragmentation, and its chaos. And the work shows it negatively. The opposite of

---

[6] Terry Eagleton, *The Ideology of the Aesthetic* (Oxford: Blackwell, 1990), 369–70.
[7] To truly understand Eagleton's arguments on postmodern aesthetics and artwork, we recommend reading the chapter "From the Polis to Postmodernism" in *The Ideology of the Aesthetic* (our philosophical position differs from that of the British theorist).

this truth content and authenticity is a tour de force. This tour de force is an artificial, affirmative, static, prefabricated, immanent musical work whose material is not released. However, the musical form should not try to hide the incompleteness that constitutes its material. In other words, the work of art becomes art by denying itself. The work of art denies itself; a determined denial, reflecting the constitutive impossibility of the union between, or perfect harmonization of, form and content, between language and meaning, and between the artistic form and empirical reality. For this reason, the work of art is opposed to being defined and, at the same time, it is constantly redefined, as it also a process of becoming, proceeding by way of negation of its own previously existing concept.[8] In a nutshell, the truth content of an authentic work of art is this constitutive negation and this historically changing constellation of moments,[9] as Max Paddison explains.

Obviously, the content of the work is always mediated by the system. Although art and empirical reality are irreconcilable—their harmonization is impossible, or their languages are different—the social is always reflected in musical material. This is the second moment in which the content of truth is revealed: the reflection of society in musical material. Although the musical language is different from that of the empirical, the musical work derives from the empirical, speaks of it, and at the same time always opposes it. If a piece of music reflects this content of the social, we speak of authentic music and the content of the work is true. Otherwise, we are defining a tour de force or a musical commodity. In summary, art and society converge in content, and this content is also the result of its form.

Now, we must question the form of Pearl Jam's work, and why art and society converge in their musical pieces. Take *Ten* (1991) and *Vs.* (1993) as examples. The musical forms of these albums, published in the United States in the early 1990s, but composed some time before, seem at least in part to reflect a disenchanted America. The aim of our inquiry here will be to attempt to justify the claim that the grunge sound of Pearl Jam is a sedimentation of historical and social tendencies. This musical form reveals the disenchantment of a large group in American society that is confused under the threat of Star Wars. In Reaganist America (with Bush around the corner), defense and militarization expenditures, and also the foreign debt, had doubled. Yet concurrently, Reagan had reduced aid programs for the poor, given impressive tax breaks to the rich, reduced the

---

[8] Paddison, *Adorno, Modernism and Mass Culture*, 57.
[9] Ibid.

power of unions, and had fired the starter pistol on the governmental practice of bailing out national banks. Moreover, one of the symbolic foundations of the American affluent society suddenly collapsed: Wall Street. Indeed, the middle class was weakened and economic inequality grew. Americans could see the disparity between rich and poor with increasing clarity, and how middle-class living conditions were worsening.

To these grim circumstances must be added a powerful crisis of information: ideological bias had returned to the United States by the end of the 1980s, when the repeal of the Fairness Act of 1940 opened the floodgates for conservative spin and opinion news, themselves quickly dominating informational media. In short, the American population of the time bore witness to this chronicle of a death foretold, and their experience is tangible in the novel sounds of the era, as in the case of grunge.

Why then does this grunge aesthetic express social content or real content? Because the musical form of Pearl Jam necessarily derives from and reflects this historical moment. This is why the harmonies of "Go," "W.M.A.," "Blood," "Once," or "Even Flow" (and so on) are dirty and partially out of tune. The classical sound of "perfect chords" falls away, or falls to pieces. The chords are neglected. It is also very relevant that this work is composed in a minor tone which contributes to this tragic feeling. Likewise, the presence of the percussion stands out, which is not concerned with creating a kind of balance or equilibrium with the other vocal and/or instrumental elements. On the contrary, the drums resonate strongly to make the sound dirtier. It is the aesthetics of dirt. Here, the sordid sound of the bass becomes important. The harmonic progressions of the bass are linear, with little variation and much constancy, yet again contributing to the somber aspect of grunge (this theme will return again in post-punk). The rhythm of the piece is moderate. The dynamics and tempo vary suddenly to give the piece a violent character. Vedder's timbre, texture, and vocal technique are decisive. In fact, the low timbre of Vedder's voice favors the somber character of the piece. The presence of screams and the neglected technique of the vocalist also contribute to this feeling of dirtiness (from this comes the term grunge, precisely). Obviously, the semantic content of the work is fundamental. The lyrics explicitly denounce issues of a political nature, such as police violence and racism in American society.

In conclusion, the form-content of this work reflects society and it rebels against it. In so doing, it becomes a subversive work of art. As Eagleton wrote, this piece of art just allows us a glimpse of what it might conceivably be like to be free in late capitalism, in the most extreme *Kulturindustrie*. In this way, these albums sustain their social content in a kind of silent subversion. There is a secret subversion, always mediated by mass culture, but this piece of art is still subversive.

Why is the music of Pearl Jam silently subverted? Because it formally reflects disenchantment and the *Zeitgeist*. It doesn't imitate empirical reality, but it represents it. Consequently, Pearl Jam's musical aesthetic is concerned with colonizing other areas of the human, and therein lies its social and subversive content. In other words, their music disturbs and invites critical reflection. That is their silent cry. They reveal the disenchantment of a society that is in large part defenseless, disillusioned, and desolate.

In the same way in which Adorno saw that the musical material of the beginning of the twentieth century responded to some historical demands (the emancipation of dissonance or the end of tonality), something similar occurs in popular music. In the case of popular music, history has also penetrated its musical material and has made some demands. For this reason, Pearl Jam fights against the musical appearance of pop: against the perfect luminous tonality, the clean sonority, the extreme rigidity of the hit, the optimistic lyrics, the pleasant texture, the catchy rhythms, etc. To this end, let us recall an important paragraph in *Philosophy of New Music*:

> The dissonances arouse as the expression of tension, contradiction, and pain. They were sedimented and became material. They are no longer media of subjective expression. Still, they do not thus disavow their origin. They become characters of objective protest.[10]

Certainly, dissonances were necessarily emancipated to become true representations of the pain, cruelty, and poverty of a war period; as well as the rise of totalitarianism and the decline of a culture. In the case of popular music, we also find particular cases of authenticity, social content, and negativity. Pearl Jam's music presents configurations that are a historical requirement of the material. For example, this music articulates the expressive aspect of the subject and its objectification in musical structures. Their work is expressed in objective forms of protest.

---

[10] Theodor W. Adorno, *Philosophy of New Music* (Minneapolis: University of Minnesota Press, 2019), 68.

In addition, to express oneself negatively is also a form of resistance to the order of establishment. As Deborah Cook writes, "resistance to the social totality is possible because the 'totally administered world' can be transcended in thought. Negative dialectics, itself a type of ideology critique, involves thinking against prevailing identitarian (or descriptive-explanatory) modes of thought. It discloses that what exists does not have to be what it is, of what might yet become other than what it is now."[11] Faced with Adorno's theory, can Pearl Jam's music transgress the evident? Can it transgress identity thinking? Does the music of Pearl Jam contain any kind of dialectical moment?

Identity thinking/critical thinking: Pearl Jam as a critique of culture?

This music, which secretly resists, shares space with other musical phenomena of a different nature, but still distributed by the music industry. They are very popular and catchy and instead of revealing a content of truth or authenticity, rather than subverting the dominant ideology, they adhere to it. As Max Paddison would say in *Adorno, Modernism and Mass Culture*, the sphere of music can be something of a pathway to emancipation from the dominant ideology, and from the dominant mode of instrumental and administered rationality.[12] Or, sometimes it simply cannot. Some music contributes to critical thinking, other music to identity thinking.

The idea of identity thinking undoubtedly evokes the notion of one-dimensional thinking, coined by Herbert Marcuse around the 1940s. At this time the philosopher of the Frankfurt School lived in the United States, and became a faithful witness to the rise and development of American capitalism and to such important social conflicts as the struggle for civil rights, the end of segregation, or the Vietnam War. In 1964, the German philosopher wrote *One-Dimensional Man*. Marcuse explains that Western societies of this period are characterized by their one-dimensional nature, painting the picture of an advanced industrial society that represses the emancipation of the subject and critical thinking using its ideological apparatus. On the one hand, the

---

[11] Deborah Cook, *The Culture Industry Revisited: Theodor W. Adorno on Mass Culture* (Lanham, MD: Rowman & Littlefield, 1996), 81.
[12] See the chapter "Truth-content, Authenticity and Musical Self-reflection," in Paddison, *Adorno, Modernism and Mass Culture*, 57–67.

one-dimensional man is gestated in a new society that is constructed between a synergy of two apparently opposed elements: the welfare state and the war state. On the other hand, one-dimensional thinking contributes to the loss of the negative thought of the individual, that is, the loss of his critical power of reason. We are talking, then, about the homogeneous and integrating thinking that generates an immediate identification between the subject and the dominant ideology. It is the ideology of the administered world.

In this way, the possibility of oppositional thinking is lost, one-dimensional thinking annuls any private space. This private space would be a space of inner freedom of the subject that allows him to distance himself from the predominant forms of social control. And, to paraphrase Hegel in the *Phenomenology of the Spirit*, in the distancing there is the authentic act of negativity, and, therefore, freedom. The problem here is that this space of distancing does not exist because one-dimensional thinking embraces everything. That is to say, one-dimensional thinking is not only present in speech. The ideology of the *administered world* is also inserted (without explicit coercion) in products and cultural goods. All of them carry a prescribed behavior. Hence the one-dimensional man believes that he lives, thinks, and consumes freely because he does so without terror or coercion. He also believes that he listens to music freely, yet covertly, certain music is revealed as inserted identity thinking. So, do *musiques populaires enregistrées* contribute to the perpetuation of identity thinking? Or can we find certain pieces of music distributed by *Kulturindustrie* which induce critical thinking?

Surely, there are certain types of music that contribute to this false uniformity of taste and thought, namely, musical commodities. On the one hand, we have these musical commodities that show an evident connection between identity thinking and cultural commodities. They are cultural goods that reinforce affirmative culture. In *The Culture Industry Revisited: Theodor Adorno on Mass Culture*, Deborah Cook explains the mechanisms of these models of imitation, behavior, and ideology:

> By reanimating the superego introjects and infantile defense mechanisms characteristic of the narcissism prevalent within late capitalist societies, the culture industry strengthens the psychological regression symptomatic of that pathology. But it also serves to promote the socio-economic conditions which led to narcissism in the first place. It does so through its positivist ideology.[13]

---

[13] Cook, *The Culture Industry Revisited*, 84.

A brief example can be useful here, to illustrate the how this psychoanalytic process functions. Recently, Ariana Grande released the song "7 Rings." It was a hit that revisited the Sound of Music's infamous tune, "My Favorite Things." Some listeners will remember Julie Andrews singing this song, while other listeners will recall John Coltrane's saxophone playing a free version of this piece. In 2019, Grande reinterprets this song "affirmatively," making it a successful hit. In the formal aspect, Adorno was absolutely right: there is no innovative aspect to the song, it respects a schematic and repetitive structure, there is no independence between the parts, nor is there a perceived connection between them and the whole, there is no speculative or negative moment, etc. And according to the process described by Cook, "7 Rings" represents and reinforces the effects of reification, the values of late capitalist societies, and a narcissistic and infantile attitude. In short, Grande (or her producer) rewrites the lyrics[14] of someone else's song, and makes a music video to seal the deal. According to Cook, "the economic interests which lie behind the production of cultural commodities are now openly expressed."[15] All this contributes, therefore, to identity thinking and affirmative culture.

On the other hand, there exist musical works within the culture industry which afford critical abstraction, to act negatively and to grant a space of freedom (here resides the critical force of reason). On this point, Gert Keunen talks about "pop mainstream," "underground," and "alternative mainstream." According to this division, we consider that the first category would contribute to identity thinking, the second would collaborate in critical thinking, and the third, being a hybrid between pop mainstream and underground, could contribute to either of the two.[16]

In *Alternative Mainstream: Making Choices in Pop Music*, Keunen points to the existence of these three segments within the popular music circuit. He proposes a dynamic scheme that allows the artist to change from one segment to another. First, "pop mainstream" or "entertainment mainstream" is accessible, hit-prone, and often melodic music for a large audience.[17] Mainstream listeners are not necessarily music lovers, according to Keunen. They are consumers of

---

[14] "Yeah, breakfast at Tiffany's and bottles of bubbles / Girls with tattoos who like getting in trouble / Lashes and diamonds, ATM machines / Buy myself all of my favorite things (yeah)."
[15] Cook, *The Culture Industry Revisited*, 86.
[16] Even if this appears sound, it is nevertheless necessary to evaluate the aesthetic—and not exclusively sociological—characteristics of each piece (popularity, production, financing, form of distribution and consumption, cultural values, etc.).
[17] Gert Keunen, *Alternative Mainstream: Making Choices in Pop Music* (Amsterdam: Valiz, 2015), 32.

entertainment. Music for them is a distraction, and so this music is comprised of songs. These songs must be accessible, with no real formal innovations, easily memorized, and with familiar sounds. This is why this music is intentionally conformist, in Keunen's words. The music of pop mainstream is repeated incessantly in the media, on the charts, in supermarkets, or in bars. People are always exposed to these hits due to their omnipresence in daily life, even if this presence is not always invited. Pop mainstream then seems to be equivalent to *Leichte Musik*; and, like *Leichte Musik*, these hits are also distributed by the biggest music industries. This implies that pop mainstream or entertainment mainstream becomes something of a common space, a sort of space where economic, political, or cultural barriers are blurred. Here then, taste definitely becomes uniform.

The second segment of the popular music circuit is "underground." The main goal of these artists, who always compose their own work, is not lucrative. Their albums are distributed by small labels with relatively little marketing and communication. Obviously, there is no broad audience. Although this music may be more or less accessible, depending on the genre and the time, the sounds are undoubtedly less familiar than those of pop mainstream. Underground requires the listener to consciously seek out this music. The listener chooses this music, instead of surreptitiously encountering it in a department store or in another public space. Since underground is not an invasive musical commodity, Keunen emphasizes its authentic character, in opposition to conventional pop. While the latter manufactures universal feelings and emotions to obtain premeditated reactions in the listener through musical recipes, underground does not prefabricate the aesthetic experience, and it is for this reason that Keunen notes its authenticity.[18]

Contrary to the uniformity of mainstream pop, the underground encompasses numerous subgenres that vary according to the context and period (metal, hardcore, techno, progressive rock, punk, country, experimental music, hip-hop, etc.). Consequently, underground music is never a hegemonic genre. On many occasions these musical subgenres bring with them an urban subculture and, therefore, a particular way of consuming music: consumption on a smaller scale,

---

[18] The term "authenticity" is problematic. We use this concept according to the theory of Hegel and Adorno. We value whether the musical material is expressed authentically in relation to the historical context. However, we consider that "to express oneself authentically" means in this case that the underground artist composes with a certain freedom, without adapting to mainstream formulae or recipes to reach a wider audience.

creating small alternative market niches, etc. But the most interesting thing about the relative autonomy of underground and its distance from the dominant mainstream is its potential for innovation. The musical form of underground is a sort of *tabula rasa*, a terrain for formal experimentation, uprooting, and progress.

Finally, between pop mainstream and underground lies the third segment of this popular music circuit: alternative mainstream. It is a category that shares characteristics of the two other segments, so hybridization is its most distinctive feature. Genres, listeners, concert halls, or market niches are intermingled. Music is composed by artists, but is distributed by powerful record companies. In addition, an alternative mainstream group can emerge in small towns or big cities and be promoted in their early days by large or small labels indifferently. Like underground, these alternative mainstream groups do not usually use music recipes, but their records are promoted. They can include new and risky sounds, but at the same time their music reaches a wider audience. And Keunen also points out that they are respected and praised by music professionals. In fact the term "alternative mainstream" "echoes that of 'alternative rock,' coined in the music press at the start of 1990s to refer to various, somewhat harder playing rock groups that had become successful since the grunge hype."[19] Doesn't this definition remind us of the life and work of Pearl Jam?

Pearl Jam is a hybrid and paradoxical example. Vedder's band is born from the underground segment of the popular music circuit in Seattle, and progressively moves to the alternative mainstream segment. In a few words, Pearl Jam is one of those *rara avis* of alternative mainstream that participates in the birth of the segment itself as well. From pop mainstream, Pearl Jam borrows some elements such as mass distribution, a wide audience, and the rationalization of the work of a big record company (promotion, production, etc.). From underground, they still maintain the authorship of their pieces, the less familiar sound of grunge, and the rejection of the use of musical recipes. Therefore, Pearl Jam is a grunge band that the mass culture internationalizes and deterritorializes, although they always stay more or less faithful to their origins, thus maintaining their underground aura. In this sense, their work contributes to critical thinking since it moves away from the commodities of mainstream pop. It also favors critical thinking because it is the result of an evolution of musical material, and

---

[19] Keunen, *Alternative Mainstream*, 44.

the product of the dialectic between subjectivity and empiricism. This favors the expression of community and/or objectivity. As contradictory as it sounds, Pearl Jam builds a "subcultural capital," in Bourdieu's terms. And how might we listen to this "subcultural capital"?

Structural listening/easy listening: How to listen to *Vitalogy, Pearl Jam*, or *Riot Act*?

How do the listeners of Pearl Jam's music behave? How adequate is the listening of the Pearl Jam listener-type? Obviously the type of listening is related to critical thinking or identity thinking; in other words, the higher the adequacy of listening, the higher the understanding of the musical work. Therefore, the absolutely adequate musical behavior is one that structurally listens to the musical work. To listen structurally means to listen consciously to a piece of music. This implies recognizing all its parts, perceiving the parts and their relationship to the whole, and reconstructing the sound architecture of the piece. The expert listener, then, has this structural-listening; which means that he thinks with his ear and listens with his mind. Music is for him a network of sense, as Adorno considers. In his musical theory, the expert listener is not as cold as he seems. In fact, in *Dissonanzen* the German philosopher makes it clear that listening consciously should not be understood as cold and outwardly reflective behavior.

It seems that this type of listening and musical behavior defines the attitude of music professionals. At the antipodes of this musical excellence, we have easy listening. This type of listening is distracted. It is characterized by inattention, dispersion, or lack of concentration. Sometimes, the listener concentrates on some part of the piece, usually the "catchy hooks." These catchy hooks are brief, and therefore, the behavior of this type of listener is also brief and irregular. Their listening is atomistic and interrupted. According to Adorno, easy listening is the mode of listening encouraged by the music industry, which makes songs like the textile industry makes bikinis. Hence, the listeners hear how they consume (compulsively). In a few words, music is an instrument for something else rather than an aim in itself. For example, this musical behavior corresponds to the attitude of the emotional listener, the entertained listener, or the cultural consumer.

On the one hand, Pearl Jam's albums demand a partially elevated listening, listening that is halfway between easy listening and structural listening. The music of Pearl Jam demands an attentive and adequate listening, although surely not as much as Webern's *String Trio* might.[20] On the other hand, although their music is not exclusively an instrument to liberate our libido or to manage our instinctive economy, the emotional component is a *conditio sine qua non*. In fact, on many occasions, unbridled passion is a constitutive element of the work. Finally, the Pearl Jam listener understands the historical violence of the Pearl Jam chords. For all these reasons, we consider that the listener of this Seattle-based group is usually "a good listener,"[21] in Adornian terms. He is the good listener whose listening is adequate, though not absolutely adequate. He listens to the echoes of history and its form-content, and does so with passion and reflection.

The Pearl Jam listener is also a negotiator. In his lecture entitled "Prêter l'oreille," Peter Szendy says that "to listen is to negotiate (*écouter c'est négocier*)." Proper listening to Pearl Jam's popular music requires negotiation. This listener is constantly negotiating between intellectualism and catharsis, between adequate and structural listening and enjoyment (*jouissance*). Without falling into cultural conformism, this listener is a progressive good listener. Consequently, this type of listening leads to ethical-aesthetic behavior: critical thinking. For simplicity, let us call this behavior "postmodern listening," which we will claim embodies the spirit of the Pearl Jam listener. So, this "postmodern listening" is a true hybridization. It is an active and structured listening, but sometimes a relaxed one. It is reflective, but brutally emotional and sensory.

In conclusion, Adorno prudently maintained that what he describes are pure ideals and categories of listeners, or types of musical behavior, that do not always coincide with reality. Today, the development and quality of mass music clearly shows that the strict separation between listeners and types of musical behavior is more complicated than ever. Agnès Gayraud knows this, and so she has reinterpreted these categories.

In *Dialectique de la pop*, the French philosopher asks herself how to analyze pop music material through listening. Gayraud's first claim consists in the simple fact of talking about pop music material (*le matériau musical de la pop*) instead

---

[20] In *Dissonanzen* Adorno uses this example because he believes that this difficult and fragmented piece by Webern demands the virtuosity of an expert listener.
[21] According to Adorno, the good listener is a category superior to the cultural consumer and inferior to the expert listener. He/she is not absolutely aware of the structure of the musical work, but he/she is able to connect the parts with the whole. Moreover, he/she can evaluate the piece of music, beyond the arbitrariness of taste.

of relegating the hit to a commodity. To this end, she presents three moments of listening. The first moment of listening (*la première écoute*) focuses on the specific registers of musicality, i.e., the form-song, the tonality, the colors, the sounds, the possibilities of innovation, etc. The second moment of listening (*la deuxième écoute*) studies the alteration, modulation, or distortion of sound. In other words, it analyzes how popular music sounds, mediated by the diffusion and production technologies characteristic of the modern era. Finally, the third mode of listening (*la troisième écoute*) examines *l'appropiation omnivore de la pop*, that is, Gayraud reflects on how a pop material relates musically to other pop material. She points out the porosity between the different subgenres of popular music, the inspiration in classical music compositions, the use of techniques such as sampling, etc.

In short, Gayraud restructures the types (or moments) of listening to popular music to dignify or elevate it, displaying the complexity and diversity that it has acquired throughout the twentieth century. Moreover, she demonstrates the existence of pop music material and opens the door to a new debate: can popular music be seen to progress?

Another precision concerning musical listening in the postmodern era seems pertinent: *la jouissance idéologique*, a term coined by Slavoj Zizek. This postmodern listening is the kind of hybrid listening required by certain musical works of the *Kulturindustrie*, such as Pearl Jam songs. They offer pleasure, but they unabashedly reveal the ideological mechanisms in charge of structuring the everyday, the real, and history. In other words, a song crystallizes the dialectic functioning through which the post-modern ideological effectiveness operates. The listener perceives this reality between reflection, pleasure, and fury. In this way, these artists produce subversively because they reveal the strategy of ideology/non-ideology. But they also produce symptomatically because, despite the fact that the listener is aware of ideological fantasy, he nevertheless enjoys the symptom.

Conclusion. The two faces of musical postmodernity: The dark side of grunge, also called radical popular music

For this reason, the effects of the new conditions of the postmodern era invite us to reflect upon—or think seriously about—a number of novel aesthetic problems. Are Pearl Jam masterpieces autonomous art, peripheral art, or simple commodities? Does popular music maintain its original function? Can Pearl

Jam's work be popular, radical, and self-reflective at the same time? Can popular music material be seen to progress?

Certainly, nowadays especially this rigid categorical division does not help us reflect on certain types of popular music, and from this first conclusion other statements can be derived. Musical postmodernity has two very different faces: musical merchandise and peripheral musical works. All of them are distributed by the *Kulturindustrie* and all of them invite *la jouissance idéologique*. But only the peripheral works behave radically and critically. Indeed, the cultural industry distributes musical merchandise, but also musical works that must be commercialized in order to survive in late capitalism. They all belong to the same circuit of popular music, but each of these categories constitutes a different segment of this circuit.

In Romantic aesthetics, the work of art was the result of the artist's talent, ingenuity, and excellent knowledge. The work is coherent, harmonious, and reflects the genius and virtuous subjectivity of the artist. For this reason, the public had to admire and learn from the gift of the artist's genius. Hence, art was considered vocational: the artist did not intend to make a profit, only to display his need for expression in an authentic way. However, throughout the twentieth century, many art theorists have analyzed mass music in this romantic spirit, concluding that the musical work distributed by the *Kulturindustrie* is anti-art, anti-romantic, and inauthentic. They are simply homogeneous cultural commodities, produced in a standard way that lacks originality or innovation, and whose purpose is commercialization. Certainly today it is impossible to escape the force of the cultural industry; in this Adorno was not wrong. Nevertheless, mass music has shown from its beginnings until today that it can be responsible and authentic. This is the case with Pearl Jam.

In Pearl Jam's musical work, art and society converge in content. Their grunge sound mirrors the sedimentation of historical and social tendencies. It is evident that their sound is not prefabricated, nor is the aesthetic experience planned (characteristics constantly enunciated in "On Popular Music" or "On the Fetish Character in Music and the Regression of Listening"). The formal content of the commented albums reveals and rebels, although without pain. It rebels with *jouissance idéologique*. It does not seem to resemble the artificiality and rationalization of musical merchandise. Still, there is an element of rationalization, automation, or standardization in their work: the method of distribution (and its atomized division of labor). This, however, is the only characteristic that is truly shared with musical merchandise.

This observation shows that in postmodernity, critical art is not outside the system or outside mass culture, but on the periphery of this system. The music of Pearl Jam is critical art, but it is the critical art of today (*art périphérique*). Artistic subversion is silent, it is secret resistance, and it is a muffled scream. Therefore, the lucidity of the work of groups like Pearl Jam denies that mass music constitutes a tragedy of culture. Instead, it conveys the need to rethink and dignify popular music, turning it into music elevated in entertainment or into alternative mainstream that demands a provisional aesthetic, a theory in constant movement.

Perhaps it is time to leave aside the stigma that remains latched on to mass music to this very day. Perhaps it is time to stop insisting on the pedagogical failure of the cultural industry, and to deny some of the errors that were at the root of precisely these considerations, such as the disregard for aesthetic pleasure and the opposition between entertainment and *loisir*. Thus, Christian Bethune reminds us that entertainment (*anapausis*) and leisure (*scholê*) are very different. Appealing to Aristotle's *Politics*, he explains that "in contrast to leisure which is autotelic, seeming to 'contain in and of itself pleasure, happiness or life's bliss,' amusement alone is nothing but a remedy for the exhaustion that a laborious life brings, dissociating man from his very being."[22] The problem is that Adorno associates popular music to simple amusement, and jazz to a remedy for a mutilated life. Yet, what if the songs of Pearl Jam leant themselves rather to leisure, and indeed, what to do if they don't?

Bibliography

Adorno, Theodor W. *Philosophy of New Music*, transl. by Robert Hullot-Kentor. Minneapolis: University of Minnesota Press, 2019.

Béthune, Christine. *Adorno et le jazz. Analyse d'un déni esthètique*. Paris: Klincksieck, 2003.

Cook, Deborah. *The Culture Industry Revisited: Theodor W. Adorno on Mass Culture*. Lanham, MD: Rowman & Littlefield Publishers, 1993.

Eagleton, Terry. *The Ideology of the Aesthetic*. Oxford: Blackwell, 1990.

Gayraud, Agnès. *Dialectique de la pop*. Paris: Éditions La Découverte, 2018.

---

[22] "...au contraire du loisir qui possède sa fin en soi et semble 'contenir en lui-même le plaisir, le bonheur et la félicité de vivre,' le simple amusement n'est en revanche qu'un remède à l'épuisement qu'entraine une vie laborieuse qui dissocie l'homme de son être" (Béthune, *Adorno et le jazz*, 140: my translation).

Keunen, Gert. *Alternative Mainstream: Making Choices in Pop Music*. Amsterdam: Valiz, 2015.

Paddison, Max. *Adorno, Modernism and Mass Culture: Essays on Critical Theory and Music*. London: Kahn &Averill, 2009.

Smith, Chris. *101 Albums That Changed Popular Music*. Oxford-New York: Oxford University Press, 2009.

11

Pearl Jam/Nirvana: A Dialectical Vortex that Revolves Around the Void

Alessandro Alfieri

Philosophical history as the research of origin is the form that, in the most remote extremes, in the apparent excess of development, reveals the configuration of the idea as the configuration of the totality, characterized by the possibility of a meaningful juxtaposition of these extremes.[1]

Theodor W. Adorno started *Philosophy of New Music* with this quote by Walter Benjamin. In his thought, the "extremes" that activate the dialectical dynamic were the artists of the early twentieth century, Arnold Schönberg and Igor Stravinsky. Sure, it is a heretical act, starting from this Adornian perspective, to understand a specific phenomenon of rock of the 1990s like Grunge, considering above all that popular music was anathema to Adorno.[2] Pearl Jam and Nirvana were the Grunge dialectical polarities in opposition. If we can speak of "opposition," this must be seen as the result of two mutual and complementary figures, in the sense of the spiral or "vortex" of which Benjamin speaks in these words ("meaningful juxtaposition of these extremes"). This spiral swirls around a fire: an abyssal void that is symbol of the Generation X of the 1990s, the same generation of grunge, a cultural and musical movement born in Seattle in the same decade, which represented the voice of an era.

The relation of dialectical complementarity between Pearl Jam and Nirvana is a vortex where the two bands often exchanged their parts. It is impossible to place them on opposite fronts in a definitive and clear way. It would be a mistake

---

[1] Theodor W. Adorno, *Philosophy of New Music* (Minneapolis-London: Minnesota University Press, 2007), 7.
[2] Theodor W. Adorno, "On Popular Music," *Studies in Philosophy and Social Science* 9, no. 1 (1941): 17–48. It is also true that the relation between Adorno's philosophy and popular music is more complex than it seems: see Colin J. Campbell, Samir Gandesha, and Stefano Marino (ed.), *Adorno and Popular Music: A Constellation of Perspectives* (Milano-Udine: Mimesis International, 2019).

to relegate the "vitalistic" dimension to the commercial circuit and the nihilistic dimension to the sphere of independent production connected to more spontaneous circuits. The message of death and catastrophe of the imaginary of many rock bands of the nineties was well received by the market, and was sometimes used to create and pilot products designed and planned ad hoc:

> In the world of rock music these are often connected to the perceived honesty, or authenticity, of the performer, and are grounded in the centuries-old division between "art" and commerce. In the case of grunge, the tension between these was often made explicit by the main players involved in the scene, but this "knowing" and ironic approach had surprisingly little impact on the way in which notions of authenticity have still been used to determine the worth of grunge. Of particular note is the way that academic enquiry into grunge has been surprisingly dismissive of the movement, often because of its commercial success or because it is constructed as not being "political" enough.[3]

The 1980s, after the intense political passions that characterized the 1960s and 1970s, represented the full realization of the consumerist-hedonistic utopia in the social sphere. Revolutionary and political violence was translated into extravagance, and political commitment was replaced by a season based on the principles of stylization and theatricality. The void of the 1990s expressed the sense of dissatisfaction of a whole generation, who were as far from political passions as they were from "yuppies' way of life" and "party style": Grunge created a community composed of individuals isolated from each other, and disinterested in communicating with the outside world.

Entertainment was the essence of 1980s' culture, satisfying the need for pleasure and easing social tensions. In the plasticized worlds of the first Metal bands (Judas Priest, Iron Maiden) and the New Romantic bands (Duran Duran, Spandau Ballet), and as with the impetuosity of Guns N' Roses, the most important norm was the "law of fun." In those years the English New Wave (Joy Division) posed a deeper and sharper sensibility to that imaginary, because New Wave reflected the frustration of those who could not identify with the consumerist triumph of the 1980s. Grunge was born from this dimension, as a musical and cultural movement that defined the closure of the 1980s and the advent of the 1990s. Grunge bands responded to the hedonistic hyper-semiotization with a return to essentiality, in terms of image and in the musical construction of the songs. Compared to the cult

---

[3] Catherine Strong, *Grunge: Music and Memory* (Farnham: Ashgate, 2011), 15.

of the excess of the 1980s, there is a reduction of the adrenalinic intensity of rock. The new bands (Nirvana, Pearl Jam, Alice in Chains, etc.) sing about the depression and the nihilism of the end of the millennium. They are introverted and intimistic, and their stylistic sobriety is the opposite of the exaggerations of Metal.

Drugs, from amplification of the "doors of perception" and from the beginning of "high fun," became means of self-harm: a nihilistic escape for those who find no sense in what surrounds them or in what past generations of young people believed. The diffusion of the phenomenon of depression in the 1990s paradoxically arose in an era of expansion of well-being. The society of well-being became sick by developing pathologies such as bulimia, anorexia, various forms of new addictions and mental disorders that lead to the abuse of legal drugs and synthetic substances. In the happy phase of the global economy, Kurt Cobain's music was the only mirror where existential dissatisfaction recognized itself. The paradox was represented by the international success of the message of grunge, a message of pain and death, compare to that of pop stars like Madonna and Michael Jackson.

In the whole history of rock there are rivalries and dichotomies; often they are products of gossip, or of personal dislikes and envies from artists constantly at risk of losing the "throne." Nirvana's frontman Kurt Cobain, in an interview for MTV News, says he has "always hated" Pearl Jam's music but that he and Eddie Vedder have:

> had a few conversations on the phone, and he's a person I really like. I didn't like him then when I was talking shit about him all the time. Well, now I can appreciate him. I realize that the same people that like our band like their band. So why create some kind of feud over something as trite as that?[4]

Often, these dichotomies turn into musical style and composition techniques, the spirit infused in the texts and the different imaginaries. The "rivalry" or permanent tension, however latent, that characterized the careers of the two most successful bands of the Seattle grunge scene, especially at the beginning of their careers, offers us significant elements. On the one hand Pearl Jam—today one of the most celebrated and significant active rock bands—could be considered, with some reservations, to be on the side of the "vitalistic" dynamic rock of the 1990s and 2000s:

---

[4] Eddie Vedder, quoted in Jonathan Cohen and Mark Ian Wilkerson (ed.), *Pearl Jam Twenty* (New York: Simon & Schuster, 2011), 116.

Pearl Jam has continued to release albums but their music now bears less resemblance to grunge. They have, however, more than any other band, attempted to adhere to the grunge anti-commercial ethos, through refusing to co-operate with typical corporate rock strategies such as releasing film clips and singles.[5]

On the other hand, there is the experience of Nirvana, including the tragic end of their frontman Kurt Cobain. It was perhaps the crudest and most disruptive manifestation of nihilistic rock carried out by self-destructive impulse. It is very important to understand how original grunge at the turn of the 1980s and 1990s condensed at the same time as the opposing forces that unraveled in isolation in Pearl Jam and Nirvana. In other words, even if the roots were common and shared, the fact that the artistic and existential choices and experiences were practically opposed better explains the reasons for the "rivalry" of the two bands.

Jennifer Le Zotte talks about the centrality of the concept of cynicism for grunge: "Cynicism was the tenor and tone of the so-called Generation X ... In 1990, *Time* magazine described a subset of young Americans as 'lacking in ambition,' 'indecisive,' and 'obsessed with blaming their parents' generation for economic and political disarray.'"[6] Peter Sloterdijk in 1983 published a classic of contemporary philosophy, *Critique of Cynical Reason*, where he highlighted how cynicism was the fundamental element for understanding modern and postmodern cultures. Sloterdijk highlighted the dialectic of the concept of cynicism, a dialectic very close to our reflection on the comparison between Nirvana and Pearl Jam. It is a hard dialectical dimension: it may seem that Nirvana represents the image of the ancient *kinical* profile like Dyogenes, and its revolutionary dimension, linked to the rejection of success and social prestige, while Pearl Jam, with their triumph during several decades, would represent the modern dimension of cynicism, because of their international achievements. But, as in every real dialectical spiral, the figures change their positions: we know that Kurt Cobain was very interested in the good commercial results of Nirvana, and his band brought grunge to world fame. This is the reason for the tragic end of the Nirvana project and Cobain's life. In the time of *Nevermind*, Pearl Jam were the less commercial dimension of grunge: if Nirvana's cynicism became a self-destructive impulse—the same impulse of late capitalism—Pearl Jam's

---

[5] Strong, *Grunge: Music and Memory*, 20.
[6] Jennifer Le Zotte, *From Goodwill to Grunge: A History of Secondhand Styles and Alternative Economies* (Chapel Hill: University of North Carolina Press, 2017), 230.

kinism is the way they chose to survive during these years. Thanks to their nostalgic and melancholic vision, they survived, paradoxically becoming one of the more important rock bands of the new millennium.

The disagreements in the grunge community of Seattle were immediately evident from the beginning, in a city considered the third pole of American rock production after the duopoly represented by West Coast (Los Angeles) and East Coast (New York). Seattle, in the extreme northwest close to Canada, is an industrial city, gloomy and grey without the sun of L.A. and the cultural ferment of New York. As well as being isolated among the rocky mountains, "because it is relatively small, located at the edge—both literally and figuratively—of the cultural front, Seattle has often been a sort of also-ran, ruler of a region but a perennial runner-up in terms of national profile. This was true until grunge hit it big."[7] In this environment, the tradition of grunge had useful ground to root and then spread as a phenomenon on a global scale.

Grunge is a reinterpretation of punk, a style that fights the euphoric and false image of Reagan's America, like hardcore and straight edge movements that assumed an extreme configuration of rejection and reaction of detachment to the cult of death, of consumerism, and of appearance:

> The genre had style, sure, but it was a complete rejection of what had passed for rock chic in previous eras. Hairspray and carefully feathered locks felt fake and showy next to built-for-comfort flannels and white-boy dreads. Who needed to bathe in a tub when you could bathe daily in your own angst and ennui?[8]

The pioneers of grunge were particularly close to the experience of hardcore bands such as Minor Threat and Fugazi. In the period of the release of the album *Bleach* (1989) Nirvana undoubtedly represented the most intransigent part of grunge. Nirvana was the band that refused to come to terms with the music industry, their sound was heavy, noisy, and radically aggressive. But the idea of Kurt Cobain, that we—as consumers—are all being immersed since birth into capitalism and market rules, would have been clearly expressed on the famous cover of the album *Nevermind* (where a newborn baby swims towards a hook lured by a banknote). For Nirvana there is only the desire to rebel *tout court*, without philosophical elucubrations. Their intransigence does not express any

---

[7] Justin Henderson, *Grunge: Seattle* (Albany, NY: Roaring Forties Press, 2010), 22.
[8] Gael Fashingbauer Cooper and Brian Bellmont, *The Totally Sweet 90s: From Clear Cola to Furby, and Grunge to Whatever: The Toys, Tastes, and Trends That Defined a Decade* (New York: TarcherPerigee-Penguin, 2013), 276.

political or ideological intention. Rather, there is only the tragic awareness that it is impossible to completely get out of the dynamics that structured the consumer society of late capitalism. For this reason, the "release from pain" that should be professed by the name of the band (Nirvana) sounds almost ironic, because there is the ruthless awareness of the absence of a possible escape route.

Nirvana, contrary to what many think, did not adapt their style and music over the years to the music industry's demands; instead, the music industry and aesthetic capitalism reconfigured themselves out of their own success and their ability to speak to new generations. With grunge, the alternative culture becomes an international mass phenomenon, through the unsolvable contradiction of the fame that characterizes the approach of Kurt Cobain. Cobain claimed to detest success, while at the same time maniacally following the airings of singles on radio, and music videos on MTV, and developing paranoia when the numbers showed a slowdown. The philosopher Mark Fisher clearly focuses on the paradox of Kurt Cobain:

> In his dreadful lassitude and objectless rage, Cobain seemed to give wearied voice to the despondency of the generation that had come after history, whose every move was anticipated, tracked, bought and sold before it had even happened. Cobain knew that he was just another piece of spectacle, that nothing runs better on MTV than a protest against MTV; knew that his every move was a cliché scripted in advance, knew that even realizing it is a cliché. . . . Cobain's death confirmed the defeat and incorporation of rock's Utopian and promethean ambitions. . . . Here, even success meant failure, since to succeed would only mean that you were the new meat on which the system could feed.[9]

Nirvana came from Mudhoney's intransigence and radicality more than Pearl Jam, even if Eddie Vedder's band had closer creative relations with them; in addition to Mudhoney, from a creative point of view, Nirvana had within them more Melvins than the great bands of the history of rock. From Melvins, Nirvana acquired not only the heavy style of the rhythmic sessions and the essential crudeness of the sound, but above all the ironic and grotesque vision, a renewed exaltation of the "I don't mind" attitude of American Punk, which translates into suffered litanies or in equally inconclusive cries of anger. There is nothing to build because nothing can be built on emptiness. So "I don't mind" becomes precisely "Nevermind." This message was perfect for the imaginary of the

---

[9] Mark Fisher, *Capitalist Realism: Is There No Alternative?* (Alresford: John Hunt Publishing-Zero Books, 2009), 9–10.

popular culture of the 1990s: hence the dialectical contortion determined by the release of *Nevermind*, and Kurt Cobain and Nirvana became a worldwide phenomenon. The suicidal and self-destructive impulse, the exaltation of drugs as a self-injurious instrument; the scruffy and dirty outfit without the theatricality of punk and metal, which are much more similar to the style of clochards, all became powerful factors of the visual and expressive grunge proposal. We are talking about Generation X: young people who cannot take anything from the yuppie hedonism and the excessive extravagance of the 1980s. Generation X was conscious of its own impotence, perpetually bored and disgusted by reality, indifferent to the fate of society, cynically bound to its own mediocre everyday life. Intransigence became an effective commercial product, and self-destruction became a vehicle of commercial seduction.

Ten is the debut studio album by Pearl Jam. It was released one month before *Nevermind*. *Ten* was originally viewed with suspicion by the pioneers of grunge because it was more conciliatory and closer to rock tradition; more "intellectual." Musically, it appeared more moderate and attentive to production and arrangements—in some ways, it seemed more "bourgeois": "The guys in Pearl Jam—Eddie Vedder, Stone Gossard, Mike McCready, Jeff Ament, and Matt Cameron—have turned grunge into good and into gold, and they've done it right, generously and consistently giving back to the community and the world."[10] Pearl Jam didn't come from Melvins but they came from Led Zeppelin, Bruce Springsteen, and Neil Young. The tracklist of *Ten* had more ballads than any other grunge albums and it immediately demonstrated a more pronounced social and political attitude than Nirvana ("Jeremy"). However, it became immediately clear that the real star (the only real star in the history of rock music of the 1990s) was Kurt Cobain. Cobain was the one who spread his face massively across the five continents, mass media talked about him and his private life. Conversely, any request for an interview sent to Vedder was destined to be cancelled or refused. The two dialectical figures changed their position, like a vortex: Pearl Jam represented the less commercial line of grunge, which was more sophisticated and artistic, while Nirvana, precisely because of their intransigence, became a commercial fashion and social phenomenon. When Cobain said that he wanted to record a pop music album, he considered that he understood the demonic and deleterious side of his project, because the intentionality of the global market had changed in relation to the model he

---

[10] Henderson, *Grunge: Seattle*, 248–9.

created with Nirvana. It was a perverse contamination of late capitalism, a consumerist symbolic universe, and the music industry. Pearl Jam's higher maturity allowed them to protect themselves from the destructive and self-destructive processes represented by aesthetic and cultural capitalism. Nirvana was more related to metropolitan culture, while Pearl Jam represented the most "lumberjack" and ascetic dimension.

But the dialectical vortex did not stop: when Cobain shot himself in the head leaving the whole world and two generations completely bewildered, Nirvana became and remains to this day an absolute cult. The diabolical coherence and cynicism of Cobain responds to the lost intransigence of Nirvana's music. The tragic death of Cobain was the answer to his "guilty" world and media fame: he returned to be the authentic opponent and the real and unique enemy of the same system under which he had remained a victim. The divinization of Kurt Cobain is comparable only to the figure of Jim Morrison. We could speak about a really "Christical sacrifice" in that his suicide could be interpreted as having redeemed the whole of Generation X, because people who found themselves in the post-Cobain emptiness preferred not to continue with that way of self-destruction, and had become "real," and no longer merely theatrical and proclaimed. After Cobain's death, Generation X reconsidered their cultural identity and looked for new stimuli and new opportunities of "sense," as we will see with the Foo Fighters project by Nirvana's drummer Dave Grohl.

In the period after Nirvana, the scene was largely dominated by Pearl Jam. With punctual record releases of excellent workmanship, and with products made by professional musicians, Pearl Jam recorded dizzying numbers in all the last decades. The current success of Pearl Jam comes precisely from here: nostalgia and *memoria* (which Cobain sang in "Come As You Are" as a font of suicide) of a betrayed generation become the extreme element for the creation of a new sense. It is a melancholic sense, to react to the catastrophe that everyone is experiencing day by day. These are two profoundly different visions of music and existence. Nirvana were the strongest manifestation of self-destructive rock. Paradoxically, Pearl Jam were able to get out of this infernal self-destructiveness thanks to nostalgia, and also to "retromania," rejected in a particular way. Nirvana sank into the void and Kurt Cobain sought escape into self-destruction; Pearl Jam, starting from their first album *Ten*, immediately returned to the "past," finding a refuge in the melancholic projection of memories, and redeeming the drama in the narrative approach. Nostalgia and melancholy could become a social evil, as well as an opportunity to transfigure the pain and the void in a narrative form. Show business knows well this opportunity, which is also a phenomenon: consider the triumph of bands like Pearl Jam and Radiohead, which have survived the decades and the passage of the millennium, defying the abyss of self-destruction to get to the present day in different ways. This tendency to recover the past, in addition to the nostalgic afflatus, finds another way of expression in the projection and the attraction to primeval origin, an absolute past that precedes our existence itself. The tribal dimension, as a refuge from the catastrophe of the present and the void of sense, is the solution of several band of the Nu Metal scene (Sepultura, Soulfly, Incubus) but it is also part of the imaginary of Pearl Jam, evident in a lot of songs, and overall in albums such as *No Code*.

Every new album release, new tour, and the surrounding events, are based on the attraction for an "immediate past," especially for Pearl Jam, because it is not, each and every time, the return of an "old rock band." The career of Pearl Jam has never been interrupted, and has renewed its nostalgic potential during the band's creative experience. Aged fans enjoy the music they already know, and the band enjoy their own legend and re-establish contact with fans.[11] Pearl Jam's proposal, both on the occasion of live sets and the release of new albums, is always full of melancholy. As Justin Henderson says, the live dimension has always been the great paradox of grunge culture, because live concerts of grunge bands were the recovery of energetic and "vitalistic" impulses:

> This is one of the paradoxes of grunge: while so many of the songs from the period can be tortured downers, what people got from seeing these bands play—what the bands put out, onstage—was the opposite. The shows were celebrations, parties, carnivals. There was plenty of rage and mania, howling mad stage diving, and thrashing, but ask anyone if they had a good time at an early Pearl Jam or Nirvana show and the answer is always an unqualified YES! This is life-affirming music about anguish and rage.[12]

Today, live concerts of the few bands surviving the millennium passage, like Pearl Jam, don't have "rage," and shows are not a celebration of affirmative tendency. They are "requiems," where the vital fervor of their music refers dialectically to the dramatic sense of history and the experience of their audience. "Nostalgia" is a search for help in the narrative transfiguration and in the

---

[11] See Fernando Rennis, *Politics. La musica angloamericana nell'era di Trump e della Brexit* (Roma: Arcana, 2018).
[12] Henderson, *Grunge: Seattle*, 170.

celebration of the mythical past; for this reason, once again nostalgia could be an impulse of death rather than of life. And yet, paradoxically, nostalgia is the opportunity that Pearl Jam found for surviving and to avoid perishing tragically like their "rivals," because, as Marcuse says, "[t]he authentic utopia is grounded in recollection."[13] In 2000, for Eddie Vedder and his band, the catastrophe became real: the death and tragedy broke into life and music, with the terrible incident at Roskilde Festival in Denmark. How could it have been possible to continue singing about the past and nostalgia now they had been contaminated by horror? The guilt for this terrible event, for Pearl Jam, is similar to the guilt that some people feel when they lose someone. Since this incident, the band found a "way of redemption" in the organization of multiple charity events in the fans' names. In this way, they didn't become victims of mourning, but tried to create a purpose from these senseless deaths, through the "memory" of these lives, highlighting the themes of special and immortal. Vedder wrote the lyrics of "I Am Mine," before the first live show by Pearl Jam since the incident. The song reflects his point of view and his endeavor to grieve, because it was the only way to make their music survive; in the lyrics, Vedder laments the lack of empathy for the tragedy, but then he gets over the blame, focusing instead on the feeling of loss: "And the feeling, it gets left behind / All the innocence lost at one time / . . . / There's no need to hide . . . / We're safe tonight."[14]

Death drives and self-destructive trends were deep in Nirvana. Pearl Jam adopted the "nostalgia for the present" that characterizes the current thirty to forty year old: a vision between anhedonic nihilism and vitalism, because the attempt to answer the tragedy of Nirvana is immediately bent to melancholy, like a "rearview mirror" ("Rearviewmirror," 1993), or like a desperate sense of "immortality" ("Immortality," 1994). The death and dark imaginary of many rock bands of the Nineties was well received by the global market, and driven and determined by the market itself in the creation of products designed and planned ad hoc, such as for the neo-emo season at the end of the first decade of the 2000s. As Walter Benjamin said at the beginning of the twentieth century, the market knows well the "sex appeal of the inorganic," and the ability of goods and cultural productions to turn the mortuary and the destructive impulse to their advantage. This deathly imaginary is perfect for adolescents, and perfect in

---

[13] Herbert Marcuse, *The Aesthetic Dimension: Towards a Critique of Marxist Aesthetics* (Boston: Beacon Press, 1978), 73.
[14] Pearl Jam, "I Am Mine," in *Riot Act* (2002).

relation to the sense of void of the 1990s. Depression, hatred of life, and the exaltation of self-harm and death become tools of social recognition; they are figures of the spirit of the market, even when they would seem functional in opposing the status quo. It is the dialectical movement of capitalism, which incorporates its own negation. In the musical and visual grunge style, the proverbial aversion to the establishment becomes the best brand for the establishment itself. The denial of mercantile vitalism is a further strengthening of the global, commercial, and cultural order: "the market, which absorbs equally well (although with often quite sudden fluctuations) art, anti-art, and non-art, all possible conflicting styles, schools, forms."[15] As Fisher says: "an effective anti-capitalism must be a rival to Capital, not a reaction to it; there can be no return to pre-capitalist territorialities. Anti-capitalism must oppose Capital's globalism with its own, authentic, universality."[16]

Thus, it often happens that the most destructive music, the one most inspired by messages of defeatism and death, finds a dominant position in mass culture. Self-destruction and death represent the fires of the elliptical orbit of late-capitalism, so it is not strange that nihilism through popular culture is perfectly at ease in this self-destructive path. On the other hand, there are some small bastions that are useful against the suffocating machine of consumption. For Cobain's orphans, the sense of despair and death circulated in different ways throughout rock towards the second half of the 1990s: 1994 was the year of the release of Beck's schizophrenic citation game of *Black Mellow*, Jeff Buckley's litanic yearning of *Grace*, but also *Live Through This* by Hole, and *The Downward Spiral* by Nine Inch Nails. We also think about *Dookie* by Green Day, *Smash* by Offspring, and *Punk in Drublic* by NOFX, essential albums of the Neo-Punk wave where the sense of catastrophe and violent impetuosity is present. The release of Pearl Jam's album *Vitalogy* comes up against these "negative" forces in the same year as Cobain's death. Another capital album of hard rock and grunge of that year is *Superunknown* by Soundgarden. In the Seattle scene, Soundgarden were the expression of the most precious and sophisticated heavy rock from a technical perspective, without ever crossing the border of metal as Alice in Chains, did but lying in the orbit of the hard rock tradition (Deep Purple, Led Zeppelin). Chris Cornell's tragic parable is indicative: *Superunknown*'s tracklist

---

[15] Herbert Marcuse, "Repressive Tolerance," in *A Critique of Pure Tolerance*, ed. Robert Paul Wolff and Barrington Moore Jr. (Boston: Beacon Press, 1969), 88.
[16] Fisher, *Capitalist Realism*, 79.

testified a clear depressive and nihilistic disposition ("The Day I Tried to Live," "Fell on Black Days," "Like Suicide," and "Black Hole Sun").

In the following years, we find the myth of the bands that "survived" the 1990s (precisely, "immortality"). Outside the period of their best productions, beginning from the early 2000s, there is exclusively the endeavor of procrastinating this myth, projecting it nostalgically on the past. It is a past-not-too-past (Pearl Jam as adolescence's rock band, but still in activity): it is useful for the "regret industry," which today offers products already widely distributed, without the need to invest in originality. *Memoria* and "nostalgia" to try to fill the void of the present, a psychological strategy for resisting the dispersion of sense and death drive, but applied to the past and not able to project the present and the future. As Mark Fisher says, our culture "is excessively nostalgic, given over to retrospection, incapable of generating any authentic novelty. ... The inability to make new memories: a succinct formulation of the postmodern impasse."[17]

This is the catastrophe of a generation that has never really become adult, and is linked to the "retro-maniac" cult professed by Simon Reynolds. Nostalgia is present from the first songs of Pearl Jam, both in the arrangements and in the lyrics of Vedder: "Nothingman" (1994), "Better Man" (1994), "Rearviewmirror" (1993), "Elderly Woman Behind the Counter in a Small Town" (1993: "I swear I recognize your breath"),[18] or "Black" (1991), where in the chorus we find everything "tattooed" even if it is a debut song. "Daughter"'s ending (1993) insists on the image of "[t]he shades [that] go down,"[19] and gradually the song fades away to silence. Even a song like "Present Tense" (1996), which seems an invocation not to fall into remorse, in reality doesn't have a sunny and proactive dimension at all. The lyrics say that it "[m]akes much more sense, to live in the present tense,"[20] but these words witness negatively how Pearl Jam's inspiration is always derived from the past. It is demonstrated by the cavernous musical effects lost in the space of the electric guitar in the ending refrain; after the docile arpeggio of the verse, we have a very long instrumental tail, which expresses a sort of impossible resolution and final conciliation of the song.

The melancholy dimension of regret becomes structural to the music of Pearl Jam. If Nirvana directly and ruthlessly embodied the sense of disorientation of the "void" that characterized the 1990s, Pearl Jam stemmed the self-destructive

---

[17] Ibid., 59–60.
[18] Pearl Jam, "Elderly Woman Behind the Counter in a Small Town," in *Vs.* (1993).
[19] Pearl Jam, "Daughter," in *Vs.* (1993).
[20] Pearl Jam, "Present Tense," in *No Code* (1996).

impulse. They covered the atrocity of the void of the 1990s with a veil, on several occasions through the adoption of a tribal imaginary that projected their work onto an absolute and primordial past, as a refuge from the misfortunes of the contemporary age. But above all, they survived thanks to the adoption of a typical blues sensitivity—linked above all to the tradition of Neil Young's folk blues. Their nostalgia represented the opportunity for a transfiguration of pain in a narration, often declined in the past. The vortex of the two perspectives has continued to rotate incessantly around an indefinable fire that can never be translated into music: it is what has always been lost, the impossibility of full adhesion to existence, looked directly into the eyes on one side, quenched in the heartbreaking tale pointing back to the past on the other.

Bibliography

Adorno, Theodor W. "On Popular Music." *Studies in Philosophy and Social Science* 9, no. 1 (1941): 17–48.

Adorno, Theodor. W. *Philosophy of New Music*, translated by Robert Hullot-Kentor. Minneapolis-London: University of Minnesota Press, 2007.

Campbell Colin J., Samir Gandesha, and Stefano Marino (eds). *Adorno and Popular Music: A Constellation of Perspectives*, Milano-Udine: Mimesis International, 2019.

Fashingbauer Cooper, Gael and Brian Bellmont. *The Totally Sweet 90s: From Clear Cola to Furby, and Grunge to Whatever: The Toys, Tastes, and Trends That Defined a Decade*. New York: TarcherPerigee-Penguin, 2013.

Fisher, Mark. *Capitalist Realism. Is There No Alternative?* Winchester-Washington: Zero Books, 2009.

Henderson, Justin. *Grunge: Seattle*. Albany, NY: Roaring Forties Press, 2010.

Le Zotte, Jennifer. *From Goodwill to Grunge: A History of Secondhand Styles and Alternative Economies*. Chapel Hill: University of North Carolina Press, 2017.

Marcuse, Herbert. "Repressive Tolerance." In *A Critique of Pure Tolerance*, edited by Robert Paul Wolff and Barrington Moore, 81–117. Boston: Beacon Press, 1969.

Marcuse, Herbert. *The Aesthetic Dimension: Towards a Critique of Marxist Aesthetics*. Boston: Beacon Press, 1978.

Rennis, Fernando. *Politics. La musica angloamericana nell'era di Trump e della Brexit*. Roma: Arcana, 2018.

Sloterdijk, Peter. *Critique of Cynical Reason*, translated by Michael Eldred. Minneapolis-London: University of Minnesota Press, 1987.

Strong, Catherine. *Grunge: Music and Memory*. Ashgate: Farnham, 2011.

Wilkerson, Mark Ian and Jonathan Cohen (eds). *Pearl Jam Twenty*. New York: Simon & Schuster, 2011.

12

The Tide on the Shell: Pearl Jam and the Aquatic Allegories of Existence

Andrea Schembari

To my brother Alessandro, my uncle Salvo and my friend Marco, who shared with me their small, dreamy, heroic cassettes; and to Luigi, the "same old friend."

Introduction

Since their debut album *Ten*, a significant part of the lyrics of Pearl Jam has explicitly made reference to spaces and geographies, animated and inanimate beings, natural events, and human actions variously connected to the element of water. Seas and rivers, ships and whales, and also waves, currents, and the human interactions with them, they all form a concrete imagery, which seems to be drawn "directly from matter," and according to which "[t]he eye assigns them names, but only the hand truly knows them" and "[a] dynamic joy touches, moulds, and refines them."[1]

These aquatic epiphanies—in their declinations and in their intense plasticity—although sometimes carrying metaphors,[2] are part of continuous poetic-narrative structures that are best suited to be read in an allegorical key,[3]

---

[1] Gaston Bachelard, *Water and Dreams. An Essay on the Imagination of Matter* (Dallas: The Pegasus Foundation, 1999), 1.
[2] While any attempt to fully explain the mechanism of the best known among rhetorical figures proves unsatisfactory, here we use the term "metaphor" according to the most common and current definitions of "substitution of one word with another whose literal sense bears some resemblance to the literal sense of the substituted word"; see Bice Mortara Garavelli, *Manuale di retorica* (Milano: Bompiani, 2004), 160 (my translation).
[3] That is to say that, even in the absence of metaphors, they can be composed "of words all used in the proper sense, and yet represent (symbolize) something else"; see Mortara Garavelli, *Manuale di retorica*, 259 (my translation).

as possible figurations of certain aspects of existence. Possible, let me reiterate it: as the present contribution certainly does not claim to reveal the true meaning of the band's lyrics (born with and for music, so that the instrumental line influences the measure and rhythm of the verses and, consequently, the lexical choices), but rather aims to seek an *intentio operis* (work's purpose) that does not call into question the *intentio auctoris* (author's purpose), and indeed integrates it while respecting the text that transmits it.[4]

From Heraclitus' *panta rhei* to Baumann's "modern liquidity," the history of Western thought has often evoked water and its contexts to generate analogies and models of existence, which art and literature—for their part—have then helped to spread, intentionally or not. In my view, Pearl Jam have also been participating in this effort of interpretation and sharing for thirty years, and their lyrics frequently revolved around three large tropes that—with different variations and lexical and rhetorical combinations—depict fundamental issues of the experience of living: navigation, the ocean, the river. This chapter aims to propose a first (and certainly not exhaustive) attempt to illuminate these three dimensions or emblems of the aquatic world in the lyrics of Pearl Jam, through the selected and focused words of philosophers, poets, and storytellers who recognized in those dimensions the mighty evocative force of our "fragile thing / This life we lead."[5]

To sail, to live (to live, perchance to shipwreck)

There is something paradoxical and at the same time extraordinarily intuitive in the fact that "human beings living on land nevertheless prefer, in their imagination, to represent their overall condition in the world in terms of a sea voyage."[6] This correlation has known, throughout the history of Western thought, several declinations. There was a time when voluntarily embarking on a sea voyage amounted to the "transgression of a mythical prohibition,"[7] chosen by human beings at their own peril; and if this subversive choice was not avoidable,

---

[4] See Umberto Eco, *On Literature* (Orlando-Austin-New York-San Diego-Toronto-London: Harcourt, 2004), 121.
[5] Pearl Jam, "Sirens," in *Lightning Bolt* (2013).
[6] Hans Blumenberg, *Shipwreck with Spectator* (Cambridge, MA-London: The MIT Press, 1997), 8.
[7] Remo Bodei, "Distanza di sicurezza," in Hans Blumenberg, *Naufragio con spettatore* (Bologna: il Mulino, 1985), xii (my translation).

"the representation of danger on high seas serve[d] only to underline … the safety and serenity of the harbor in which a sea voyage reache[d] its end."[8]

If we look at the texts of the first songs composed by Pearl Jam (and we leave out for the time any consideration on the specific means used to face the sea), already the protagonist of "Oceans" seems to confirm Blumenberg's assumption, when he asserts his confidence in the return to shore and the expectation of reuniting with those waiting for him: "The sea will rise… / Please stand by the shore… / … / I will be… / There once more."[9] A few years later, that same protagonist annotated on a list the wish (unachievable, at that point?) to be "a sailor with someone who waited for [him]," implicitly acknowledging navigation as a perennial state of existence but still relying on the hope that there will be *teloi* along the way, a port to moor or someone to rejoin. His attitude oscillates between needs of security and stability ("the evidence … the grounds … the pedal brake") and desires for exceptions and discontinuity with respect to a pre-established order ("a neutron bomb [which] once … could go off / … a sacrifice, … somehow still lived on"[10]).

That sailor, by the way, had already made an appearance in 1994, in a song showing him "[w]inded … drifting by the storm";[11] and it is in that situation of extreme danger that he relies on a kind of "chancy hope, a wager,"[12] based on awareness of the immanent turbulence of life ("[l]ittle secrets, tremors…turned to quake… / The smallest oceans still get…big, big waves…"[13]), and declined in terms of a new resolution ("[I]'ll decide…take the dive"[14]), of the choice of a new route: "Turns the bow back, tows and…drops the line…"[15]

In short, in the years between *Ten* and *Vitalogy* Pearl Jam's lyrics show the emergence of a new attitude, inspired by the "*vous êtes embarqué*" of the mathematician and philosopher Blaise Pascal, who is credited with one of the most significant crystallizations of the nautical metaphor as a paradigm of existence. The most famous, and in some ways "scandalous," of his *Pensées* (*Thoughts*) invites indeed human beings to solve the dilemma of faith in God in terms of a bet that no one can escape: "wager you must; there is no option, you

---

[8] Blumenberg, *Shipwreck with Spectator*, 7.
[9] Pearl Jam, "Oceans," in *Ten* (1991).
[10] Pearl Jam, "Wishlist," in *Yield* (1998).
[11] Pearl Jam, "Tremor Christ," in *Vitalogy* (1994).
[12] Bodei, "Distanza di sicurezza," xiii (our translation).
[13] Pearl Jam, "Tremor Christ."
[14] Ibid.
[15] Ibid.

have embarked on it."[16] But in navigation, Pascal asserts, the sea man must always perceive the imminence of the shipwreck:

> We sail over a vast expanse, ever uncertain, ever adrift, carried to and fro. To whatever point we think to fix and fasten ourselves it shifts and leaves us; and if we pursue it escapes our grasp, slips away, fleeing in eternal flight. Nothing stays for us. That is our condition, natural, yet most contrary to our inclination; we have a burning desire to find a sure resting place and a final fixed basis whereon to build a tower rising to the Infinite; but our whole foundation cracks, and the earth yawns to the abyss.[17]

More than a Pascalian bet of faith, however evoked by its last emblematic line, "Thremor Christ" already contains the seed of the meditation on the "all-encompassing trip," on how to "live in the present tense," neither "re-digesting past regrets"[18] nor building the future on the obsessive implementation of an already established and preplanned program.[19] Not by chance, in other lines of *Vitalogy* itself the ocean is invoked so that it "swell, dissolves 'way [the] past,"[20] to the point that "[w]on't even know [we]'ve left";[21] however, consciously and willingly accepting the immanent experience of navigation and its alternate fortunes is above all an experience of extreme awareness of our finiteness.

As Pascal urged to "cease to look for security and stability"[22] because "[o]ur reason is ever cheated by misleading appearances,"[23] so Pearl Jam—a few years after the reference to the new "existential paradigm" that has emerged from *Vitalogy*—expressed their afterthought ("I had a false belief / I thought I came here to stay / We're all just visiting / All just breaking like waves"[24]). This seems to testify a new awareness that would have been defined more precisely in *Yield* and *Binaural*.

---

[16] Blaise Pascal, *Pascal's Pensées* (New York: Routledge, 2020), 115. And again: "So which will you have? What. Since you must choose, let us see what concerns you least. You have two things to lose: truth and good, and two things to stake: your reason and your will, your knowledge and your happiness. And your nature has two things to shun: error and misery. Your reason does not suffer by your choosing one more than the other, for you must choose. That's one point cleared. But your happiness? Let us weigh gain and loss in calling heads that God is. Reckon these two chances: if you win, you win all; if you lose, you lose naught. Then do not hesitate, wager that He is" (ibid.).
[17] Ibid., 29.
[18] Pearl Jam, "Present Tense," in *No Code* (1996).
[19] In addition to those already mentioned, see the line "Take my time. . .not my life" (Pearl Jam, 'Tremor Christ').
[20] Pearl Jam, "Last Exit," in *Vitalogy* (1994).
[21] Ibid.
[22] Pascal, *Pascal's Pensées*, 29.
[23] Ibid.
[24] Pearl Jam, "Push Me, Pull Me," in *Yield* (1998).

In the two albums that close the band's first decade of activity, in fact, the Pascalian opposition between our "natural" status of sailors, on the one hand, and our inclination to stability, on the other hand, configures itself as a condition or, say, a matter of fact that we cannot escape and we have to live with. So, whereas in *Grievance* we can read "I want to run into the sea / I only want life. . . . to be. . . / I just want to be. . .,"[25] it is anyway evident that the individual expresses this intention starting from a precise and indeed explicit physical place, chosen for its ideal existence (not only for when earthly life will end, as the letter of the song's lyrics suggests): there, where "the land meets high tide."[26]

According to the classical tradition, from the shoreline, "on the boundary between land and sea, . . . a mis*step* into the inappropriate and the immoderate was first taken."[27] However, if we follow Pascal, this can be read as the most perfect allegory to express the contrast between our inescapable "burning desire . . . to build a tower" and the natural erosion to which the building is destined. In fact, in the abovementioned fragment Pascal first postulated the need to accept the possible falls and sufferings of navigation as the first way out of our existential enigma, since "nothing can fix the finite between the two Infinites which enclose it and fly from it."[28]

For Pascal, the results of this inference were—as has been already mentioned—the argument of the bet and the "convenience" that is inherent in the choice to live in faith in God: a seemingly unavoidable choice ("you *must* choose") but implying at least a "finite freedom, . . . the intervention of freedom in the order of knowledge."[29] In my interpretation, Pearl Jam "humanistically" assume and rely on Pascalian assumptions, but after recognizing the need to accept the tribulations of existence (still with an image connected to the element of water: "The ocean is full 'cause everyone's crying / . . . / The sorrow grows bigger when the sorrow's denied"[30]) they claim the freedom to choose one's conduct to be held in this irreversible proceeding, that leads us from one infinity to another: "I know I was born and I know that I'll die / The in between is mine."[31]

---

[25] Pearl Jam, "Grievance," in *Binaural* (2000).
[26] Pearl Jam, "Push Me, Pull Me."
[27] Blumenberg, *Shipwreck with Spectator*, 9.
[28] Pascal, *Pascal's Pensées*, 115.
[29] Claudio Ciancio, "La libertà in Blaise Pascal," conference at Cooperativa Cattolico-democratica di Cultura, Brescia (Italy), 10 April 2015 (my translation).
[30] Pearl Jam, "I Am Mine," in *Riot Act* (2002).
[31] Ibid.

Getting into the existential condition of perennial navigation and the ever-imminent shipwreck, implies the periodic and renewed renunciation of the Epicurean position of wise and shrewd spectator of life, as it was iconically handed down by the Roman poet Lucretius.[32] In fact, this condition of salvation that we instinctively seek (and that we will always pursue, anyway) is no longer enough to transmit the stillness of detachment, not even the pleasure of being sheltered from suffering. This is something that, for example, the man of whom it is told in "Force of Nature" apparently knows (following again the diachronic development of Pearl Jam's lyrics): still shaken and aching for a broken love, he "stands the edge of the ocean / . . . / In the sand . . . upon the shore / Forevermore," while the "[h]urricane has the trade winds blowing."[33]

However, abandoning the position of safety—where one falsely supposes to be sheltered and safeguarded from the turbulence of life, and indifferent to the processes of construction and destruction of nature—does not mean letting oneself go passively with the fatal flow of the currents and the other oceanic motions that alter the course of existence. The laws of physics, after all, assure us that the sea waves, so recurrent in the lyrics of the band, in their materiality oscillate and do not advance—not referring here to the waves understood as an ontological entity that results from the perceptual experience of our eye, but rather to the water molecules that concretely substantiate them. As a result, a signage buoy left adrift we'll see rise and descend, as the wave passes, much more clearly than it progresses (and its progress will not be due to the wave motion).[34]

The sea is therefore—at the same time—a reservoir and a conductor of energy which can only be transformed and exploited by means of our movements of opposition, participation, construction, even if this requires a bet on the unknown or choices that never cease to transcend our supposed limits. Whereas

---

[32] See Titus Lucretius Carus, *Titi Lucretii Cari De Rerum Natura Libri Sex. Vol. 1* (New York: Cambridge University Press, 2009), 62: "Suave, mari magno turbantibus aequora ventis, / e terra magnum alterius ship laborem; / not quia vexari quemquamst iocunda voluptas, / sed quibus ipse malis careas quia cernere suave est . . . It is sweet, when on the great sea the winds trouble its waters, to behold from land another's deep distress; not that it is a pleasure and delight that any should be afflicted, but because it is sweet to see from what evils you are yourself." See also Blumenberg, *Shiprewck with Spectator*, 26–8.

[33] Pearl Jam, "Force of Nature," in *Backspacer* (2009).

[34] Only approaching the coast does vertical oscillation become horizontal, and the wave is able to translate its own matter (and the sandy sediment, and floating bodies) as a result of a composite action, a clash of frictions, and pressures into the increasingly emerging seabed (I am grateful to Francesco Romano for his explanation on this matter). The man of "Given to Fly" experiences the strong productive force of the subcoastal wave, which "came crashing like a fist to the jaw [and] / Delivered him wings" (Pearl Jam, "Given to Fly," in *Yield*, 1998). In the supernatural experience of the flight, that man discovers the revelation of the energies offered by the "wave-events" of life, even the most probative and painful.

"Oceans" and "Release" still seemed to attribute to that energy the power of leading or not to a desired goal, according to a fatal and inscrutable nature's plan ("The currents will shift / Glide me towards you / ... / And we're all allowed / to dream of the next / ... time we touch";[35] "I'll ride the wave / Where it takes me"[36]), the lyrics of the songs from the subsequent albums build step by step the mature awareness that "[t]his time ... will not permit any unmoving or static setting," and "[a]ll objects—the sun, the stars, the hearth, the sea and so forth—are present to man ... exclusively as part of the collective process of labor ... becom[ing] living participants in the event of life."[37]

In the manifold forms that sea voyage can take, what is required from those who choose to face it is an active cooperation in movement, a symbiotic approach to those "wave events" that—as much as it may seem an atypical navigation—is embodied in a peculiar and indeed unique way by surfing. In fact, "[s]urfing ... is always tracing routes, exploiting—constantly composing and breaking down—the strength of the wind, waves and sailor."[38] A song like "Big Wave" is a kind of manifesto of this rule of life, inasmuch as it hinges on the longest and most complex evolutionary story of humanity ("I surf in celebration / Of a billion adaptations"[39]) in order to verify it then in the field of individual experiences and in terms of a necessary and conscious reaction to bewilderments and impediments that we experience ("I scream in affirmation / Of connecting dislocations / And exceeding limitation."[40])

It is no coincidence that literature has often expressed this form of humankind's "conscious adaptation" by means of marine images or, rather, through the "chronotope"[41] of blue water. Taking up this Bakhtinian concept and applying it to some examples of the English and French novel, Margareth Cohen pointed out that:

> Bluewater is the world of the open ocean, which embodies the immense and violent forces of atmospheric elements and matter (currents, deep tides) ... [It], while unsinkable and ungovernable, is not entirely arbitrary. Although beyond any human norm, it is still subject to the laws of nature, which have their own

---

[35] Pearl Jam, "Oceans."
[36] Pearl Jam, "Release," in *Ten*.
[37] Mikhail Bakhtin, *The Dialogic Imagination* (Austin: University of Texas Press, 1981), 209.
[38] Luciano De Fiore, *Anche il mare sogna. Filosofie dei flutti* (Roma: Editori Internazionali Riuniti, 2013), 263 (my translation).
[39] Pearl Jam, "Big Wave," in *Pearl Jam* (2006).
[40] Ibid.
[41] See Bakhtin, *The Dialogic Imagination*, 84.

predictability... Those who are able to decipher these natural laws succeed only by virtue of direct experience ... This ability does not obey the laws of conventional morality, but the idea of survival of the most suitable."[42]

Direct lived or first-hand experience, that is, the abandonment of the condition of spectator, is also a necessity suggested—from Pascal onwards—by other intellectuals and philosophers, also in reference to historical processes in which we are typically actors and authors at the same time. As the Swiss historian Jacob Burckhardt put it, "[w]e would like to know the waves on which we sail across the ocean; but we ourselves are these waves";[43] or rather, in a second and more detailed version: "As soon as we rub our eyes, we clearly see that we are on a more or less fragile ship, borne along on one of the million waves that were put in motion by the revolution. We are ourselves these waves. Objective knowledge is note made easy for us."[44]

What is expressed in Burckhardt's abovementioned quotation is an "aquatic" and less syncretic version of the famous image used more than a century later by the historian Howard Zinn for the title of his book *You Can't Be Neutral on a Moving Train*[45] (which, as is well-known, is also mentioned in the lines of the song "Down"[46]). The relationship between the two assertions and the peculiarity of their meaning are evident: abandoning the state of spectator is equivalent, at a personal as well as a civil perspective, to "searching for our better way / ... thinking with our different brains," trying to "[f]ind a lighthouse in the dark stormy weather" (because—let us not forget this aspect—our inclination to safe harbor will never cease), but putting "all hands on deck"[47] (a line that will occur again in the poignant invocation to hope and participation of "Seven O'Clock").[48]

In the Pearl Jam catalogue of songs the most explicit appeal not to close in one's own enclosure—pulling a straight line from Pascal to Burckhardt—is all contained in the ironic overthrow of "Infallible,"[49] a text denouncing the arrogance and distortions of an economic progress disjointed from a true social

---

[42] Margareth Cohen, "Il mare," in *Il romanzo. IV. Temi, luoghi, eroi*, ed. Franco Moretti (Torino: Einaudi, 2003), 432 (my translation).
[43] Quoted in Blumenberg, *Shiprewck with Spectator*, 69.
[44] Quoted in Blumenberg, *Shiprewck with Spectator*, 69–70.
[45] See Howard Zinn, *You Can't Be Neutral on a Moving Train: A Personal History* (Boston: Beacon Press, 2002).
[46] See Pearl Jam, "Down," in *Lost Dogs* (2003).
[47] Pearl Jam, "Getaway," in *Lightning Bolt*.
[48] Pearl Jam, "Seven O'Clock," in *Gigaton* (2020).
[49] See Pearl Jam, "Infallible," in *Lightning Bolt* (especially the first six lines).

and cultural progress, as a result of which "[o]ur ship's come in / And it's sinking."⁵⁰ However, the exhortation is not only aimed at making individual and collective efforts of greater participation in public life. As other lines of the same song suggest,⁵¹ it is necessary that the individual's willingness to engage and participate is inspired by higher qualities, which are often neglected: not least the development of a more complete "intelligence of emotions" (freely quoting here Martha Nussbaum), which teaches us to manage in a better way the relationships between individuals or groups, and without which it will always be arduous to pursue a "progress [that] could be plausible."⁵²

In this sense, it is neither an abstract navigation nor surfing (that even teaches at "[r]iding high among the waves"⁵³) but rather swimming that probably represents the best aquatic allegory to depict the complex dynamic that incessantly weaves and dissolves one's own and others' emotions, starting with those on which the feeling of love is hinged. In order to sanction its saving power, the voice of "Amongst the Waves" invites the loved one to "go swim tonight, darling," reminding us that "[i]f not for love [we] would be drowning."⁵⁴ Once broken down in its single movements, the complex gesture of swimming reveals to us how much we should devote care and sensitivity to the composition of our relationships with others (not necessarily only with our sentimental partners), as luminously showed by these word by Paul Valéry:

> to plunge into the mass and the movement, to be active from head to toe, to roll in that pure and deep element, breathe in and breathe out the divine saltness- this for me is nearest to love ... Here ... I am the man I wish to be. My body becomes the immediate instrument of my mind, and yet the author of all its ideas. All is clarified for me. I understand to the full what love might be ... Caresses are knowledge. The lover's acts would be model of works. I know, swim! Plunge your head into the wave rolling toward you, breaking over you and rolling you.⁵⁵

---

[50] Ibid.
[51] See ibid.: "Of everything ... possible / In the hearts and minds of men / ... the biggest things / ... keep on slipping / Right through our hands."
[52] Ibid.
[53] Pearl Jam, "Among the Waves," in *Backspacer* (2009).
[54] Ibid. The fact that love is the guiding feeling to rely on in the frequent shipwrecks of life is an assertion that had already emerged in "Tremor Christ," as already seen, and in "Love Boat Captain" which claims that "towards the clear ..." while " ... Earthquakes making waves / ... / Once you hold the hand of love, ... it's all surmountable" (Pearl Jam, 'Love Boat Captain', in *Riot Act*, 2002).
[55] Paul Valéry, "Mediterrenean Impressions," in *Collected Works of Paul Valéry: Moi. Vol. 15* (New York: Princeton University Press, 2015), 26-7.

The refinement of the senses, emotions, and intellect, enclosed in the gesture of the swimmer lovers, as well as the practical, adaptive, and experiential intuition of the surfer, erase from Pearl Jam lyrics the risk that—in the middle of a shipwreck—on our "comfortable ship we do not have the courage anymore to jump into the water and start all over again from the beginning,"[56] from the "swimming *status naturalis*."[57] Those qualities, nourished and cultivated, even make it possible—far beyond the fate assigned to us as passing entities, disposable bodies in navigation—to identify oneself with the medium of water, in the claim to have lived (and in the hope of being able to live) "[a]ll this life / Like an ocean / In disguise":[58] in the lightning and fatal necessity—as one can argue—of an uninterrupted re-creation of oneself.

"The sea, the sea, perpetually renewed,"[59] as Valéry sings; or more extensively, as in Eugenio Montale's verses addressed to the Mediterranean Sea: "It was you who first told me / the petty ferment of my heart was no more / than a moment of yours; that deep in me / was your hazardous law: to be vast / and yet various fixed."[60] Once navigation and shipwreck have been accepted as parts of its own destiny, it just remains for humanity to recognize itself in the law of the sea, perhaps the only one that is capable of giving shape to the ineffable intuition with which we try to represent the first factor in our evolution: time.

"The river is within us, the sea is all about us": A matter of time

The dazzling synthesis offered by Valéry's and Montale's lyrics attempts to crystallize the inexpressible definition of time in the paradox of an unmoving motion, perpetual and mutable, in the effigy of a *sub specie maris* existence. Pearl Jam have soon begun to wonder about the "rocking horse of time,"[61] fascinated

---

[56] Blumenberg, *Shiprewck with Spectator*, 78. See also Pearl Jam, "Infallible": "Time we best begin / Here at the ending."
[57] Ibid.
[58] Pearl Jam, "Can't Keep," in *Riot Act* (2002).
[59] Paul Valéry, "Graveyard by the Sea," in *Collected Works of Paul Valéry: Poems. Vol. 1* (New York: Princeton University Press, 2015), 213. Although using here the official English translation of Valéry's poems, I would like to point out that no translation succeeds in fully rendering the logical-semantic short circuit of the original French verse, "La mer, la mer toujours recommence," which would literally play as: "The sea, the sea, *is* always recommenced."
[60] Eugenio Montale, "Mediterranean," in *Collected Poems 1920-1954* (New York: Farrar, Straus and Giroux, 1999), 67, 69.
[61] Pearl Jam, "Release."

by the constant aporias that human thinking must undergo at every attempt to delimit and fix the sense of such an elusive dimension. When compared with it—as some lyrics of Pearl Jam suggest—our existence appears as negligible ("You know time is long, and life is short"),[62] and it seems clear that there's "[n]o time to question…why'd nothing last…"[63] What really matters is, as already mentioned, to "live in the present tense,"[64] also in order not to fall into the trap of habits, like the one that cages the protagonist of "Sleight of Hand." He manages to guess—like each of us—how decisive it is to give value and quality to our time, but in the end he becomes entangled in the repetitiveness of everyday events, postponing any intention of change to the point of no return ("Til he had more time,… more time…"):[65] where he only has "[t]ime to dream"[66] what he would have wanted to be and he can only "[wave] goodbye, / To himself."[67]

However, the question concerning the understanding of time and the good use of it has been recently re-proposed, with greater complexity, by the aquatic allegories that are present in some lyrics from *Gigaton*. Here, in fact, a significant recurring of marine and river images also calls into question a very precise season in early twentieth-century European thought and poetry. In the album's first single released in January 2020, the passage that reads "[w]hen the past is the present and the future's no more / When every tomorrow is the same as before"[68] recalls the inescapable acknowledgment of the indissolubility of time which opens the first of Thomas Stearn Eliot's *Four Quartets*: "Time present and time past / Are both perhaps present in time future, / And future time contained in time past."[69]

Those lines in "Dance of the Clairvoyants"—as well as those in the "Present Tense" manifesto, in which arboreal allegories replace the aquatic ones—cannot in any way be mistaken for a declaration of nihilism. In fact, they are not meant to banish past and future from the individual's consciousness, nor do they intend to banish past and future from his/her system of ethical values or from his/her poetic imagery. This is clearly testified, for example, by a song like "Future Days" that

---

[62] Pearl Jam, "Bee Girl," in *Lost Dogs* (2003).
[63] Pearl Jam, "Last Exit," in *Vitalogy* (1994).
[64] Pearl Jam, "Present Tense."
[65] Pearl Jam, "Sleight of Hand," in *Binaural* (2000).
[66] Ibid.
[67] Ibid.
[68] Pearl Jam, "Dance of the Clairvoyants," in *Gigaton* (2020).
[69] Thomas Stearn Eliot, "Burnt Norton," in *Four Quartets* (London: Faber and Faber, 2009, ebook edition), 8.

celebrates "[o]ur future days" even if "hurricanes and cyclones raged / ... winds turned dirt to dust / ... floods they came or tides they raised ... ."[70]

Rather, what the abovementioned lines from "Dance of the Clairvoyants" convey is a full acknowledgment of the existence of a "phenomenological time" à la Husserl, in which "each actual mental process ... is necessarily an enduring one" and "find its place in an infinite continuum of duration," and in which "each *Now* of the mental process ... necessarily has its *horizon of Before* ... and also has its necessary horizon of *After*," involved in "*one* endless stream of mental processes."[71]

It is a "time of consciousness,"[72] as a long tradition of Western thought—from Augustine to Heidegger and beyond, passing through Bergson and Husserl—has defined it, the only one that humans can intuitively grasp the essence of, the "duration"[73] that substantiates it, in which the past and the future of our possibilities merge as if in an uninterrupted cross-dissolve. In this context, the present—as Husserl's original insight shows—has no *instantaneous* and therefore overtakable nature, but *nunc fluens et nunc stans* (now flowing, now standing):[74] a condition that sea and river waters clearly illustrate.

Returning to Pearl Jam, already some really short and lilting lines from "Big Wave" read: "Can't you see / The oceans size? / Defining time / And tide / Arising."[75] However, it is precisely in Pearl Jam's last studio album that this issue gets structured by showing its references to Eliotian poetry and—by reflection— to Husserl's phenomenological inquiry. "We cannot think of a time that is oceanless," Eliot wrote in the third of the *Four Quartets*, entitled "The Dry Salvages" (entirely focused on marine imagery as an allegory of time), nor "of an ocean not littered with wastage / Or of a future that is not liable / Like the past,

---

[70] Pearl Jam, "Future Days," in *Lightning Bolt* (2013). As it has been already noted for "Amongst the Waves" and "Love Boat Captain," also in this song, widely focused on the allegory of the shipwreck, the feeling of love (in this case, love understood as a sentimental relationship between two partners) offers a place for hope and new routes after the drifts of our existence.

[71] Edmund Husserl, *Ideas Pertaining to a Pure Phenomenology and to a Phenomenological Philosophy. First book: General Introduction to a Pure Phenomenology*, in *Collected Works. Vol. II* (Dordrecht, Boston, London: Kluwer Academic Publishers) 194–5, *passim* (italics in the original text).

[72] See Matteo Silva, 'Tempo della coscienza e tempo della scienza', *Rivista di Filosofia Neo-Scolastica* 94, no. 4 (2002): 707–23.

[73] See Henri Bergson, *Duration and Simultaneity* (Indianapolis: Bobbs-Merril, 1965).

[74] I'm using in his proper function of adverb the substantivized *nunc* of a well-known argument, traditionally attributed to Boethius by Thomas Aquinas: "*Nunc fluens facit tempus, nunc stans facit aeternitatem*" ("The flowing now makes time, the standing now property makes Eternity"). See Boethius, *De consolatione philosophiae*, (London: B. Oates and Washbourne, 1925), 158. See also Silva, "Tempo della coscienza e tempo della scienza," 709.

[75] Pearl Jam, "Big Wave."

to have no destination."[76] This is exactly what the protagonist of "Seven O'Clock" seems to have in mind, when he claims: "We saw the destination, got so close before it turned / Swim sideways from this undertow and do not be deterred / Floodlight dreams go drifting past / All the lives we could've had."[77]

The risk of idealizing the future (evoked here by the "floodlight dreams") is that of "[d]rifting out of the present / Sucked by the undertow and pulled out deep,"[78] as stated over time by other lyrics of the band. And this is how the current of undertow (the "past regrets" of "Present Tense") ends up overwhelming us, inasmuch it provides us with a convenient excuse for the missing landings in life. On the other hand, fighting to avoid being carried away brings us closer to the beneficial disillusionment that makes the care of the present appear as the only guarantee of a future without fear and a past without regrets.

But what is it that, most of the time, makes us want (and operate accordingly) to be infallible sailors, along a route always verifiable in its previous stages and programmable for those to come ("our inclination" to safety, according to Pascal)? It is the convention according to which we measure the so-called "objective" time, what Husserl calls "the cosmic time,"[79] or—as in a note added to one of the manuscripts of his lectures—the "space-time":[80] it is the "time of science," which we treat as a physical extension available to our sensory perception (as for the colors and shapes of objects) and which, for this reason, we consider knowable and understandable.

Already in "I Am Mine" one line explicitly declared the irreconcilability between cosmic time and phenomenological time: "The North is to South what the clock is to time."[81] Yet we are all somehow forced to decompose and compute the same dimension or, so to speak, entity that shapes our earthly existence, on the assumption that we are able to tame its impalpable "matter"; whereas all we do is cooperate actively and necessarily in its own dissipation, without ever

---

[76] Eliot, "The Dry Salvages," in *Four Quartets*, 30.
[77] Pearl Jam, "Seven O'Clock."
[78] These lines are taken from a text which, to this day, is difficult to give an exact location to, but which is quite well-known to Pearl Jam fans with the apocryphal title "I'm Still Here." According to the most accredited version, it would be a "song" (a sort of prose poem) that appeared in a promo version for the Japanese market of the *Lost Dogs* compilation. The text is quoted here from the transcription offered by the website Pearljamonline.it, an important reference point for Italian supporters of the band.
[79] Husserl, *Ideas Pertaining to a Pure Phenomenology. First book: General Introduction to a Pure Phenomenology*, 192.
[80] Ibid., 192n.
[81] Pearl Jam, "I Am Mine," in *Riot Act* (2002).

grasping its intrinsic quality. "Only through time time is conquered,"[82] here's the paradox. In Eliot's verses it takes the form of the Mississippi: the river of space-time "[i]s a strong brown god—sullen, untamed and intractable / . . . Keeping his seasons and rages, destroyer, reminder / Of what men choose to forget. Unhonoured, unpropitiated."[83] But, hopelessly, "[h]is rhythm was present in the nursery bedroom."[84]

The objective passage of time, understood as the placement of events according to the criteria of before and after, is something almost "instinctive" and inborn for us, related to the analogy between the flow of our blood and that of the river. However, it is actually nothing more than a continuous series of "empirical apperception[s],"[85] linked to a dimension or an entity—ultimately the only truly objective one—that we can seize (always by means of the data of reality) only by intuition: "What becomes constituted here as objectively being valid is finally the one infinite objective time in which all things and events—bodies and their physical qualities, psyches and their psychic states—have their definite temporal positions, which we can determine by means of a chronometer."[86] In other words, as Eliot would say, "[t]he river is within us, the sea is all about us":[87] if the worldly and measurable time is something necessary and "instinctive" for us ("something temporal that is *sensed*"[88]), this depends on the fact that it "exists" as part of the "vast, various, yet fixed" time of which we have consciousness by intuition ("something temporal that is *perceived*"[89]).

Now, it is by an awareness of this kind that a song like "River Cross" is apparently inspired. The song seems to conclude a long path of reflection by Pearl Jam on the meaning of the "all-encompassing trip" that we lead, thus contemplating the enigmas that the band had tried so far to highlight: the inherent evanescence of future goals and the danger of the currents of regret; the waiver of the condition of shipwreck's spectator and the natural oscillation between illusion and disillusionment in landing;[90] finally arriving to face the most disorienting aporia, namely the irreducibility of the inner time of our

---

[82] Eliot, "Burnt Norton," 11.
[83] Eliot, "The Dry Salvages," 28.
[84] Ibid.
[85] Edmund Husserl, *On the Phenomenology of the Consciousness of Internal Time (1893–1917)*, in *Collected Works. Vol. IV* (Dordrecht, Boston, London: Kluwer Academic Publishers, 1991), 7.
[86] Ibid.
[87] Eliot, "The Dry Salvages," 28.
[88] Husserl, *On the Phenomenology of the Consciousness of Internal Time (1893–1917)*, 7.
[89] Ibid.
[90] In order to make explicit this part, readers can refer to the entire first two verses of the song.

consciousness to the time of science, the impossibility to reduce the "perpetually renewed" time of oceans and storms to the "shadow-sundial" and measurable time of rivers that the protagonist wishes to be able to overcome:

> I always thought I'd cross that river / ... / I used to tell time by my shadow / Til the thunderclouds, they took the stage / These days will end as do the light's rays / Another read of the same page ...[91]

The intuition, transfigured into a dream, has the function to sustain the hope that human time is not limited to that of physical processes, to Husserl's daily "empirical apprehensions," and that it is possible to "lengthen our time" and that it is only "a lie that all futures die."[92] For this reason, instead of abandoning itself to the ethereal memory of a dreamlike revelation, "River Cross" turns into a poignant paraenesis: an exhortation not to be conditioned by adverse events (which in the quoted line appear as aberrations of political power), nor by the necessary exiguity of our existence, but rather to choose to put daily commitment, quality, and value into our actions, and to share them with others.[93]

The true and inner sense of this wish emerges even in the most recent and apodictic incitement by Eddie Vedder, perhaps the epigraph that is most in tune with the considerations that I have made so far: "When your time is limited / Well, nothing happens too soon / Navigate, come find a way."[94] This is the only seemingly contradictory key to the enigma of "our" river time, the possibility that we are given to expand it and attune it to the fundamental norm of oceanic time. And this finds its detailed and definitive explication in the third movement of "The Dry Salvages":

> Fare forward, travellers! not escaping from the past / Into different lives, or into any future; / You are not the same people who left that station / Or who will arrive at any terminus, / While the narrowing rails slide together behind you; / And on the deck of the drumming liner / Watching the furrow that widens behind you, / You shall not think "the past is finished" / Or "the future is before us". / At nightfall, in the rigging and the aerial, / Is a voice descanting (though not to the ear, / The murmuring shell of time, and not in any language) / "Fare

---

[91] Pearl Jam, "River Cross," in *Gigaton* (2020).
[92] Ibid.
[93] This assertion is testified, in my interpretation, by the last verse of the song, which furthermore has been often interpolated with new lines by Eddie Vedder in some live solo performances (such as the one in Firenze on June 15, 2019, which the two editors of the present book personally attended): "Live it out / Let it out / Get it out / Shout it out / ... / Share the light / Won't hold us down."
[94] Eddie Vedder, "Matter of Time," in *Matter of time* (2020).

forward, you who think that you are voyaging; / You are not those who saw the harbor / Receding, or those who will disembark. / Here between the hither and the farther shore / While time is withdrawn, consider the future / And the past with an equal mind. / ... / Do forward. / O voyagers, O seamen, / You who come to port, and you whose bodies / Will suffer the trial and judgment of the sea, / Or whatever event, this is your real destination." / So Krishna, as when he admonished Arjuna / On the field of battle. / Not do well, / But do forward, voyagers.[95]

The hollow of the seashell as the end of the voyage (and of this essay too)

"The murmuring shell of time, and not in any language," as Eliot sang. Suggestive and iconic, the figure of the shell frequently recurs in twentieth-century literature. Its significant allegorical/existential function is configured in that form of apparent geometric order that hides the abyss of mystery that created it. The same happens in the one—in an essay of 1937—that Paul Valéry puts in the hands of an imaginary mathematician, soon convinced that all the figures that, as he knew, could represent it "suddenly broke off or degenerated: whereas the cone, the helix, the spiral can well go on 'indefinitely,' the shell suddenly wearies of following them";[96] and the same also happens in the one that Italo Calvino, in *Cosmicomics*, let grow on the back of his metamorphic character Qfwfq, a gastropod endowed with will, judgment, and self-consciousness:

> So I can say that my shell made itself, without my taking any special pains to have it as out one way rather than another, but this doesn't mean that I was absent-minded during that time; I applied myself, instead, to that act of secreting, without allowing myself a moment's distraction, never thinking of anything else, or rather: thinking always of something else, since I didn't know how to think of the shell, just as, for that matter, I didn't know how to think of anything else either, but I accompanied the effort of making the shell with the effort of thinking I was making something, that is anything: that is, I thought of all the things it would be possible to make. So it wasn't even a monotonous task, because the

---

[95] Eliot, "The Dry Salvages," 33.
[96] Paul Valéry, "Man and the Sea Shell," in *Paul Valéry. An Anthology*, (London: Routledge & Keegan Paul 1977), 116.

effort of thinking which accompanied it spread toward countless types of thoughts which spread, each one, toward countless types of actions that might each serve to make countless things, and making each of these things was implicit in making the shell grow, turn after turn...["]97

I don't know how much the "seed, wondering why it grows"98 that Pearl Jam once identified themselves with would settle for Qfwfq's solution about the meaning of life. Maybe Pearl Jam would prefer the one indicated by the spiral that a Bedouin offers to the ear of William Wordsworth, in the nightmare about the imminent end of the cosmos in which one day the poet—as he informs us—had fallen, while he was reading by the sea. From the hollow of the shell, an unknown but comprehensible language sings the apocalypse, while the man of the desert confides his mission to him: to save the arts and sciences. The stone he carries under his arm is Euclid's *Geometry*, the shell is the poetry from all over the world, and both are books: and—in the proteiform reality of dreams—the shell-book "was a god, yea many gods, / Had voices more than all the winds, with power to exhilarate the spirit, and to soothe, / through every clime, the hearth of human kind."99

The "[s]hell of the man from the sea," evoked in "Help Help" was a "[s]torybook [that] keeps from hurting"100 anesthetized citizens by a sweetened, hyperbolic, and emphatic political narrative. But I like to think that the shell—in the imagination of the band that shaped the furors and mildnesses of my early youth, and still attracts me magnetically to its concerts—can contain much more than the daily fable of power told to a childish people.

Rather, in my interpretation Pearl Jam aim to remind us that "[a]n empty shell *seems* so easy to crack," but it *is not*. And when we "[g]ot [a whole] of questions" and we "don't know who [we] could even ask,"101 we can always pick up a shell left ashore by the tides, extract its immaterial and incorruptible content made of knowledge and beauty, art and thought, and recognize our unique and distinctive "voice inside / so drown out."102

---

97 Italo Calvino, "The Spiral," in *The Complete Cosmicomics* (London: Penguin e-book, 2010), 130.
98 Pearl Jam, "Education," in *Lost Dogs* (2003).
99 William Wordsworth, *The Prelude: The Four Texts (1798, 1799, 1805, 1850)* (London-New York: Penguin Book 1995), 177.
100 Pearl Jam, "Help Help", in *Riot Act* (2002).
101 Pearl Jam, "I Got Id," in *Merkin Ball* (1995).
102 Pearl Jam, "Faithful," in *Yield* (1998).

Bibliography

Bachelard, Gaston. *Water and Dreams: An Essay on the Imagination of Matter*, translated by Edith R. Farrell. Dallas: The Pegasus Foundation, 1999.

Bakhtin, Mikhail. *The Dialogic Immagination*, translated by Caryl Emerson and Michael Holquist, edited by Michael Holquist. Austin: University of Texas Press, 1981.

Bergson, Henry. *Duration and Simultaneity*, translated by Leon Jacobson. Indianapolis: Bobbs-Merril, 1965.

Blumenberg, Hans. *Shipwreck with Spectator*, translated by Steven Rendall. Cambridge, MA-London: The MIT Press, 1997.

Bodei, Remo. "Distanza di Sicurezza." In Hans Blumenberg, *Naufragio con spettatore*, translated by Francesca Rigotti, vii–xxv. Bologna: il Mulino, 1985.

Boethius. *De consolatione philosophiae*, edited by Adrian Fortescue. London: B. Oates and Washbourne, 1925.

Calvino, Italo. *The Complete Cosmicomics*, translated by Martin McLaughlin, Tim Parks, and William Weaver. London: Penguin e-book, 2010.

Ciancio, Claudio. "La libertà in Blaise Pascal." Conference at Cooperativa Cattolico-democratica di Cultura, Brescia (Italy), 10 April 2015. Available online: https://www.ccdc.it/documento/il-problema-della-libert-in-blaise-pascal-testo (accessed December 13, 2020).

Cohen, Margareth. "Il mare." In *Il romanzo. IV. Temi, luoghi, eroi*, edited by Franco Moretti, 429–47. Torino: Einaudi, 2003.

De Fiore, Luciano. *Anche il mare sogna. Filosofie dei flutti*. Roma: International Publishers Gathered, 2013.

Eco, Umberto. *On Literature*, translated by Martin McLaughlin. Orlando-Austin-New York-San Diego-Toronto-London: Harcourt, 2004.

Eliot, Thomas S. *Four Quartets*. London: Faber and Faber Digital ebook, 2009.

Husserl, Edmund. *Ideas Pertaining to a Pure Phenomenology and to a Phenomenological Philosophy: First book: General Introduction to a Pure Phenomenology*. In *Collected Works. Vol. II*, translated by Fred Kersten, edited by Rudolf Bernet. Dordrecht-Boston-London: Kluwer Academic Publishers, 1982.

Husserl, Edmund. *On the Phenomenology of the Consciousness of Internal Time (1893–1917)*. In *Collected Works. Vol. IV*, translated by John Barnett Brough, edited by Rudolf Bernet. Dordrecht-Boston-London: Kluwer Academic Publishers, 1991.

Lucretius, Titus Carus. *Titi Lucreti Cari De Rerum Natura Libri Sex*: *With a translation and notes by Hugh Andrew Johnstone Munro. Vol. 1*. New York: Cambridge University Press, 2009.

Montale, Eugenio. *Collected Poems 1920–1954*, bilingual edition, translated and annotated by Jonathan Galassi. New York: Farrar, Straus and Giroux, 1999.

Mortara Garavelli, Bice. *Manuale di retorica*. Milano: Bompiani, 2004.

Pascal, Blaise. *Pascal's Pensées: With an English Translation, Brief Notes and Introduction by Hugh Fraser Stewart*. New York: Routledge, 2020.

Silva, Matteo. "Tempo della coscienza e tempo della scienza." *Rivista di Filosofia Neo-Scolastica* 94, no. 4 (2002): 707–23.

Valéry, Paul. *Paul Valéry: An Anthology*, edited by James R. Lawley. London: Routledge & Keegan Paul, 1977.

Valéry, Paul. *Collected Works of Paul Valéry: Moi*. Vol. 15, translated by Marthiel and Jackson Mathews. New York: Princeton University, 2015.

Valéry, Paul. *Collected Works of Paul Valéry: Poems*. Vol. 1, translated by David Paul. New York: Princeton University, 2015.

Wordsworth, William. *The Prelude: The Four Texts (1798, 1799, 1805, 1850)*. London-New York: Penguin Book, 1995.

Zinn, Howard. *You Can't Be Neutral on a Moving Train: A Personal History*. Boston: Beacon Press, 2002.

Notes on Contributors

Alessandro Alfieri is Professor of Theory and Methodology of Mass Media at the Academy of Fine Arts of Roma, Professor of Theory and History of Digital Culture at the University of Camerino, and Research Fellow in Aesthetics at the Department of Philosophy of the "Sapienza" University of Roma. His main fields of research are cultural studies, philosophy of popular culture, and audiovisual aesthetics. Among his most recent publications: *Video Web Armi* (2021), *Che cos'è la video-estetica* (2019), *Rocksofia* (2019), *Galassia Netflix* (2019), *Lady Gaga. La seduzione del mostro* (2018).

Laura M. Bernhardt (PhD, MLIS) is a philosopher, an information professional, and an occasional musician. She currently works as a Research & Instruction Librarian in the David L. Rice Library at the University of Southern Indiana, having turned to librarianship after sixteen-odd years as the Philosophy half of a Philosophy and Religion Department at a small private university in Iowa. Her scholarly interests include aesthetics (especially the philosophy of music and the philosophy of popular culture), applied ethics, and information literacy.

Mihail-Valentin Cernea teaches Philosophy, Business Ethics, and Social Psychology at the Bucharest University of Economic studies and his research interests could easily be expressed using Pearl Jam songs: what do we see when we look through science's "Rearviewmirror" (history and philosophy of science), what kind of beings actually "Do the Evolution" (multi-level selection in the philosophy of biology), understanding what "Jeremy" had spoken about in class during that infamous day (ethics, moral sanctions, and non-ideal political philosophy), and "World Wide Suicide" with robots (the ethics of autonomous weapon systems). His publications include: "The Ethical Troubles of Future Warfare: On the Prohibition of Autonomous Weapon Systems," "Tales of a Failed Scientific Revolution: Wynne-Edwards' Animal Dispersion," and "The Clash Between Global Justice and Drug Patents: A Critical Analysis" (alongside Radu Uszkai).

Theodore Gracyk is Professor of Philosophy at Minnesota State University Moorhead and (since 2013) the co-editor of *The Journal of Aesthetics and Art*

Criticism. He is the author of four philosophical books on music, including *Rhythm and Noise: An Aesthetics of Rock* (1996) and *On Music* (2013). Another of his books was co-recipient of the 2002 Woody Guthrie Award (the 2002 IASPM/US Book Award). With Andrew Kania, he co-edited *The Routledge Companion to Philosophy and Music* (2011), and with Lee B. Brown and David Goldblatt co-wrote *Jazz and the Philosophy of Art* (2018). He has published many articles on philosophy of music and the history of aesthetics.

Stephanie Kramer is Adjunct Professor at the Fashion Institute of Technology, where she teaches a sociology course entitled "Youth Subcultures, Fashion, and Identity," and Research Assistant at The Metropolitan Museum of Art's Costume Institute. Prior to joining the Costume Institute team, she was the Research Assistant on The Museum of Modern Art's exhibition *Items: Is Fashion Modern?* She received an MA in Visual Culture: Costume Studies from New York University, following a career in the fashion industry as the Director of Fabric R&D at Nicole Miller. She currently combines her experience as a practitioner with her research, and has a focus in the sociological underpinnings of subcultural fashion.

Stefano Marino is Associate Professor of Aesthetics at the University of Bologna. His main research interests are focused on critical theory, hermeneutics, neopragmatism and somaesthetics, philosophy of music, and aesthetics of fashion. He is the author of several books on Adorno, Gadamer and Heidegger, and Frank Zappa. He has translated from German into Italian three books by Adorno and Gadamer, and from English into Italian a book by Carolyn Korsmeyer. He has published as co-editor several collections (books and special issues in journals) on Kant, Nietzsche, Gadamer, Adorno, deconstruction, aesthetics and affectivity, fashion, popular culture and feminism.

Sam Morris is Assistant Professor of English at the University of South Carolina Beaufort. He researches and writes about adolescent literature, secondary English education, literacy theory and pedagogy, utopian theory, and popular culture. He advocates for the incorporation of music as text in the high school classroom. He has written previously about utopian theory in adolescent literature for *The Lion and the Unicorn* and is currently working on a larger project that includes a lyrical analysis of Paramore and Hayley Williams' music.

Jacqueline Viola Moulton is an interdisciplinary artist, writer, and PhD candidate in Philosophy and Aesthetics at the Institute for Doctoral Studies in the Visual Arts. Moulton's creative work focuses on public, performative, and participatory poetry practices. Philosophically, Moulton works within queer, post-humanist, and new materialist theories with attention to the narratives of ghosts, monsters, and all manner of border-creatures. Moulton as well makes experimental philosophy zines under the moniker, The Depressed Waitress.

Cristina Parapar is PhD candidate in Aesthetics and Philosophy of Music at the Sorbonne University of Paris, Lecturer of History and Political Art in Spain and Latin America at the Sorbonne University, Lecturer of Spanish and Hispanic Culture at the Catholic University of Paris, and Teacher of History of Spain at the France National Education. Her research focuses on history, ideology, and popular music. Selected musical writings have been published in French ("I wanna be sedated: entre musique et violence") and Spanish ("¿O la trampa sintomática o la música en los márgenes?"), among others. Between 2012 and 2016, she also worked as a music critic for classical music magazines and popular music magazines.

Andrea Schembari earned his PhD in Modern Philology at the University of Catania, and is currently Researcher and Assistant Professor at the Institute of Literature and New Media of the University of Szczecin, where he teaches Comparative Literature, Contemporary Italian Literature, and also holds courses on Italian songwriting. He is visiting professor at the Department of Human Sciences of the University of Catania, Italy. He is the author of several book chapters, articles in peer-reviewed journals, and edited volumes on Leonardo Sciascia's work, on eighteenth-century literature in Sicily, and on women's writing in the twentieth century.

Alberto L. Siani is Associate Professor of Aesthetics at the University of Pisa. He has done research mostly on the aesthetics of Hegel and German Idealism, and its relevance for the self-understanding of the modern Western world. In addition, he has research interests in contemporary political philosophy. Among his recent publications are the book *Morte dell'arte, libertà del soggetto. Attualità di Hegel* (2017), the co-edited volume *Women Philosophers on Autonomy. Historical and Contemporary Perspectives* (2018), and the article "Antisubjectivism and the End of Art: Heidegger on Hegel" in *The British Journal of Aesthetics* (2020).

Paolo Stellino is a Researcher and Invited Professor at the Nova Institute of Philosophy, New University of Lisbon. His main fields of research interest are the history of nineteenth- and twentieth-century philosophy, ethics, and philosophy of cinema. He has published many articles in international peer-reviewed journals and has authored several book chapters. He is the author of the books *Nietzsche and Dostoevsky: On the Verge of Nihilism* (2015) and *Philosophical Perspectives on Suicide: Kant, Schopenhauer, Nietzsche, and Wittgenstein* (2020).

Enrico Terrone is Associate Professor of Aesthetics at the University of Genoa. He works on philosophical issues concerning fiction and depiction. His primary area of research is philosophy of film. He has published papers in international journals such as *The British Journal of Aesthetics, The Journal of Aesthetics and Art Criticism, Erkenntnis, Ergo, The Monist, Dialectica*. His last book, co-authored with Luca Bandirali, is *Concept TV—An Aesthetics of Television Series* (2021).

Radu Uszkai teaches Philosophy and Business Ethics at the Bucharest University of Economic Studies, where he works as an Assistant Lecturer at the Department of Philosophy and Social Sciences. He is also a researcher at the Research Center in Applied Ethics, University of Bucharest. His research focuses mostly on applied ethics, political philosophy, and philosophy in pop culture. He has a passion for spinning the black circle and began collecting grunge vinyls, and has presented papers at international conferences in places where Pearl Jam had concerts like New Orleans or Budapest. He is the co-author of a chapter published in the book *How I Met Your Mother and Philosophy*, of "The Use of Torrents in Society," and (with Mihail-Valentin Cernea) of "Unfit for the Market? The Case for Moral Enhancement for Managers."

Copyright Notices

Alive
Words by Eddie Vedder
Music by Stone Gossard
Copyright © 1991 INNOCENT BYSTANDER, WRITE TREATAGE MUSIC and UNIVERSAL MUSIC WORKS
All Rights administered by UNIVERSAL MUSIC WORKS
All Rights Reserved. Used by Permission.
Reprinted by Permission of Hal Leonard Europe Ltd.

All Or None
Words by Eddie Vedder and Stone Gossard
Music by Stone Gossard
Copyright © 2002 INNOCENT BYSTANDER and WRITE TREATAGE MUSIC
All Rights administered by UNIVERSAL MUSIC WORKS
All Rights Reserved. Used by Permission.
Reprinted by Permission of Hal Leonard Europe Ltd.

Amongst The Waves
Words by Eddie Vedder
Music by Stone Gossard
Copyright © 2009 INNOCENT BYSTANDER and WRITE TREATAGE MUSIC
All Rights administered by UNIVERSAL MUSIC WORKS
All Rights Reserved. Used by Permission.
Reprinted by Permission of Hal Leonard Europe Ltd.

Better Man
Words and Music by Eddie Vedder
Copyright © 1994 INNOCENT BYSTANDER
All Rights administered by UNIVERSAL MUSIC WORKS
All Rights Reserved. Used by Permission.
Reprinted by Permission of Hal Leonard Europe Ltd.

Big Wave
Words by Eddie Vedder
Music by Jeff Ament
Copyright © 2006 INNOCENT BYSTANDER and SCRIBING C-MENT SONGS
All Rights administered by UNIVERSAL MUSIC WORKS
All Rights Reserved. Used by Permission.
Reprinted by Permission of Hal Leonard Europe Ltd.

Bushleager
Words by Eddie Vedder and Stone Gossard
Music by Stone Gossard
Copyright © 2002 INNOCENT BYSTANDER and WRITE TREATAGE MUSIC
All Rights administered by UNIVERSAL MUSIC WORKS
All Rights Reserved. Used by Permission.
Reprinted by Permission of Hal Leonard Europe Ltd.

Can't Keep
Words and Music by Eddie Vedder
Copyright © 2002 INNOCENT BYSTANDER
All Rights administered by UNIVERSAL MUSIC WORKS
All Rights Reserved. Used by Permission.
Reprinted by Permission of Hal Leonard Europe Ltd.

Corduroy
Words by Eddie Vedder
Music by Eddie Vedder, Stone Gossard, Jeff Ament, Mike McCready and Dave Abbruzzese
Copyright © 1994 INNOCENT BYSTANDER, WRITE TREATAGE MUSIC, SCRIBING C-MENT SONGS, JUMPIN' CAT MUSIC and PICKLED FISH MUSIC
All Rights for INNOCENT BYSTANDER, WRITE TREATAGE MUSIC, SCRIBING C-MENT SONGS and JUMPIN' CAT MUSIC administered by UNIVERSAL MUSIC WORKS
All Rights Reserved. Used by Permission.
Reprinted by Permission of Hal Leonard Europe Ltd.

Daughter
Words by Eddie Vedder
Music by Eddie Vedder, Stone Gossard, Jeff Ament, Mike McCready and Dave Abbruzzese
Copyright © 1993 INNOCENT BYSTANDER, WRITE TREATAGE MUSIC, SCRIBING C-MENT SONGS, JUMPIN' CAT MUSIC, PICKLED FISH MUSIC and UNIVERSAL MUSIC WORKS
All Rights for INNOCENT BYSTANDER, WRITE TREATAGE MUSIC, SCRIBING C-MENT SONGS and JUMPIN' CAT MUSIC administered by UNIVERSAL MUSIC WORKS
All Rights Reserved. Used by Permission.
Reprinted by Permission of Hal Leonard Europe Ltd.

Deep
Words by Eddie Vedder
Music by Stone Gossard and Jeff Ament
Copyright © 1991 INNOCENT BYSTANDER, WRITE TREATAGE MUSIC, SCRIBING C-MENT SONGS and UNIVERSAL MUSIC WORKS
All Rights administered by UNIVERSAL MUSIC WORKS
All Rights Reserved. Used by Permission.
Reprinted by Permission of Hal Leonard Europe Ltd.

Dissident
Words by Eddie Vedder
Music by Eddie Vedder, Stone Gossard, Jeff Ament, Mike McCready and Dave Abbruzzese
Copyright © 1993 INNOCENT BYSTANDER, WRITE TREATAGE MUSIC, SCRIBING C-MENT SONGS, JUMPIN' CAT MUSIC, PICKLED FISH MUSIC and UNIVERSAL MUSIC WORKS
All Rights for INNOCENT BYSTANDER, WRITE TREATAGE MUSIC, SCRIBING C-MENT SONGS and JUMPIN' CAT MUSIC administered by UNIVERSAL MUSIC WORKS
All Rights Reserved. Used by Permission.
Reprinted by Permission of Hal Leonard Europe Ltd.

Do The Evolution
Words by Eddie Vedder
Music by Stone Gossard
Copyright © 1998 INNOCENT BYSTANDER and WRITE TREATAGE MUSIC
All Rights administered by UNIVERSAL MUSIC WORKS
All Rights Reserved. Used by Permission.
Reprinted by Permission of Hal Leonard Europe Ltd.

Down
Words by Eddie Vedder
Music by Eddie Vedder, Stone Gossard and Michael McCready
Copyright © 2002 INNOCENT BYSTANDER, WRITE TREATAGE MUSIC and UNIVERSAL MUSIC WORKS
All Rights administered by UNIVERSAL MUSIC WORKS
All Rights Reserved. Used by Permission.
Reprinted by Permission of Hal Leonard Europe Ltd.

Education
Words and Music by Eddie Vedder
Copyright © 2003 INNOCENT BYSTANDER
All Rights administered by UNIVERSAL MUSIC WORKS
All Rights Reserved. Used by Permission.
Reprinted by Permission of Hal Leonard Europe Ltd.

Even Flow
Words by Eddie Vedder
Music by Stone Gossard
Copyright © 1991 INNOCENT BYSTANDER, WRITE TREATAGE MUSIC and UNIVERSAL MUSIC WORKS
All Rights administered by UNIVERSAL MUSIC WORKS
All Rights Reserved. Used by Permission.
Reprinted by Permission of Hal Leonard Europe Ltd.

Faithfull
Words by Eddie Vedder
Music by Mike McCready
Copyright © 1998 INNOCENT BYSTANDER and JUMPIN' CAT MUSIC
All Rights administered by UNIVERSAL MUSIC WORKS

All Rights Reserved. Used by Permission.
Reprinted by Permission of Hal Leonard Europe Ltd.

Force Of Nature
Words by Eddie Vedder
Music by Mike McCready
Copyright © 2009 INNOCENT BYSTANDER and JUMPIN' CAT MUSIC
All Rights administered by UNIVERSAL MUSIC WORKS
All Rights Reserved. Used by Permission.
Reprinted by Permission of Hal Leonard Europe Ltd.

Future Days
Words and Music by Eddie Vedder
Copyright © 2013 INNOCENT BYSTANDER
All Rights administered by UNIVERSAL MUSIC WORKS
All Rights Reserved. Used by Permission.
Reprinted by Permission of Hal Leonard Europe Ltd.

Garden
Words by Eddie Vedder
Music by Stone Gossard and Jeff Ament
Copyright © 1991 INNOCENT BYSTANDER, WRITE TREATAGE MUSIC, SCRIBING C-MENT SONGS and UNIVERSAL MUSIC WORKS
All Rights administered by UNIVERSAL MUSIC WORKS
All Rights Reserved. Used by Permission.
Reprinted by Permission of Hal Leonard Europe Ltd.

Getaway
Words and Music by Eddie Vedder
Copyright © 2013 INNOCENT BYSTANDER
All Rights administered by UNIVERSAL MUSIC WORKS
All Rights Reserved. Used by Permission.
Reprinted by Permission of Hal Leonard Europe Ltd.

Given To Fly
Words by Eddie Vedder
Music by Mike McCready
Copyright © 1998 INNOCENT BYSTANDER and JUMPIN' CAT MUSIC

All Rights administered by UNIVERSAL MUSIC WORKS
All Rights Reserved. Used by Permission.
Reprinted by Permission of Hal Leonard Europe Ltd.

Gods' Dice
Words and Music by Jeff Ament
Copyright © 2000 SCRIBING C-MENT SONGS
All Rights administered by UNIVERSAL MUSIC WORKS
All Rights Reserved. Used by Permission.
Reprinted by Permission of Hal Leonard Europe Ltd.

Gone
Words and Music by Eddie Vedder
Copyright © 2006 INNOCENT BYSTANDER
All Rights administered by UNIVERSAL MUSIC WORKS
All Rights Reserved. Used by Permission.
Reprinted by Permission of Hal Leonard Europe Ltd.

Green Disease
Words and Music by Eddie Vedder
Copyright © 2002 INNOCENT BYSTANDER
All Rights administered by UNIVERSAL MUSIC WORKS
All Rights Reserved. Used by Permission.
Reprinted by Permission of Hal Leonard Europe Ltd.

Grievance
Words and Music by Eddie Vedder
Copyright © 2000 INNOCENT BYSTANDER
All Rights administered by UNIVERSAL MUSIC WORKS
All Rights Reserved. Used by Permission.
Reprinted by Permission of Hal Leonard Europe Ltd.

Help Help
Words and Music by Jeff Ament
Copyright © 2002 SCRIBING C-MENT SONGS
All Rights administered by UNIVERSAL MUSIC WORKS
All Rights Reserved. Used by Permission.
Reprinted by Permission of Hal Leonard Europe Ltd.

I Am Mine
Words and Music by Eddie Vedder
Copyright © 2002 INNOCENT BYSTANDER
All Rights administered by UNIVERSAL MUSIC WORKS
All Rights Reserved. Used by Permission.
Reprinted by Permission of Hal Leonard Europe Ltd.

I Got ID
Words and Music by Eddie Vedder
Copyright © 1995 INNOCENT BYSTANDER
All Rights administered by UNIVERSAL MUSIC WORKS
All Rights Reserved. Used by Permission.
Reprinted by Permission of Hal Leonard Europe Ltd.

I'm Open
Words by Eddie Vedder
Music by Eddie Vedder and Jack Irons
Copyright © 1996 INNOCENT BYSTANDER and MR. BROOTZ MUSIC
All Rights for INNOCENT BYSTANDER administered by UNIVERSAL MUSIC WORKS
All Rights Reserved. Used by Permission.
Reprinted by Permission of Hal Leonard Europe Ltd.

In My Tree
Words by Eddie Vedder
Music by Eddie Vedder, Stone Gossard and Jack Irons
Copyright © 1996 INNOCENT BYSTANDER, WRITE TREATAGE MUSIC and MR. BROOTZ MUSIC
All Rights for INNOCENT BYSTANDER and WRITE TREATAGE MUSIC administered by UNIVERSAL MUSIC WORKS
All Rights Reserved. Used by Permission.
Reprinted by Permission of Hal Leonard Europe Ltd.

Indifference
Words by Eddie Vedder
Music by Eddie Vedder, Stone Gossard, Jeff Ament, Mike McCready and Dave Abbruzzese

Copyright © 1993 INNOCENT BYSTANDER, WRITE TREATAGE MUSIC, SCRIBING C-MENT SONGS, JUMPIN' CAT MUSIC, PICKLED FISH MUSIC and UNIVERSAL MUSIC WORKS
All Rights for INNOCENT BYSTANDER, WRITE TREATAGE MUSIC, SCRIBING C-MENT SONGS and JUMPIN' CAT MUSIC administered by UNIVERSAL MUSIC WORKS
All Rights Reserved. Used by Permission.
Reprinted by Permission of Hal Leonard Europe Ltd.

Infallible
Words by Eddie Vedder
Music by Stone Gossard and Jeff Ament
Copyright © 2013 INNOCENT BYSTANDER, WRITE TREATAGE MUSIC and SCRIBING C-MENT SONGS
All Rights administered by UNIVERSAL MUSIC WORKS
All Rights Reserved. Used by Permission.
Reprinted by Permission of Hal Leonard Europe Ltd.

Insignificance
Words and Music by Eddie Vedder
Copyright © 2000 INNOCENT BYSTANDER
All Rights administered by UNIVERSAL MUSIC WORKS
All Rights Reserved. Used by Permission.
Reprinted by Permission of Hal Leonard Europe Ltd.

Last Exit
Words by Eddie Vedder
Music by Eddie Vedder, Stone Gossard, Jeff Ament, Mike McCready and Dave Abbruzzese
Copyright © 1994 INNOCENT BYSTANDER, WRITE TREATAGE MUSIC, SCRIBING C-MENT SONGS, JUMPIN' CAT MUSIC and PICKLED FISH MUSIC
All Rights for INNOCENT BYSTANDER, WRITE TREATAGE MUSIC, SCRIBING C-MENT SONGS and JUMPIN' CAT MUSIC administered by UNIVERSAL MUSIC WORKS
All Rights Reserved. Used by Permission.
Reprinted by Permission of Hal Leonard Europe Ltd.

Leash
Words by Eddie Vedder
Music by Eddie Vedder, Stone Gossard, Jeff Ament, Mike McCready and Dave Abbruzzese
Copyright © 1993 INNOCENT BYSTANDER, WRITE TREATAGE MUSIC, SCRIBING C-MENT SONGS, JUMPIN' CAT MUSIC, PICKLED FISH MUSIC and UNIVERSAL MUSIC WORKS
All Rights for INNOCENT BYSTANDER, WRITE TREATAGE MUSIC, SCRIBING C-MENT SONGS and JUMPIN' CAT MUSIC administered by UNIVERSAL MUSIC WORKS
All Rights Reserved. Used by Permission.
Reprinted by Permission of Hal Leonard Europe Ltd.

Life Wasted
Words by Eddie Vedder
Music by Stone Gossard
Copyright © 2006 INNOCENT BYSTANDER and WRITE TREATAGE MUSIC
All Rights administered by UNIVERSAL MUSIC WORKS
All Rights Reserved. Used by Permission.
Reprinted by Permission of Hal Leonard Europe Ltd.

Lightning Bolt
Words and Music by Eddie Vedder
Copyright © 2013 INNOCENT BYSTANDER
All Rights administered by UNIVERSAL MUSIC WORKS
All Rights Reserved. Used by Permission.
Reprinted by Permission of Hal Leonard Europe Ltd.

Love Boat Captain
Words by Eddie Vedder
Music by Eddie Vedder and Kenneth "Boom" Gaspar
Copyright © 2002 INNOCENT BYSTANDER and SUNNY HI MUSIC
All Rights for INNOCENT BYSTANDER administered by UNIVERSAL MUSIC WORKS
All Rights Reserved. Used by Permission.
Reprinted by Permission of Hal Leonard Europe Ltd.

Low Light
Words and Music by Jeff Ament
Copyright © 1998 SCRIBING C-MENT SONGS
All Rights administered by UNIVERSAL MUSIC WORKS
All Rights Reserved. Used by Permission.
Reprinted by Permission of Hal Leonard Europe Ltd.

Mind Your Manners
Words by Eddie Vedder
Music by Mike McCready
Copyright © 2013 INNOCENT BYSTANDER and JUMPIN' CAT MUSIC
All Rights administered by UNIVERSAL MUSIC WORKS
All Rights Reserved. Used by Permission.
Reprinted by Permission of Hal Leonard Europe Ltd.

No Way
Words and Music by Stone Gossard
Copyright © 1998 WRITE TREATAGE MUSIC
All Rights administered by UNIVERSAL MUSIC WORKS
All Rights Reserved. Used by Permission.
Reprinted by Permission of Hal Leonard Europe Ltd.

Not For You
Words by Eddie Vedder
Music by Eddie Vedder, Stone Gossard, Jeff Ament, Mike McCready and Dave Abbruzzese
Copyright © 1994 INNOCENT BYSTANDER, WRITE TREATAGE MUSIC, SCRIBING C-MENT SONGS, JUMPIN' CAT MUSIC and PICKLED FISH MUSIC
All Rights for INNOCENT BYSTANDER, WRITE TREATAGE MUSIC, SCRIBING C-MENT SONGS and JUMPIN' CAT MUSIC administered by UNIVERSAL MUSIC WORKS
All Rights Reserved. Used by Permission.
Reprinted by Permission of Hal Leonard Europe Ltd.

Nothingman
Words by Eddie Vedder
Music by Jeff Ament
Copyright © 1994 INNOCENT BYSTANDER and SCRIBING C-MENT SONGS
All Rights administered by UNIVERSAL MUSIC WORKS
All Rights Reserved. Used by Permission.
Reprinted by Permission of Hal Leonard Europe Ltd.

Oceans
Words by Eddie Vedder
Music by Eddie Vedder, Jeff Ament and Stone Gossard
Copyright © 1991 INNOCENT BYSTANDER, SCRIBING C-MENT SONGS, WRITE TREATAGE MUSIC and UNIVERSAL MUSIC WORKS
All Rights administered by UNIVERSAL MUSIC WORKS
All Rights Reserved. Used by Permission.
Reprinted by Permission of Hal Leonard Europe Ltd.

Off He Goes
Words and Music by Eddie Vedder
Copyright © 1996 INNOCENT BYSTANDER
All Rights administered by UNIVERSAL MUSIC WORKS
All Rights Reserved. Used by Permission.
Reprinted by Permission of Hal Leonard Europe Ltd.

Once
Words by Eddie Vedder
Music by Stone Gossard
Copyright © 1991 INNOCENT BYSTANDER, WRITE TREATAGE MUSIC and UNIVERSAL MUSIC WORKS
All Rights administered by UNIVERSAL MUSIC WORKS
All Rights Reserved. Used by Permission.
Reprinted by Permission of Hal Leonard Europe Ltd.

Pendulum
Words by Eddie Vedder
Music by Stone Gossard and Jeff Ament
Copyright © 2013 INNOCENT BYSTANDER, WRITE TREATAGE MUSIC and SCRIBING C-MENT SONGS
All Rights administered by UNIVERSAL MUSIC WORKS
All Rights Reserved. Used by Permission.
Reprinted by Permission of Hal Leonard Europe Ltd.

Present Tense
Words by Eddie Vedder
Music by Mike McCready
Copyright © 1996 INNOCENT BYSTANDER and JUMPIN' CAT MUSIC
All Rights administered by UNIVERSAL MUSIC WORKS
All Rights Reserved. Used by Permission.
Reprinted by Permission of Hal Leonard Europe Ltd.

Push Me, Pull Me
Words by Eddie Vedder
Music by Jeff Ament
Copyright © 1998 INNOCENT BYSTANDER and SCRIBING C-MENT SONGS
All Rights administered by UNIVERSAL MUSIC WORKS
All Rights Reserved. Used by Permission.
Reprinted by Permission of Hal Leonard Europe Ltd.

Red Mosquito
Words by Eddie Vedder
Music by Stone Gossard, Jeff Ament, Mike McCready and Jack Irons
Copyright © 1996 INNOCENT BYSTANDER, WRITE TREATAGE MUSIC, SCRIBING C-MENT SONGS, JUMPIN' CAT MUSIC and MR. BROOTZ MUSIC
All Rights for INNOCENT BYSTANDER, WRITE TREATAGE MUSIC, SCRIBING C-MENT SONGS and JUMPIN' CAT MUSIC administered by UNIVERSAL MUSIC WORKS
All Rights Reserved. Used by Permission.
Reprinted by Permission of Hal Leonard Europe Ltd.

Release
Words by Eddie Vedder
Music by Eddie Vedder, Stone Gossard, Jeff Ament, Mike McCready and Dave Krusen
Copyright © 1991 INNOCENT BYSTANDER, WRITE TREATAGE MUSIC, SCRIBING C-MENT SONGS, JUMPIN' CAT MUSIC, 3 KICK HEADS and UNIVERSAL MUSIC WORKS
All Rights for INNOCENT BYSTANDER, WRITE TREATAGE MUSIC, SCRIBING C-MENT SONGS and JUMPIN' CAT MUSIC administered by UNIVERSAL MUSIC WORKS
All Rights Reserved. Used by Permission.
Reprinted by Permission of Hal Leonard Europe Ltd.

Save You
Words by Eddie Vedder
Music by Eddie Vedder, Stone Gossard, Jeff Ament, Mike McCready and Matt Cameron
Copyright © 2002 INNOCENT BYSTANDER, WRITE TREATAGE MUSIC, SCRIBING C-MENT SONGS, JUMPIN' CAT MUSIC and THEORY OF COLOR
All Rights administered by UNIVERSAL MUSIC WORKS
All Rights Reserved. Used by Permission.
Reprinted by Permission of Hal Leonard Europe Ltd.

Severed Hand
Words and Music by Eddie Vedder
Copyright © 2006 INNOCENT BYSTANDER
All Rights administered by UNIVERSAL MUSIC WORKS
All Rights Reserved. Used by Permission.
Reprinted by Permission of Hal Leonard Europe Ltd.

Sirens
Words by Eddie Vedder
Music by Mike McCready
Copyright © 2013 INNOCENT BYSTANDER and JUMPIN' CAT MUSIC
All Rights administered by UNIVERSAL MUSIC WORKS
All Rights Reserved. Used by Permission.
Reprinted by Permission of Hal Leonard Europe Ltd.

Sleight Of Hand
Words by Eddie Vedder
Music by Jeff Ament
Copyright © 2000 INNOCENT BYSTANDER and SCRIBING C-MENT SONGS
All Rights administered by UNIVERSAL MUSIC WORKS
All Rights Reserved. Used by Permission.
Reprinted by Permission of Hal Leonard Europe Ltd.

Sometimes
Words and Music by Eddie Vedder
Copyright © 1996 INNOCENT BYSTANDER
All Rights administered by UNIVERSAL MUSIC WORKS
All Rights Reserved. Used by Permission.
Reprinted by Permission of Hal Leonard Europe Ltd.

State Of Love And Trust
Featured In The Motion Picture SINGLES
Words by Eddie Vedder
Music by Eddie Vedder, Jeff Ament and Mike McCready
Copyright © 1992 INNOCENT BYSTANDER, SCRIBING C-MENT SONGS, JUMPIN' CAT MUSIC and UNIVERSAL MUSIC WORKS
All Rights administered by UNIVERSAL MUSIC WORKS
All Rights Reserved. Used by Permission.
Reprinted by Permission of Hal Leonard Europe Ltd.

Supersonic
Words by Eddie Vedder
Music by Stone Gossard
Copyright © 2009 INNOCENT BYSTANDER and WRITE TREATAGE MUSIC
All Rights administered by UNIVERSAL MUSIC WORKS
All Rights Reserved. Used by Permission.
Reprinted by Permission of Hal Leonard Europe Ltd.

Thumbing My Way
Words and Music by Eddie Vedder
Copyright © 2002 INNOCENT BYSTANDER

All Rights administered by UNIVERSAL MUSIC WORKS
All Rights Reserved. Used by Permission.
Reprinted by Permission of Hal Leonard Europe Ltd.

Tremor Christ
Words by Eddie Vedder
Music by Eddie Vedder, Stone Gossard, Jeff Ament, Mike McCready and Dave Abbruzzese
Copyright © 1994 INNOCENT BYSTANDER, WRITE TREATAGE MUSIC, SCRIBING C-MENT SONGS, JUMPIN' CAT MUSIC and PICKLED FISH MUSIC
All Rights for INNOCENT BYSTANDER, WRITE TREATAGE MUSIC, SCRIBING C-MENT SONGS and JUMPIN' CAT MUSIC administered by UNIVERSAL MUSIC WORKS
All Rights Reserved. Used by Permission.
Reprinted by Permission of Hal Leonard Europe Ltd.

Unthought Known
Words and Music by Eddie Vedder
Copyright © 2009 INNOCENT BYSTANDER
All Rights administered by UNIVERSAL MUSIC WORKS
All Rights Reserved. Used by Permission.
Reprinted by Permission of Hal Leonard Europe Ltd.

Who You Are
Words by Eddie Vedder
Music by Stone Gossard and Jack Irons
Copyright © 1996 INNOCENT BYSTANDER, WRITE TREATAGE MUSIC and MR. BROOTZ MUSIC
All Rights for INNOCENT BYSTANDER and WRITE TREATAGE MUSIC administered by UNIVERSAL MUSIC WORKS
All Rights Reserved. Used by Permission.
Reprinted by Permission of Hal Leonard Europe Ltd.

Wishlist
Words and Music by Eddie Vedder
Copyright © 1998 INNOCENT BYSTANDER

All Rights administered by UNIVERSAL MUSIC WORKS
All Rights Reserved. Used by Permission.
Reprinted by Permission of Hal Leonard Europe Ltd.

Who Ever Said
Words and Music by Eddie Vedder
Copyright © 2020 INNOCENT BYSTANDER
All Rights administered by UNIVERSAL MUSIC WORKS
All Rights Reserved. Used by Permission.
Reprinted by Permission of Hal Leonard Europe Ltd.

Superblood Wolfmoon
Words and Music by Eddie Vedder
Copyright © 2020 INNOCENT BYSTANDER
All Rights administered by UNIVERSAL MUSIC WORKS
All Rights Reserved. Used by Permission.
Reprinted by Permission of Hal Leonard Europe Ltd.

Dance Of The Clairvoyants
Words by Eddie Vedder
Music by Eddie Vedder, Stone Gossard, Jeff Ament, Mike McCready and Matt Cameron
Copyright © 2020 INNOCENT BYSTANDER, WRITE TREATAGE MUSIC, SCRIBING C-MENT SONGS, JUMPIN' CAT MUSIC and THEORY OF COLOR
All Rights administered by UNIVERSAL MUSIC WORKS
All Rights Reserved. Used by Permission.
Reprinted by Permission of Hal Leonard Europe Ltd.

Quick Escape
Words by Eddie Vedder
Music by Jeff Ament
Copyright © 2020 INNOCENT BYSTANDER and SCRIBING C-MENT SONGS
All Rights administered by UNIVERSAL MUSIC WORKS
All Rights Reserved. Used by Permission.
Reprinted by Permission of Hal Leonard Europe Ltd.

Seven O'clock
Words and Music by Eddie Vedder, Stone Gossard, Jeff Ament and Mike McCready
Copyright © 2020 INNOCENT BYSTANDER, WRITE TREATAGE MUSIC, SCRIBING C-MENT SONGS and JUMPIN' CAT MUSIC
All Rights administered by UNIVERSAL MUSIC WORKS
All Rights Reserved. Used by Permission.
Reprinted by Permission of Hal Leonard Europe Ltd.

River Cross
Words and Music by Eddie Vedder
Copyright © 2020 INNOCENT BYSTANDER
All Rights administered by UNIVERSAL MUSIC WORKS
All Rights Reserved. Used by Permission.
Reprinted by Permission of Hal Leonard Europe Ltd.

Bee Girl
Words by Eddie Vedder
Music by Jeff Ament
Copyright © 2003 INNOCENT BYSTANDER and SCRIBING C-MENT SONGS
All Rights administered by UNIVERSAL MUSIC WORKS
All Rights Reserved. Used by Permission.

Fatal
Words and Music by Stone Gossard
Copyright © 2003 WRITE TREATAGE MUSIC
All Rights administered by UNIVERSAL MUSIC WORKS
All Rights Reserved. Used by Permission.
Reprinted by Permission of Hal Leonard Europe Ltd.

Wash
Words by Eddie Vedder
Music by Stone Gossard, Jeff Ament, Mike McCready and Dave Krusen
Copyright © 1991 INNOCENT BYSTANDER, WRITE TREATAGE MUSIC, SCRIBING C-MENT SONGS, JUMPIN' CAT MUSIC, 3 KICK HEADS and UNIVERSAL MUSIC WORKS

All Rights for INNOCENT BYSTANDER, WRITE TREATAGE MUSIC, SCRIBING C-MENT SONGS and JUMPIN' CAT MUSIC administered by UNIVERSAL MUSIC WORKS
All Rights Reserved. Used by Permission.
Reprinted by Permission of Hal Leonard Europe Ltd.

I'm Still Here (Untitled)
Words by Eddie Vedder
Music by Eddie Vedder, Stone Gossard, Jeff Ament, Mike McCready and Matt Cameron
Copyright © 1998 INNOCENT BYSTANDER, WRITE TREATAGE MUSIC, SCRIBING C-MENT SONGS, JUMPIN' CAT MUSIC and THEORY OF COLOR
All Rights administered by UNIVERSAL MUSIC WORKS
All Rights Reserved. Used by Permission.
Reprinted by Permission of Hal Leonard Europe Ltd.

Index

Abbruzzese, D. 63, 68, 70, 76, 77, 83n, 148, 151–3
Adorno, Th. W. viii, 13, 15, 16, 22, 23, 30, 38, 169, 170, 172, 173, 183–9, 192, 193, 195, 198, 199, 201, 202
Aiello, L. 3n
Alfieri, A. 6
Alice in Chains 4, 48, 62, 73, 74, 207, 215
Ament, J. vii, 43, 44, 56, 57, 82n, 140, 145–8, 150, 151, 153, 211
Amos, T. 3
Andrews, J. 195
Aquinas, T. 230n
Aristotle 18, 18n, 33n, 202
Augustine 28, 28n
Azerrad, M. 151n

Bachelard, G. 219n
Bad Radio 66
Bakhtin, M. 225n
Baumann, Z. 220
Beall, Jc 116n
Beatles viii
Beck 215
Bell, R.H. 89, 89n, 90n
Bellmont, B. 209n
Benjamin, W. 16, 16n, 30, 38, 38n, 205, 214
Bennington, C. 62
Berg, A. 185
Berger, A. 87n
Bergson, H. 230, 230n
Bernhardt, L.M. 6
Béthune, C. 186, 186n, 202, 202n
Betts, K. 162n
Bieber, J. 76
Bicknell, J. 86n
Big Brother and the Holding Company vii
Black Sabbath 66, 73, 74
Blake, W. 44, 47, 47n, 48, 48n, 49, 49n, 51–3, 56, 56n, 58, 58n
Blasengame, B. 112n

Bloch, E. 44, 50, 50n, 51, 52, 52n, 53, 53n, 54, 54n, 55, 55n
Blumenberg, H. 220n, 221, 221n, 223n, 224n, 226n, 228n
Bodei, R. 220n, 221n
Boehlert, E. 112n
Boethius 230n
Bollas, C. 97
Bon Jovi, J. 71
Bondarchuk, J. 63, 66n
Bordone, A. 3n
Borradori, G. 173, 173n
Bourdieu, P. 198
Bourgault, S. 91n
Brad 4
Bremer, M. 68, 68n
Buckley, J. 215
Burckhardt, J. 226
Bush, G.H.W. 147, 177, 190
Bush, G.W. 80n, 169, 174, 175, 175n, 176, 178
Byrne, A. 99n

Calvino, I. 234, 235n
Cameron, M. 56, 57, 61, 67, 70
Campbell, C.J. 3n, 32n, 35n, 205n
Cantrell, J. 62, 73
Carnap, R. 65n
Casciana, D. 3n
Cassirer, E. 17, 18n
Cave, N. 2
Celan, P. 31n
Cernea, M.-V. 6
Chamberlain, M. 68
Christgau, R. viii
Ciancio, C. 223n
Clarke, M. 92n
Clash 2
Clinton, B. 147
Cobain, K. ix, 4, 34, 35, 35n, 62, 73, 82, 88, 90, 92, 143, 151, 207–12, 215
Coddington, G. 143

Cohen, J. 80n, 82n, 83n, 174n, 207n
Cohen, L. 5
Cohen, M. 225, 226n
Cohnitz, D. 63, 68, 68n
Coleridge, S.T. 44, 46
Colomasi, E. 3n
Coltrane, J. 195
Conti, C. 37n
Cook, D. 193, 193n, 194, 194n, 195, 195n
Cook, R.F. 1n
Cook, S. 126, 126n
Cooper, G.F. 209n
Copani, C. 3n
Corbett, B.M. 5n
Cornell, C. 4, 62, 215
Cox, D. 99n
Cray, W.D. 63, 69, 69n, 73
Cross, C. 156n
Crowe, C. 81n, 87n, 158, 158n

Danto, A.C. 120n
Deep Purple 215
De Fiore, L. 225n
DeMay, D. 165n
Dennett, D. 98
Derrida, J. 170, 170n, 171, 171n, 172, 173, 179, 179n
Descartes, R. 20
Di Dia, N. 80
Di Pasquale, L. 3n
Dixie Chicks 174n, 175n
Dodd, J. 105n
Dotto, S. 5n, 16n
Drive-By Truckers vii
Duran Duran 206
DuVall, W. 62
Dylan, B. 2, 5
Dyogenes 208

Eagleton, T. 189, 189n, 191
Eco, U. 8n, 120n, 220n
Egli, S. 136
Eliot, T.S. 229, 229n, 230, 231n, 232, 232n, 234, 234n
Ellington, D. 186
Ellis, P. 143
English Beat 81
Euclid 235

Farrugia, F. 3n
Ferber, M. 45, 45n, 46
Ferraris, M. 7n
Fillioley, P. 3
Fisher, M. 34, 34n, 35, 35n, 210, 210n, 215, 215n, 216
Foo Fighters 212
Forman, O. 177n
Foucault, M. 84, 124
Fraistat, N. 46, 46n
Franz, R. 132, 135
Freud, S. 97, 167, 167n, 168, 169
Fricke, D. 121n, 174n, 175n
Fripp. R. 36, 36n
Fromm, E. 126, 127n, 133, 133n, 134
Fugazi 2, 3n, 209

Gadamer, H.-G. 14, 15n, 18, 18n, 20, 28n, 30, 31n
Galella, R. 53
Gandesha, S. 3n, 205n
Garavelli, B.M. 219n
Garufi, R. 3n
Gaspar, B. 62, 68
Gayraud, A. 187, 187n, 188, 199, 200
Gemunden, G. 11n
Geoghegan, V. 50, 50n
Ginsberg, A. 52, 52n
Givony, R. 5n
Glanzberg, M. 116n
Gödel, K. 65n
Goodman, B. 186
Gossard, S. vii, 43, 44, 56, 57, 71, 73, 82n, 146–8, 151, 153, 158
Gracyk, T. 4n, 6, 87, 87n, 88, 88n, 89, 90, 105n
Gramsci, A. 37, 38n
Grande, A. 195
Grant, J.E. 47n
Grateful Dead vii
Green Day 215
Green River 62, 66, 68, 140, 146
Greer, J. 81, 81n
Grohl, D. 212
Guns N' Roses 68, 206
Gutt, J. 62

Habermas, J. 15n, 36n
Halmi, N. 46n

Hannan, J. 132, 133
Hanssen, C. 124, 125n
Haraway, D.J. 166, 166n, 172, 172n, 174
Harkins, T.E. 5n
Hebdige, D. 140, 140n, 141, 142, 142n, 154n, 155, 155n
Hegel, G.W.F. 25, 33, 120n, 194, 196n
Heidegger, M. 19, 19n, 20, 25, 26, 26n, 30, 120n, 230
Hell, R. 153, 153n, 154, 155
Henderson, J. 209n, 211n, 213, 213n
Heraclitus 61, 220
Herzog, W. 136
Hilburn, R. 87n
Hinson, M.P. 188
Hitler, A. 172
Hole 215
Hopkins, H. 155, 155n
Horkheimer, M. 16, 17n, 20n, 38
Horton, S. 186
Huguenard, A. 135
Husserl, E. 230, 230n, 231, 231n, 232n, 233

Iacona, A. 99n
Iemulo, C. 3n
Incubus 213
Iommi, T. 66
Iron Maiden 206
Irons, J. 43, 44, 67, 68
Irwin, W. 66n, 68n

Jackson, M. 207
Jacobs, M. 143
James, W. 128, 128n, 129, 129n, 130, 131, 131n
Jameson, F. 54, 54n, 141, 154, 154n, 155, 157, 157n
Jaspers, K. 15, 15n, 17, 17n
Johnson, M.L. 47n
Joplin, J. viii
Joy Division 67, 206
Joyce, J. 157
Judas Priest 206
Jurgens, D. 186

Kania, A. 105n
Kant, I. 17, 17n, 103, 103n
Keunen, G. 195, 195n, 196, 197, 197n

Kierkegaard, S. 19
Kim, J. 98
Kivy, P. 95, 95n
Koselleck, R. 27, 27n, 30
Krakauer, J. 123n, 124, 124n, 125, 125n, 126n, 127, 129n, 130, 130n, 131n, 133, 134, 134n, 135n, 136
Kramer, S. 6
Kripke, S. 67
Krüger, H.-P. 23, 23n
Krusen, D. 61, 66, 68, 69

La Bella, L. 18n
Lamothe, R. 127
Lavine, M. 144, 145, 148, 151
Led Zeppelin 67, 211, 215
Leigh, M. 35n
Lennon, J. 5
Leonti, G. 3n
Letkemann, J. 46n
Letterman, D. 61
Levine, M.P. 99n
Le Zotte, J. 208, 208n
Limer, A. 3n, 9
London, J. 125
Löwith, K. 26, 27, 27n, 30
Lucretius 224, 224n
Lukin, M. 62

McCandless, Carine 134, 135
McCandless, Christopher J. 123–36
McCready, M. vii, 43, 44, 56, 57, 73, 148, 150, 151-3, 211
McDowell, J. 150
McLaren, M. 154
Mad Season 4
Madonna 207
Maione, F. 3
Marcuse, H. 20, 20n, 189, 193, 214n, 215
Marin, R. 139, 139n, 156
Marino, S. 3n, 9, 23n
Marks, C. 81, 81n, 82, 82n, 83n, 87n
Martin, M.G.F. 99n
Marx, K. 38n, 155, 189
Mason, E. 51, 52n
Mehldau, B. 35n
Mellor, H. 97
Melvins 62, 210, 211

Mendieta, E. 36n
Mercer, L. 158, 161, 162
Metallica viii, 5, 68n, 76
Miano, L. 3n
Midolo, M. 3n
Mignosa, L. 3n
Miles, S. 89n
Minor Threat 209
Modell, J. 157n
Monk, R. 131, 131n
Monkees viii
Montale, E. 228, 228n
Mookie Blaylock 61, 66, 67, 69
Moore, B. 215n
Moore, D.W. 175n
Moretti, D. 5n
Moretti, F. 226n
Morris, S. 6
Morris, W. 189
Morrison, J. 212
Mother Love Bone ix, 6, 62, 66, 68, 146, 147
Moulton, J. 6
Mudhoney 62, 68, 143, 210
Muir, J. 134
Munch, E. 189
Muñoz, J.E. 53, 53n
Muscolino, E. 3n

Napoleon 74
Navantieri, A. 3n
Navarro, D. 70
Neely, K. 5n, 83n, 157, 157n
Nelbock, J. 65n
Neri, L. 15n
New Yardbirds 67
Nickelback 71
Nietzsche, F. 19, 25, 25n, 124, 126
Nine Inch Nails 215
Nirvana 4, 7, 35, 35n, 48, 62, 68, 73, 90, 143, 205, 207–14, 216
NOFX 215
Nozick, R. 22, 22n, 23, 29, 30, 30n, 64, 64n, 65, 68, 72, 103n
Nucifora, V. 3n
Nussbaum, M. 227

O'Brien, B. 80
Oğuz, C. 109

Osbourne, B. 62
Osbourne, O. 66
Ostriker, A. 47, 47n
Özkök, B. 109n

Pachelbel, J. 188
Paddison, M. 184, 184n, 190, 190n, 193, 193n
Paglia, C. 87, 88, 92
Pals, K. 9
Panichas, G.A. 89n
Parapar, C. 6
Parmenides 21, 29
Pascal, B. 221, 222, 222n, 223, 223n, 226, 231
Pasternak, B. 123, 135, 135n
Paul, L. 97
Pearl Jam 7 and passim
Penn, S. 4, 124, 124n, 125, 127, 128, 13, 133–6
Peterson, C. 143
Peterson, G. 130
Petty, T. 5
Picasso, P. 157
Plath, S. 47
Plato 20, 52, 53
Popper, K. 65n
Power, M. 124n, 126n, 127, 127n
Pray, D. 158n
Presley, E. 185
Puy, N.G.-C. 105

Quarry Men 67
Quine, W. 97
Quinn, D. 16n
Quinney, L. 51, 51n, 52, 52n

Radiohead 3, 5, 213
Rancière, J. 168, 168n, 170, 172, 172n, 175, 175n, 176, 178
Reagan, R. 190, 209
Red Hot Chili Peppers 70
Reed, L. 1, 2
Reed, R. 179n
R.E.M. 2
Rennis, F. 213
Reynolds, J. 177n
Reynolds, S. 216
Rhodes, Z. 142

Rietmulder, M. 165n, 170n, 171n, 172n, 179n
Ripley, D. 116n
Ritchie, K. 71n, 72
Roberts, E. 159
Robinson, J. ix
Rodman, D. 63
Rolling Stones 87
Romano, A. 3n
Romano F., 224n
Rorty, R. 36, 36n, 38, 38n
Rose, C. 124, 124n

Said, E. 124, 124n
Scalia, B. 3
Scheler, M. 32n
Schembari, A. 9, 33n
Schiller, J.C.F. 189
Schlick, M. 65, 65n
Schönberg, A. 185, 205
Schopenhauer, A. 137, 137n
Searle, J. 63
Sellars, W. 97
Sepultura 213
Sex Pistols 188
Shaggs viii
Showden, C. 84, 84n, 85-8, 90-2
Shusterman, R. 29, 29n
Siani, A.L. 6, 110n, 120n
Silva, M. 230n
Simmel, G. 141, 141n, 142
Sinatra, F. 185, 186
Siracusa, E. 3n
Siracusa, G. 3n
Sloterdijk, P. 208
Smart, J. J. C. 97, 101, 101n, 102, 102n
Smith, C. 184, 184n, 185
Smith, P. 2
Snyder, W. 2n
Socrates 18, 19
Sonic Youth 2
Sorensen, R. 21n
Soulfly 213
Soundgarden 4, 62, 67, 153, 216
Spandau Ballet 206
Speroni, E. 37n
Spielberg, S. 98
Springsteen, B. 2, 5, 211

Staley, L. 4, 62, 73, 74
Starr, E. 177
Stellino, P. 6
Stone Temple Pilots 62
Strachey, J. 167n
Stravinsky, I. 205
Strawson, P. 98
Strohmeier, D. 72, 74
Strokes vii
Strong, B. 177n
Strong, C. 206n, 208n
Swift, T. viii
Szendy, P. 199

Tamm, E. 36n
Tatarkiewicz, W. 119n
Television 153
Temple of the Dog 4, 66
Terrone, E. 6, 96n
Terzi, P. 23n
Thayil, K. 153
Thewliss, D. 35
Thomas, W. 156
Thoreau, H.D. 123, 125, 127, 130, 133, 134, 134n
Three Fish 4
Tolstoy, L.N. 123, 129, 130
Treadwell, T. 135, 136
Truman, J. 156
Trump, D. 57, 168n, 178n

U2 2, 5, 44
Uszkai, R. 6, 61n

Valéry, P. 227, 227n, 228, 228n, 234, 234n
Van Halen, E. 71
Varner, P. 126n
Vedder, E. vii, x, 1, 2, 2n, 3, 4, 13, 16n, 17, 32, 35, 37n, 38, 43, 44, 46-51, 54-7, 66, 71-4, 79, 80, 80n, 81, 81n, 82, 82n, 83, 83n, 86, 87, 92, 92n, 96, 102, 105, 106, 112n, 113n, 114, 124, 124n, 126-8, 128n, 130, 130n, 132, 133, 133n, 134, 134n, 135n, 136, 137, 137n, 147-53, 157n, 158-62, 165, 168, 170-2, 174, 174n, 175, 175n, 177, 177n, 178, 178n, 179, 179n, 180, 180n, 191, 197, 207, 207n, 210, 211, 214, 216, 233, 233n

Velvet Underground 2
Venuti, M. 3n
Venuti, S. 3n
Vera, J.S. 125, 125n
Villa, L. 5n
Vitali, R. 25n
Voidoids 153
Volpi, A. 27n
Volpi, F. 23, 23n

Wakeman, R. 188
Walters, K. 167n
Warsaw 67
Webern, A. 185, 199, 199n
Weil, S. 79, 89, 89n, 90n, 91, 91n
Weiland, S. 62
Weissman, D. 169n
Wenders, W. 1, 1n, 2, 2n
Wenner, J. 5n
West, K. 71, 72, 75, 76
Westerberg, W. 123, 129, 134
Westwood, V. 154
Whitaker, B. 143

Whitfield, N. 177n
Who 2, 5
Wilkerson, M.I. 80n, 82n, 83n, 174n, 207n
Wilson, E. 139, 139n
Wittgenstein, Helene 131
Wittgenstein, Hermine 131
Wittgenstein, L. 18, 18n, 19, 30, 65n, 130, 131
Wittgenstein, P. 131
Wolff, R.P. 215n
Wood, A. 146
Wordsworth, W. 44, 46, 46n, 48, 49, 49n, 50, 51, 51n, 52, 53, 55, 55n, 57, 57n, 58, 235, 235n

Yarm, M. 140n, 143n
Young, N. x, 2, 3, 5, 69n, 116, 211, 217
Young Pioneers 145

Zalta, E.N. 21n, 116n
Zappa, F. viii
Zinn, H. 16, 16n, 33, 226, 226n
Zizek, S. 200

www.ingramcontent.com/pod-product-compliance
Lightning Source LLC
Chambersburg PA
CBHW070752020526
44115CB00032B/1772